FRONTIERS OF EXPERT SYSTEMS:
Reasoning with Limited Knowledge

THE KLUWER INTERNATIONAL SERIES
IN ENGINEERING AND COMPUTER SCIENCE

FRONTIERS OF
EXPERT SYSTEMS:
Reasoning with Limited Knowledge

by

Chilukuri Krishna Mohan
Syracuse University, U.S.A.

KLUWER ACADEMIC PUBLISHERS
Boston / Dordrecht / London

Distributors for North, Central and South America:
Kluwer Academic Publishers
101 Philip Drive
Assinippi Park
Norwell, Massachusetts 02061 USA
Telephone (781) 871-6600
Fax (781) 871-6528
E-Mail <kluwer@wkap.com>

Distributors for all other countries:
Kluwer Academic Publishers Group
Distribution Centre
Post Office Box 322
3300 AH Dordrecht, THE NETHERLANDS
Telephone 31 78 6392 392
Fax 31 78 6546 474
E-Mail <orderdept@wkap.nl>

 Electronic Services <http://www.wkap.nl>

Library of Congress Cataloging-in-Publication Data

Mohan, Chilukuri K.
  Frontiers of expert systems : reasoning with limited knowledge / by Chilukuri Krishna Mohan.
    p. cm.-- (Kluwer international series in engineering and computer science ; SECS 552)
  Includes bibliographical references and index.
  ISBN 0-7923-7815-6 (alk. paper)
    1. Expert systems (Computer science) I. Title. II. Series

  QA76.76.E95 M64 2000
  006.3'3--dc21

                                                                00-028579

Contents

Preface

Expert systems have come a long way from their exclusive definition as rule-based systems. This book hopes to introduce the reader to the many exciting advances made in recent years, including new methodologies and new applications. It is intended as an advanced presentation of the subject of expert systems for readers at the senior undergraduate or beginning graduate levels, as well as professional engineers and computer scientists.

Beginning with the central topics of formal logic, uncertainty and rule-based reasoning, each chapter in the book presents a different perspective on how we may solve problems that arise due to limitations in the knowledge of an expert system's reasoner. Successive chapters address:

1. the fundamentals of knowledge-based systems,

2. formal inference, and reasoning about models of a changing and partially known world,

3. uncertainty and probabilistic methods,

4. the expression of knowledge in rule-based systems,

5. evolving representations of knowledge as a system interacts with the environment,

6. applying connectionist learning algorithms to improve on knowledge acquired from experts,

7. reasoning with cases organized in indexed hierarchies,

8. the process of acquiring and inductively learning knowledge,

9. extraction of knowledge nuggets from very large data sets, and

10. interactions between multiple specialized reasoners with specialized knowledge bases.

Chapters 1-2 should be read first, followed by Chapters 3-4 in any order. Chapters 5-8 and 10 can then be read, in any order. Chapter 9 relies on the material in several of the preceding chapters, and should ideally be read immediately after Chapter 8. The sequencing of chapters attempts to provide some flow between chapters, although this has implied that topics of more common interest (such as Chapter 8) occur later in the book.

Within each chapter, it is best to cover most sections in the same sequence as the text; this is not always logically necessary, but minimizes confusion. Course projects can be initiated after material in chapter 4 is covered.

For students who have already had a course in Artificial Intelligence, material in Chapters 1 and 4 may be skimmed at a fast pace. For students with a background in Probability and Statistics, little time needs to be spent on Chapter 3. For a one-semester undergraduate course that does not assume prior background in Artificial Intelligence, it is advisable to omit coverage of Chapters 5, 6, 9 and 10.

To gain experience in rule-based programming, the author recommends working with the expert systems development language *CLIPS* (or *Jess*, its Java implementation), for which source code and documentation are available over the internet. Experience using toolkits with user-friendly interfaces would be helpful in attacking large applications.

This book evolved from lecture notes for a course taught by the author at Syracuse University since 1990. I apologize for errors, particularly if I have omitted attributing credit to researchers whose work is described in this book.

I am grateful to Kishan Mehrotra for his review of Chapters 1, 3 and 9, Thirunarayan Krishnaprasad for his review of Chapters 2, 7 and 8, Tim Kovacs for his review of Chapter 5, Sudha Kailar for her comments on Chapter 7, and Wilfred Jamison for his review of Chapter 10. This book is much improved thanks to their comments. Finally, I thank and salute all the authors and researchers who have contributed to my understanding of the subject, making this book possible.

Material for transparencies may be obtained from the author, reachable at ckmohan@syr.edu. Suggestions for improvements and corrections are welcomed. Course-related material (including errata) will be available on the internet, at www.cis.syr.edu/~mohan/es.html.

Chapter 1

Knowledge-Based Systems

Although kingdoms and provinces may be wrested from the hands that
hold them ... it is the glorious prerogative of the empire of knowledge,
that what it gains it never loses. On the contrary, it increases by
the multiple of its own power; all its ends become means; all its
attainments, help to new conquests. ————Daniel Webster, 1825

The phrases *knowledge-based systems* and *expert systems* are often used in
the broad sense of systems whose main components are a set of production rules
and an inference engine that fires these rules nondeterministically. However, this
definition is much too narrow: it excludes a large number of expert systems that
are not rule-based, e.g., systems that use case-based reasoning, blackboards, and
neural networks.

A more accurate description that summarizes actual usage would be that
expert systems are *software systems for specialized applications that require ex-*
pertise, generally based on *Artificial Intelligence (AI)* techniques. This definition excludes research efforts whose goal is to develop or illustrate new concepts,
although many AI techniques will be applied in building expert systems. For example, a researcher may implement a new idea for natural language processing:
this would not be an expert system. However, one may implement an expert
system for diagnosis in internal medicine, and this expert system may exploit a
new research idea for natural language processing.

Many expert systems applications are characterized by the need to carry
out reasoning in the absence of a clear formulation of complete knowledge about
the problem domain. Learning a specific programming paradigm, such as rule-
based programming, is insufficient. The following important issues must be

understood to facilitate building successful systems:

- how formal and practical inferences can be carried out;

- how reasoning can be carried out despite uncertainty associated with problem parameters;

- how inference engines of rule-based systems work;

- how interaction with the environment can be used to evolve knowledge;

- how knowledge may be augmented by learning algorithms;

- how knowledge in the form of cases can be manipulated;

- how knowledge may be acquired;

- how knowledge can be discovered from large amounts of data; and

- how problems can be solved by invoking multiple interacting subsystems with partial knowledge.

The reader is invited to visit successive chapters of this book that address the issues mentioned above.

Section 1.1 presents a brief listing of early commercially successful and historically important expert systems. Section 1.2 discusses expert systems applications and modalities of usage. Section 1.3 describes the high level structure of most expert systems, although variations do exist. Section 1.4 presents the knowledge representation techniques most frequently applied in developing expert systems. Section 1.5 illustrates how cost-benefit analysis may be used in deciding whether to indulge in the effort of developing an expert system for a task. Section 1.6 discusses the verification and validation of knowledge-based systems. Finally, Section 1.7 introduces and summarizes the remaining chapters of this book.

1.1   Early Expert Systems

This section presents a brief list of some major expert systems that have had an impact on (and led to the development of) other expert systems; the dates mentioned indicate when each system was developed, to be distinguished from the dates associated with cited literature.

DENDRAL: Developed in 1965 by Feigenbaum *et al.* [5] for chemical synthesis, this system illustrated the feasibility of encoding expert knowledge for complex tasks.

MACSYMA: Developed in 1969 by Martin and Moses [14], this system for mathematical formula manipulation illustrated the process of developing rule-based expert systems for well-understood domains.

MYCIN: Developed in 1973 by Shortliffe *et al.* [18], this huge and complex rule-based medical diagnosis system introduced the use of certainty factors, a knowledge acquisition facility, and an explanation facility. It also led to many spinoffs, such as the EMYCIN shell for various applications, obtained by stripping MYCIN of its medical knowledge base.

HEARSAY-II: Developed in 1973 by Reddy *et al.* [15], this speech recognition system proposed what has come to be known as the "blackboard model" with the use of multiple (distributed) knowledge sources (agents) that cooperate to solve a hierarchically structured complex task.

PROSPECTOR: Developed in 1976 by Duda, Gaschnig and Hart [3], this was a system for mineral exploration using a hierarchical knowledge representation structure, applying probabilistic methods (with independence assumptions) for practical decision-making.

R1 (XCON): Developed in 1977 by McDermott *et al.* [12], this goal-driven expert system configured computer systems for Digital Equipment Corporation, illustrating most clearly the quantifiable savings (many minutes per order, translating into millions of dollars each year) resulting from the use of expert systems.

In addition to the development of specific methodologies such as rule-based programming, the most important contribution of these early systems is the notion of *separating control from knowledge*. This is an invaluable principle that makes it possible to apply the same methodology to a large number of problems, often providing design templates for new problems. The alternative to be shunned is the attempt to solve every problem from scratch, throwing away expertise gained earlier in building expert systems for other applications.

1.2   Roles, Tasks, Applications

Expert systems have been used in various *modalities* for different *tasks* in *applications*. 'Modalities' refer to how the system is used, whereas 'tasks' refer to the nature of the problem; 'applications' refer to problems that may involve multiple tasks. For instance, an expert system may be used in advisory modality, for the flight crew scheduling task, in an airline planning application.

Examples of modalities:

1. Tutoring, helping a human learn about the domain

2. Advisory, suggesting a possible solution to a human

3. Autonomous, interacting with a physical system or environment without a human in the loop

Examples of tasks:

1. Computation: to calculate the value of a desired function of given attributes

2. Diagnosis: to infer the cause from observable symptoms

3. Prognosis: to predict possible future effects

4. Configuration: to arrange components to achieve desirable properties of the whole

5. Inverse Control: to determine values of variables necessary to obtain a desired effect

6. Monitoring: to observe some variables and take actions that depend directly on the values of observed variables

7. Triage: to assign each input case to a predefined group

Applications range over practically all fields of human endeavor, including education, chemistry, biology, medicine, engineering, manufacturing, and computer science. Medical applications have constituted a particularly important area of application, for several reasons:

1. the amount of knowledge to be encoded is often very large;

2. complex cases arise, for which encoded knowledge often turns out to be inadequate (a physician may generate new rules to handle such exceptions, after such cases arise);

3. the knowledge acquisition task is difficult, since software engineers and physicians use entirely different jargon; and

4. almost every case involves considerable uncertainty.

Another major class of applications arises in the field of computer systems, where expert systems tend to be more successful because expert systems developers are familiar with the subject matter.

1.3 Structure of an Expert System

At a high level, most expert systems consist of three major components:

1. The **Knowledge Base** is generally static, and changes little during operation of the system. It is applicable to all possible cases that may arise, and is often obtained in the *knowledge acquisition* phase in the development of the expert system. In many systems, knowledge is abstracted as a set of production rules, and the knowledge base is referred to as the *production memory* or *rule base*.

2. The **Working Memory** contains transient knowledge that changes significantly during the use of the system. It is initialized with the specific attribute values relevant to one particular case currently under consideration, obtained from the user in each specific interaction. In many systems, case-specific knowledge is encoded as a set of independent facts, and the working memory is referred to as *fact base*.

3. The **Inference Engine** is the operational component that applies the knowledge base to the working memory, changing the latter. It generates results and explanations, and is generally determined by the choice of expert system development tool. If an expert system shell or tool (such as CLIPS) is used, the user will not have to program a new inference engine, but must learn how to use an existing one.

As with any computer software, the expert system must communicate with users, requiring appropriate interfaces. Three kinds of interfaces are needed (although these may be combined in some applications):

1. Developer interface: used to modify essential aspects of the system, such as search strategy.

2. Expert interface: used to acquire knowledge from an expert[1], and modify the existing knowledge base.

3. User interface: used in the operation of the expert system, to initialize working memory, send appropriate control signals to the inference engine, and receive results from the latter.

Separating the interfaces provides some protection against the modification of a knowledge base by mistake or malice.

1.4   Knowledge Representation

Expert systems generally represent knowledge using *production rules, frames, graphs,* and *trees*, sometimes in combination.

- A production rule is a two-tuple, consisting of an *antecedent (lhs)* and a *consequent (rhs)*, where the antecedent is a sequence of condition elements, and the consequent is a sequence of actions. Production rules are very widely used, and are discussed in greater detail in Chapter 4.

- A frame is a named structure consisting of *slots* (attributes) associated with specific *fillers* (values). Frames resemble record data structures in imperative programming languages. A *schema* identifies the slots describing the structure of a collection of frames, possibly with *default* fillers. Every frame that instantiates a schema has the default filler values, unless explicitly specified otherwise. Slots and fillers need not be static values, e.g., they may contain constraints to be enforced, procedures to be executed (when a filler is needed, or obtained), pointers to other frames, and graphics to assist in user interaction. Frames may be combined with rules, e.g., the antecedent of a rule may specify constraints on fillers of a frame, and the consequent may describe fillers of a new or modified frame.

- A graph (network) contains a set of *vertices* (nodes) and a set of *edges*, where each edge is a two-tuple of vertices. A graph and its edges may be *directed*, if the relationships between vertices are asymmetric; undirected graphs treat an edge as a set of two vertices, unordered. Edges are often annotated with information that explicates relationships between adjacent vertices, e.g., the strength of a connection between vertices. A *path* is a

---

[1] In this book, the word "expert" by itself refers only to a human expert, not an expert system.

sequence of edges between two nodes. Efficient graph traversal algorithms may be invoked to reason about the relationship between two concepts represented as vertices.

- A tree is a directed graph with a distinguished vertex called the *root* with no incoming edge, such that there is a unique path from the root to each node. *Leaves* are vertices with no outgoing directed edges. If a tree contains an edge (v_1, v_2), we say v_1 is a *parent* of v_2 and v_2 is a *child* of v_1. Computer implementations often assume that a tree is *ordered*, i.e., the children of each node constitute a sequence.

Trees are generally used to establish the following hierarchical relationships between entities or concepts represented as vertices:

- In *abstraction hierarchies*, the child node denotes a subclass, subset, specialization, or instance of the class or set represented by the parent node. They are sometimes referred to as *specialization-generalization hierarchies* or *subclass-superclass hierarchies*. These hierarchies permit *inheritance*: unless specified otherwise, each node inherits the properties of the nearest ancestor for which the property value is specified.

- In *part-whole hierarchies*, the child node denotes a part of the entity represented by the parent node.

Each node in a tree structure has a unique parent, but the definition of a hierarchy is sometimes generalized to violate this constraint, resulting in a *directed acyclic graph* rather than a tree. Reasoning with such hierarchies is non-trivial when there are conflicts between property values inherited along different ancestor lines.

1.5 To use, or not to use?

Expert systems are often applied to problems that are too difficult to solve using traditional algorithmic techniques. Success is achieved by understanding how humans solve such problems, and the nature of the specialized heuristic knowledge needed to solve such problems. Many AI applications may be viewed as applying heuristic search algorithms, where the heuristic is problem-specific, although the overall methodology is fairly general. Two completely different applications may use similar search algorithms, differing only in the nature of the problem-specific heuristics, wherein lies the key to successful application.

The primary factor for the deployment of the technology is economics, although political and social considerations may be important in selecting the applications of the technology and focus areas to be emphasized. There are several examples of successful expert systems that have saved millions of dollars. The question to be addressed is whether expert systems would be economically advantageous for a specific application, not whether expert systems are desirable in the abstract sense. The applicability of an expert system for a task should be evaluated in terms of the short term and long term consequences, posing three questions relevant to their *cost benefit analysis*:

1. How much effort is needed to develop the expert system?

2. How much effort is needed to maintain the expert system and upgrade it as the application (or the knowledge available about the application) changes with time?

3. How much expert effort is saved in the long term?

These considerations (that determine whether an expert system can be deployed) may be quantified using the following notation.

- c': cost per unit time of expert availability if expert system is not used, including assessment of losses when expert is not available

- t_a: estimated knowledge acquisition time

- c_e: average cost per unit time of experts needed for knowledge acquisition

- c_k: average cost per unit time of knowledge engineer needed for knowledge acquisition

- t_d: estimated time to develop software

- c_d: average cost per unit time of software developer

- t_t: estimated time for testing and evaluation of developed expert system, including time taken to perform required changes to expert system after testing

- c_t: testing, evaluation and repair cost per unit time

- c_m: maintenance cost per unit time, including costs of training multiple personnel to use the expert system

- T_b: breakeven time period, i.e., time required to recover investment, when the cost of expert system development and maintenance equals the savings achieved because of expert system usage

Until the system is deployed, i.e., for the time period $(t_a + t_d + t_t)$, the cost is the same (c') whether or not the expert system is developed.

If the expert system is developed, the total cost for time T is

$$(c_e + c_k)t_a + (c_d t_d + c_t t_t) + c_m(T - (t_a + t_d + t_t)) + c'(t_a + t_d + t_t).$$

For the same time T, the total cost if the expert system is not developed is $c'T$. Assuming $c' > c_m$, the breakeven time period T_b is obtained by solving the equation

$$c'T_b = (c_e + c_k)t_a + (c_d t_d + c_t t_t) + c_m T_b + (c' - c_m)(t_a + t_d + t_t).$$

This implies that

$$T_b = \frac{(c_e + c_k)t_a + (c_d t_d + c_t t_t) + (c' - c_m)(t_a + t_d + t_t)}{(c' - c_m)}$$

A business decision to deploy the expert system will probably be made if the breakeven time period T_b is small enough, e.g., if $T_b < 4$ years, ignoring other intangible benefits of introducing the expert system.

When decisions are made, all of these numbers are estimates, which may be revised periodically. Actual costs incurred with developing a system may be twice the costs as estimated by those who are already biased towards deciding to develop the system. Crucial factors such as equipment and overheads are often ignored in optimistic analyses, and come back to haunt the developers.

Example 1.1 An industrial unit must be in use 10 hours per day, for 250 days in a year. The skilled employees operating the unit cost $50 per hour on the average (taking into account considerations such as overtime and employer benefits). Without using an expert system, the annual expense can thus be estimated as

$$c' = \$50/\text{hr.} \times 10\text{hrs.}/\text{day} \times 250\text{days/yr.} = \$125,000/\text{yr.}$$

If an expert system is to be developed, knowledge acquisition may require more experienced subject experts costing $100,000 per year, and a knowledge engineer costing another $100,000 per year. Assuming that the knowledge acquisition process requires half a year, its total cost is

$$(c_e + c_k)t_a = \$100,000.$$

We assume that the software development takes half a year, $(t_d = 0.5$ yrs.), and incurs software development cost of $c_d = \$100,000$ per year. Similar costs are assumed for software testing, evaluation and final changes, with $t_t = 0.5$ years, and $c_t = \$100,000$ per year. These numbers must include costs of computing equipment and related overheads. Expert system maintenance costs are estimated to be \$40,000/yr. for this application. Based on these estimates, $T_b =$

$$\frac{100000 + 50000 + 50000 - 40000(0.5 + 0.5 + 0.5) + 125000(0.5 + 0.5 + 0.5)}{(125000 - 40000)}$$

$$\approx 3.9 \text{ years.}$$

In other words, if the expert system project is started immediately, it will be profitable in four years. including expert system development time. This analysis supports launching the project.

In practice, the criticality and complexity of the task dictate how much time and cost may be permitted to develop an expert system. For instance, much more time and cost may be allowed for developing an expert system to be used in a nuclear power plant, as opposed to an expert system to assist students to register for courses at a University.

1.6   Verification and Validation

Verification of software addresses its compliance with specifications, whereas *Validation* addresses the correctness of the encoded domain knowledge and the performance of the software in the context of actual usage. Software is verified with respect to its requirements (specification), and validated with the assistance of end-users. In a similar manner, the verification and validation (*V&V*) of expert systems involve experts and end users, not just the developers.

Errors and difficulties in the practical usage of expert systems stem from multiple sources, such as

- the lack of clear specifications;

- semantic and syntactic errors in implementation; and

- incorrect representation of domain knowledge.

Errors may arise because the knowledge acquisition process relies on the subjective assessments of an expert. Further, questions in the problem domain may not have a unique answer: expert opinions may be uncertain or imprecise, and different experts may disagree. Errors may also arise in the measurement of uncertainty, and the manner in which unreliable evidence from different sources is combined.

Unlike most other software, expert systems cannot easily be tested by the developers unless they test the system by interacting with the actual problem environment. Also, unlike other software, the subjective opinions of an expert may be used in evaluating the answers of the expert system.

Verification is intended to determine whether an expert system complies with its specification, and hence depends on the quality of the specification. Unfortunately, clear declarative specifications are often not developed for most expert systems. It is common to consider a natural language description of production rules as the specification. When the tasks of design and specification are confused in this manner, there is little assurance that the desired behavior of the expert system has been communicated accurately to the developers.

Expert systems must also meet some non-behavioral requirements. The system should be easily maintainable and modifiable, without requiring the presence of the original expert system developers, especially if the nature of the knowledge in the relevant domain can change with time. Change-management protocols must be laid out in advance, describing exactly how a knowledge base may be modified, and the nature of system tests needed when such modifications occur. In particular, the system must be designed such that it is easy to see which components may be affected by changes to other components of the system.

Rough guidelines may be established for the computational efficiency of the system, and these may lead to system-specific space-time tradeoffs, as well as design decisions to generate quick suboptimal solutions rather than optimal solutions requiring excessive computations. This depends on understanding the tradeoff between solution quality and computational efficiency. Care is needed to ensure that there is no needless looping in system execution, a problem to which elaborate non-deterministic systems are particularly susceptible.

If the expert system is to interact directly with external software or hardware, verification also involves examining the interfaces (e.g., formats of files created) to ensure their correctness. User interface design calls for care and expertise; an expert system may be functionally powerful but may remain little used if the non-technical user finds it difficult to use or navigate.

Unlike other software, an expert system often needs to be supplemented by an explanation facility, so that the workings of the system are not opaque to the user. Design of this facility can be guided by knowing the obvious questions that a user may ask (e.g., why the system draws a specific conclusion, or why the system asks for specific data), as discovered by other builders of expert systems.

In the world of hackers and extensive computer literacy, verification includes compliance to security specifications; these must be clearly stated, and not taken for granted.

Ensuring that the expert system meets its specification is no guarantee that the expert system will satisfy its intended users or customers, since errors of commission and omission may occur in the specification itself. In the validation step, the system's outputs are to be compared against known results, expert performance, and theoretical results, to determine whether the answers are satisfactory, and whether a sufficiently large part of the problem domain is covered by the expert system.

Validation may be performed *via* informal meetings with experts and users to discuss system conclusions, or by black-box testing, comparing system results with aggregates of multiple expert opinions. The most important validation occurs in field tests, which always uncover unexpected errors. In some cases, it may be possible to partition the knowledge base into subsystems or modules, and validate each one separately. Since considerable uncertainty and imprecision are involved in the knowledge acquisition phase, sensitivity analysis should be performed, observing variations in expert system outputs with small changes in inputs; the system must be robust enough to withstand small errors in the knowledge acquisition phase.

Some tools are available to help in V&V: these exhaustively compare components of rules, or apply graphical simulation models.

1.7   The rest of this book

This section describes the contents of the remaining chapters of this book.

Chapter 2:   Any discussion of expert systems must begin from the fundamentals of logical reasoning, and the use of inference rules, discussed in this chapter. In addition, expert systems must adopt reasoning procedures that can cope successfully with a changing external world, and make "commonsense" inferences that are uncommonly difficult for automated reasoners. This chapter examines the *non-monotonic* reasoning involved when a reasoning system has to withdraw past conclusions. The incorporation of such a reasoning process into *truth maintenance systems* is also discussed. Finally, this chapter discusses diagnostic reasoning about models of real world systems.

Chapter 3: This chapter discusses how to handle uncertainty in expert systems, emphasizing the time-tested approach of probability theory. Beginning from the basic axioms of probability and fundamental notions of conditional independence, a methodology is developed for propagating beliefs in probabilistic inference networks. The chapter also discusses how to carry out rational decision-making in the presence of uncertainty and subjective preferences. The Dempster-Shafer approach of belief masses and belief intervals is presented. Fuzzy systems are discussed, distinguishing their use from that of probability. The method of certainty factors is also described.

Chapter 4: Rule-based systems receive early attention since these are the most frequently used expert systems in practice. The basic concepts of grammar rules, rewrite rules, and Prolog-style rules for backward chaining, all provide a prelude to production rules, the staple of most expert systems. Emphasis is placed on the principles of commonly used forward-chaining inference engines (*a la* CLIPS). The chapter ends with a discussion of the difficulties in the specification, verification and validation of rule-based systems.

Chapter 5: When an expert system has to be built to interact successfully with a changing environment, there need to be mechanisms that allow the rule base itself to be modified with time. This chapter describes *classifier systems* in which rules are evolved by the system, based on positive and negative reinforcements received from the environment. These systems use credit allocation strategies that punish or reward individual rules in response to reinforcements received by the entire system. *Genetic Algorithms*, used to discover rules, are also described in this chapter.

Chapter 6: Since the 1980s, *neural networks* have gathered increasing presence among other intelligent system models. This chapter discusses how such systems have been coopted to work along with traditional expert systems. The systematic and well-understood aspects of rule-based system development (e.g., explanation facilities) are preserved, while utilizing the computational power of neural networks. Two such connectionist expert system models, KBCNN and MACIE, are discussed in this chapter, following a generic introduction to neural networks.

Chapter 7: This chapter describes the most important challenge to rule-based expert systems: *case-based reasoning (CBR)*. The processes of case retrieval and case adaptation are discussed, along with a description of how to establish and structure a case library. Several examples of existing practical CBR systems are also presented.

Chapter 8: This chapter addresses one of the greatest obstacles facing expert systems developers: knowledge acquisition. The overall knowledge engineering methodology is presented, followed by discussion of knowledge elicitation techniques, particularly when multiple experts are involved. This is followed by a discussion of the *Personal Constructs* approach from cognitive psychology, in which subjective opinions are extracted and translated into *repertory grids*, from which rules may be generated using a logic of confirmation. Finally, a methodology for mechanizing the knowledge acquisition process is presented; this involves applying an inductive learning algorithm that builds a classification tree using example data, circumventing expensive knowledge acquisition procedures.

Chapter 9: AI, statistics, and database technologies have recently come together to solve real-life application problems that involve extracting meaningful information from very large amounts of data, also known as *Data Mining*, the subject of this chapter. Methodologies for preprocessing data are first described, followed by techniques for transforming data representations to a form amenable to analysis. Approaches and recent algorithms for knowledge discovery and prediction are then discussed.

Chapter 10: The most important change in the computing world is the shift from single-machine systems to networks of many systems that communicate with each other. Distributed computing systems facilitate and hasten the distribution of experts over multiple computing systems. This chapter addresses two main paradigms in distributed expert systems: Blackboard Systems and Multiagent Systems. Blackboard Systems involve centralized communication and coordinated problem-solving activity, whereas Multiagent Systems involve much greater autonomy for experts. Complex questions of organization and communication among experts are discussed in this chapter.

To summarize, this book attempts to go beyond traditional expert systems, exploring modern methodologies that provide useful paradigms for developing knowledge-based systems. For a given problem, several of these methodologies may be usefully combined. Exciting challenges are posed by data mining problems, a new and significant application area that requires interdisciplinary understanding and multiple fields of specialization.

1.8 Bibliographic Notes

The field of AI is well described in textbooks such as those by Winston [21], Ginsberg [7], Rich and Knight [16], Russell and Norvig [17], Luger and Stubblefield [11], Tanimoto [20], and several others. The four volumes of the *Handbook of Artificial Intelligence* [2] also comprehensively discuss various topics of AI.

Stefik's book [19] provides a comprehensive treatment of many topics important to traditional expert systems, as well as reasoning methodologies. Giarratano and Riley's book [6] is recommended for its clear description of rule-based programming in CLIPS. The book by Gonzalez and Dankel [8] is recommended for its comprehensive treatment of requirements analysis, knowledge acquisition, verification and validation. Several other books provide good introductions to the topic of expert systems, such as those authored by Jackson [10], Durkin [4], and Awad [1].

Nondeterministic systems have been studied for many years in the context of communicating systems, and satisfactory solutions have been proposed for problems that arise in such systems. The solutions, specification languages and verification techniques that have emerged from this field (e.g., [9, 13]) have much to offer future expert systems developers and verifiers.

Bibliography

[1] E.M. Awad, *Building Expert Systems: Principles, Procedures, and Applications*, West Publishing Company, Minneapolis (MN), 1996.

[2] A. Barr, P.R. Cohen, E.A. Feigenbaum (Eds.) *The Handbook of Artificial Intelligence*, Volumes I-IV, Addison-Wesley, 1989.

[3] R. Duda, H. Gaschnig, and P. Hart, "Model Design in the PROSPECTOR Consultant System for Mineral Exploration," in D. Michie (Ed.), *Expert Systems in the Micro-electronic Age*, Edinburgh University Press, 1976, pp.153-167.

[4] J. Durkin, *Expert Systems: Design and Development*, Macmillan, NY, 1994.

[5] B.G. Buchanan and E.A. Feigenbaum, "Dendral and Meta-Dendral: Their Applications Dimension," *Artificial Intelligence*, 1978, 11(1):5-24.

[6] J. Giarratano and G. Riley, *Expert systems: principles and programming*, third edition, PWS Pub. Co., Boston (MA), 1998.

[7] M. Ginsberg, *Essentials of Artificial Intelligence*, Morgan Kaufmann, 1993.

[8] A.J. Gonzalez and D.D. Dankel, *The Engineering of Knowledge-Based Systems: Theory and Practice*. Prentice-Hall, 1993.

[9] C.A.R. Hoare, *Communicating Sequential Processes*, Prentice-Hall, 1985.

[10] P. Jackson, *Introduction to Expert Systems*, third edition, Addison-Wesley, 1999.

[11] G.F. Luger and W.A. Stubblefield, *Artificial Intelligence: Structures and Strategies for Complex Problem Solving*, second edition, 1993.

[12] J. McDermott and J.Bachant, "R1 Revisited: Four Years in the Trenches." *AI Magazine*, Fall 1984, 5(3):21-32.

[13] A.J.R.G. Milner, *A Calculus of Communicating Systems,* Springer Verlag LNCS 92, 1980.

[14] J. Moses, "The current capabilities of the MACSYMA system," in *Proc. of the ACM National Conference,* 1976.

[15] D.R. Reddy, L.D. Erman, R.D. Fennel, and R.B. Neely, "The Hearsay speech understanding system: an example of the recognition process," in *Proc. Third International Joint Conference on Artificial Intelligence* (IJCAI-73), 1973, pp.185-193.

[16] E. Rich and K. Knight, *Artificial Intelligence,* second edition, McGraw Hill, 1991.

[17] S. Russell and P. Norvig, *Artificial Intelligence: A Modern Approach,* Prentice-Hall, 1995.

[18] E.H. Shortliffe, *Computer-based Medical Consultations: MYCIN,* Elsevier/North Holland, NY, 1976.

[19] M. Stefik, *Introduction to Knowledge Systems,* Morgan Kaufmann, 1995.

[20] S.L. Tanimoto, *The Elements of Artificial Intelligence using Common Lisp,* second edition, Computer Science Press (Freeman and Co.), 1995.

[21] P.H. Winston, *Artificial Intelligence,* third edition, Addison-Wesley, 1992.

Chapter 2

Practical Reasoning

Science is a first-rate piece of furniture for man's upper chamber, if he has common sense on the ground floor.
_____Oliver Wendell Holmes, Sr., 1872

The whole of science is nothing more than a refinement of everyday thinking. _____Albert Einstein, 1938

The use of any expert system involves careful reasoning about a formal representation of problem-specific knowledge. It is important to begin with a clear understanding of classical propositional logic and first order logic, which are at the foundation of all symbolic intelligent systems. Practical reasoning systems also require reasoning about time, "common sense" reasoning, and model-based reasoning, which are also discussed in this chapter. These are not esoteric topics that can be ignored by the practitioner. Indeed, aspects of temporal and common sense reasoning occur even in traditional rule-based expert systems, and are generally left unexplained, leading to confusion about how to specify and verify such systems (cf. Section 4.9).

Although there is no universally accepted definition of *common sense reasoning*, we may consider this phrase to encompass reasoning with all the assumptions and inference rules used by non-specialist humans. Traditional expert systems are woefully inadequate for common sense reasoning, since they are generally built to contain a useful domain-specific body of knowledge, rather than immense collections of unrelated information accumulated by humans. Two important aspects of common sense reasoning have been identified:

- *The frame problem:* Actions are presumed not to have effects other than those explicitly specified. This implies, for instance, that objects do not change their attributes arbitrarily.

- *The qualification problem:* Humans often make a very large number of implicit assumptions when drawing conclusions. For instance, in reasoning from *Tweety is a bird*, and *Birds fly*, that *Tweety can fly*, we presume that Tweety is not a penguin, not an ostrich, its wings are not broken, it is not tied down, it is awake, not unconscious, not dead, etc. It would be infeasible (and against common sense) to attempt to enumerate all these qualifiers in reasoning about Tweety. In the absence of additional information, commonsense reasoning would allow us to draw the 'default' conclusion that Tweety can indeed fly.

Section 2.1 discusses the use of inference rules in reasoning, focusing on classical first order logic. Section 2.2 discusses a version of temporal logic, useful in reasoning about events that change over time. Conclusions drawn previously may have to be withdrawn when new information arrives, an issue addressed by systems that attempt to conduct *non-monotonic reasoning* and *truth maintenance*, addressed in Section 2.3 and Section 2.4, respectively. Other practical reasoning systems attempt to construct models of an external entity, reasoning by evaluating hypotheses that can be made about such models, as discussed in Section 2.5.

2.1   Formal Inference

Many computational systems need to carry out formal or logical reasoning. This section discusses classical logic, in which *inference rules* are successively applied to prove results.

A formal system is described in terms of three components: syntax, inference rules, and semantics, described below in greater detail with particular focus on classical first order logic.

2.1.1   Syntax

Syntax describes what constitute acceptable sequences of vocabulary elements. In first order logic, syntactic rules define *well-formed formulas (wffs)*, using a vocabulary of symbols that denote *constants, variables, functions,* and *predicates.* Each function and predicate symbol is associated with a specific integer, its *arity,* that denotes the number of permitted arguments. A *term* is defined as a constant, variable, or function symbol followed by a parenthesized sequence of as many terms as its arity permits. An *atom* is a predicate symbol followed by as many parenthesized terms as permitted by its arity. Based on these definitions, a wff in first order logic is defined inductively as follows: [1]

- An atom is a wff.

- If ϕ is a wff, ψ is a wff, and x is a variable, then each of the following is a wff: (ϕ), $\neg\phi$, $\phi\&\psi$, $\phi \vee \psi$ (to be read "ϕ or ψ"), $\phi \supset \psi$, $\exists x.\phi$ (to be read "there exists x such that ϕ"), $\forall x.\phi$ (to be read "for all x, ϕ").

The last two formulas are said to be *existentially quantified* and *universally quantified*, respectively, and occurrences of the variable x in ϕ are said to be *bound* in these formulas. A variable that has an occurrence not bound in a formula is said to be *free*.

Some of the connectives may be defined using formulas invoking other connectives, so that discussion can be restricted to only one of '$\vee$', '$\supset$' and '$\&$', and only one of the quantifiers. For example, $\forall x.\phi$ may be considered an abbreviation for $\neg\exists x.\neg\phi$, and $\phi \vee \psi$ may be considered an abbreviation for $\neg\phi \supset \psi$ or $\neg(\neg\phi\&\neg\psi)$.

Example 2.1 If x, y are variables, a, b are constants, f is a function symbol of arity 2, g is a function symbol of arity 1, and P, Q are predicate symbols of arity 2 and 1 respectively, then $f(f(x, f(x, y)), g(g(b)))$ is a term, but not $f(x)$, nor $g(a, b)$, nor any sequence that contains $g(Q(a))$.

$$Q(x) \vee (\forall x \exists y.P(x, f(a, y))\&Q(a) \supset Q(b))\&Q(y)$$

is a well-formed formula. The occurrences of variables x and y in $P(x, f(a, y))$ are bound, whereas their occurrences in $Q(x)$ and $Q(y)$ are free.

2.1.2 Inference Rules

Inference rules describe what formulas may be derived from other formulas. Each inference rule consists of two parts, *lhs* (left-hand-side) and *rhs* (right-hand-side), separated by the '$\vdash$' symbol (read 'derives' or "leads to" or "infer" or "deduce"). The *lhs* is a set of formulas, containing symbols that can be matched against elements of formulas, and the *rhs* is another formula that may

---

[1] Some authors parenthesize many more elements of the above expressions; this book omits parentheses unless required for clarity. We also use the abbreviation that the scope of a variable preceding a period extends as far as permitted by the parenthesization. Some authors use *true* and *false* as special symbols within the language of predicate logic, but these can instead be defined using formulas such as $(p \supset p)$ and $(p\&\neg p)$.

also contain some of these symbols. If some subset of the current theorems successfully match with the *lhs* of the inference rule, then the rule can be 'applied' (executed) to generate a new theorem, the appropriate instance of the *rhs* of the rule.

Example 2.2 A classic example is the *modus ponens* inference rule:

$$\{A, A \supset B\} \vdash B$$

Here, the *lhs* is $\{A, A \supset B\}$ and the *rhs* is B.

The inference rule of *substitution* in propositional logic states that any formula ϕ may be substituted for all occurrences of a propositional symbol α, i.e.,

$$\{U\} \vdash S_\phi^\alpha U$$

where $S_\phi^\alpha U$ is the result of substituting ϕ for every occurrence of α in U.

First order logic allows *instantiation* of a universally quantified variable x by a term t:

$$\{\forall x.U\} \vdash S_t^x U.$$

In these rules, symbols such as 'A' are in the metalanguage used to describe the inference rules, treated as though they can be replaced by any appropriate symbol of the language in which the formulas are stated.

Example 2.3 Given:

- Socrates is a dead man, denoted "*Dead(Socrates)*," and

- Dead men are immortal, denoted "$\forall x.\ Dead(x) \supset Immortal(x)$,"

we may instantiate x by *Socrates* and apply modus ponens, deriving *Immortal(Socrates)*, i.e., Socrates is immortal.

Example 2.4 Given two formulas

$$P \supset \neg P$$

and

$$(Q \supset R) \supset (R \supset Q),$$

we may apply modus ponens to derive

$$\neg P \supset P$$

as well as to derive

$$\neg((Q \supset R) \supset (R \supset Q)).$$

Theorems are formulas derived by repeatedly applying inference rules to existing theorems. To begin with, the set of theorems consists of a set of *axioms*, formulas that do not require proof. In practical reasoning problems, we also make certain other problem-specific assumptions without proof, and these are referred to as *premises*.

All theorems in *propositional logic* (also known as *propositional calculus*) can be obtained using the inference rules of modus ponens and substitution, and the following three axioms:

- $(p \supset (q \supset r)) \supset ((p \supset q) \supset (p \supset r))$

- $p \supset (q \supset p)$

- $(\neg p \supset \neg q) \supset (q \supset p)$

If the above three axioms are treated as *axiom schema*, i.e., describing an infinite set of axioms obtained by replacing their symbols by any formulas, then modus ponens alone is sufficient, and the substitution inference rule can be omitted.

Proofs in first order logic are obtained by modus ponens and these three axiom schema, as well as the inference rule[2]

$$\phi \vdash (\forall x)\phi$$

and two more axiom schema:

- $((\forall x)\phi \supset \psi) \supset (\phi \supset (\forall x)\psi)$ where x is any variable not free in ϕ

- $((\forall x)\phi) \supset \psi$ where ψ results from substituting a variable y for all free occurrences of x in ϕ, and ϕ contains no free occurrence of x in a subformula "$(\forall y)\ldots$".

A basic instance of the last axiom schema is $(\forall x.P(x)) \supset P(y)$.

Classical logical systems are *monotonic*: the set of theorems cannot decrease, and can only grow. When an inference rule is applied, a new theorem may be added to the current set of theorems, but existing theorems cannot be withdrawn or removed.

2.1.3 Semantics

Semantics associates meanings with elements in a language such as first order logic. Meanings for larger formulas and terms are built up by composing the

---

[2] This inference rule should not be construed as $\vdash \phi \supset (\forall x)\phi$.

meanings of components. Formulas may be associated with the special meanings *true* or *false*, treating the logical connectives and quantifiers in the usual manner.

In propositional logic, an *interpretation* is an assignment of a truth value ('true' or 'false') to every propositional symbol. An interpretation I is extended to a truth assignment to formulas, using the following rules:[3]

- $\neg\phi$ is true in I if ϕ is false in I, and conversely.

- $\phi \supset \psi$ is true in I if ϕ is false in I or ψ is true in I.

The treatment of logical connectives is the same in first order logic, but the presence of terms, predicates and quantifiers makes the semantics a little more complex. In first order logic, an interpretation I over a nonempty set D assigns values to each constant, variable, function and predicate symbol:

- I assigns an element of D to each constant and variable.

- I assigns an n-ary function f_I over the domain elements to each function symbol f with arity n. If $t_1, \ldots, t_n$ are terms assigned by I to domain elements $d_1, \ldots, d_n$, then I assigns $f_I(d_1, \ldots, d_n)$ as the meaning of the term $f(t_1, \ldots, t_n)$.

- I assigns an n-ary relation P_I over the domain elements to each predicate symbol P with arity n. If $t_1, \ldots, t_n$ are terms assigned by I to domain elements $d_1, \ldots, d_n$, then I assigns $P_I(d_1, \ldots, d_n)$ as the meaning of the atom $P(t_1, \ldots, t_n)$. We say $P_I(d_1, \ldots, d_n)$ is *true* if the n-tuple $(d_1, \ldots, d_n)$ belongs to the relation P_I, and *false* otherwise.

- The formula $\forall x.\phi$ is true in I if ϕ is true in I for every possible domain element assignment of x.

- The formula $\exists x.\phi$ is true in I if ϕ is true in I for some possible domain element assignment of x.

The notation '$A \models B$' refers to the semantic notion that 'A logically implies B,' i.e., B must be true in every interpretation in which A is true. This should not be confused with '$A \vdash B$', i.e., we can derive B from the premise A (using the axioms and inference rules). Both '$A \models B$' and '$A \vdash B$' are statements in the metalanguage, talking about the logic, whereas '$A \supset B$' is a formula in the logic. We may write '$\models B$' to denote that B is true in every interpretation.

---

[3]We ignore the rules for '&' and '∨', since those connectives can be defined in terms of '$\neg$' and '$\supset$'.

A logic is *sound* if every provable theorem is true in every possible interpretation. A logic is *complete* if it is possible to prove every formula that is true in all interpretations. The great appeal of classical propositional and first order logics is that they are sound and complete. In other words, the axioms and inference rules are precisely those needed to prove all (and only) logically implied formulas.

Example 2.5 Defined below are inference rules for two new logics with the same syntax, axiom schema, and intended semantics as classical propositional logic, but without modus ponens.

Methanol Logic: $\{P\} \vdash (\neg\neg P)$
    This logic is incomplete.

Ethanol Logic: $\{P \supset Q\} \vdash P$
    This logic is unsound.

2.2 Temporal Logic

Reasoning about real world problems and the behavior of practical expert systems often requires explicit modeling of time, as shown in the following example.

Example 2.6 The following is a nonviolent version of the *Yale shooting problem* posed by Hanks and McDermott [11].

$$
\begin{array}{rcl}
\text{Gasoline tank is non-empty} & \Rightarrow & \text{Fred drives the car} \\
\text{Fred drives the car} & \Rightarrow & \text{Gasoline tank becomes empty} \\
\text{Gasoline tank is empty} & \Rightarrow & \text{Fred cannot drive the car}
\end{array}
$$

If taken as logical implications, one would conclude from these rules that the first rule can never fire, since it results in a contradiction; hence it can never be the case that the gasoline tank is non-empty, irrespective of how hard Fred tries to fill it up!

The anomaly in this example comes from the fact that the *lhs* and *rhs* of a rule may refer to different time instants, e.g., with the gasoline tank becoming empty *after* the car is driven. Explicit reasoning about time is necessary.

Temporal logic (a simple variation of modal logic) has been used for many years to model and prove properties of concurrent programs, communicating processes and communication protocols, e.g., [17]. It also holds promise as a useful framework for specifying and understanding rule-based expert systems. The elements of a simple propositional temporal logic are presented below; details and variations may be found in the literature, e.g., [21].

- If ϕ is a formula in propositional logic, then ϕ is also a formula in propositional temporal logic.

- If ϕ and ψ are formulas in propositional temporal logic, then each of the following is also a formula in propositional temporal logic:

  $\neg\phi$; $\phi\&\psi$; $\phi \supset \psi$; $\phi \vee \psi$;

  $\circ\phi$ (read "next ϕ");

  $\Diamond\phi$ (read "eventually ϕ"), sometimes written $M\phi$;

  $\Box\phi$ (read "henceforth ϕ"), sometimes written $L\phi$; and

  $\phi U\psi$ (read "ϕ until ψ"), not to be confused with set union.

  The intended semantics is that

- $\circ\phi$ is true if ϕ is true at the next instant (assuming that time is discrete);

- $\Diamond\phi$ is true if ϕ is true at present or at some instant in the future;

- $\Box\phi$ is true if ϕ is true at present and at every future instant; and

- $\phi U\psi$ is true if ϕ continues to be true (from the present) until the first instant at which ψ becomes true.

Formal semantics for temporal logic (and its close cousins, *modal logics*) is generally given in terms of Kripke's *possible worlds*. The notion of 'interpretation' from classical logic is extended, parameterized by identifying a 'world' (state) in which formulas may be true or false. Formally, a *structure* for a propositional temporal logic formula with a set P of atomic propositions is a triple $A = (S, N, \pi)$ where S is an enumerable set of states, $N : S \rightarrow S$ is an accessibility function that associates each state with a unique next state, and $\pi : S \rightarrow 2^P$ assigns truth values to propositions in each state. An intepretation is a combination of a structure and a state. For a structure $A = (S, N, \pi)$ and a state $s \in S$,

- $\langle A, s \rangle \models p$ iff $p \in \pi(s)$

- $\langle A, s \rangle \models \phi\&\psi$ iff$\langle A, s \rangle \models \phi$ and $\langle A, s \rangle \models \psi$

- $\langle A, s \rangle \models \neg\phi$ iff not $\langle A, s \rangle \models \phi$

- $\langle A, s \rangle \models \circ\phi$ iff $\langle A, N(s) \rangle \models \phi$

- $\langle A, s \rangle \models \Box\phi$ iff $\forall i \geq 0.\langle A, N^i(s) \rangle \models \phi$ where $N^i(s)$ is defined as the result of repeatedly applying the accessibility function i times to s.

- $\langle A, s \rangle \models \Diamond\phi$ iff $\exists i \geq 0.\langle A, N^i(s) \rangle \models \phi$

- $\langle A, s \rangle \models \phi U\psi$ iff $\langle A, s \rangle \models \Box\phi$ or $\exists i \geq 0.\langle A, N^i(s) \rangle \models \psi \& \forall j.(0 \leq j < i \supset \langle A, N^j(s) \rangle \models \phi)$

Example 2.7 Some $(n \geq 2)$ philosophers are dining at a round table with n chopsticks, each placed between two philosophers. However, each philosopher needs two chopsticks to eat, and may have to wait until his neighbors lay these down. All philosophers will go hungry if each picks up one chopstick and holds it while waiting for the other chopstick to become available. One solution to this synchronization problem is that each philosopher repeatedly picks up the chopstick on his right, then picks up the one on his left, eats a little, then puts down the one on his left, and finally puts down the one on his right. A temporal logic specification for the ith philosopher follows, assuming that the chopstick on his right is numbered i, and the chopstick on his left is numbered $i \oplus 1$ (i.e., $i + 1$ modulo n).

$$\Box(pick_i \supset \circ pick_{i \oplus 1})$$

$$\Box(pick_{i \oplus 1} \supset \circ put_{i \oplus 1})$$

$$\Box(put_{i \oplus 1} \supset \circ put_i)$$

$$\Box(put_i \supset \circ pick_i)$$

The sequence of actions for the synchronizer are specified as follows, expressing that a chopstick cannot be picked up at the same time by two philosophers:

$$\Box(P_{i \oplus 1}.pick_{i \oplus 1} \supset ((\neg P_i.pick_{i \oplus 1})U(P_{i \oplus 1}.put_{i \oplus 1}))),$$

and

$$\Box(P_{i \oplus 1}.pick_{i \oplus 1} \supset ((\neg P_{i \oplus 1}.pick_{i \oplus 1})U(P_i.put_{i \oplus 1}))),$$

where $P_j.pick_i$ denotes that the jth philosopher picks up the ith chopstick.

The above presentation assumes a *linear time* model, in which there is a single temporal sequence of states of the world, and $\Diamond\phi \equiv \neg\Box\neg\phi$. Such an equivalence does not hold in *branching time* models, with many possible alternative futures: $\Diamond \phi$ is true if ϕ is true now or must eventually become true in every possible alternative future.

Time may instead be modeled using first order logic with an explicit variable representing time, included as an extra argument with every proposition or predicate, expressing the equivalent of $\Diamond P$ by the formula $\exists t.(t \geq t_0)\&P(t)$, where t_0 is a special constant that denotes the current time. In the process, however, we have moved up from simple propositional logic to first order predicate logic with arithmetic constraints, making it harder to reason about such formulas; propositional temporal logic is less expressive, but easier to work with, when compared to full first order logic.

2.3   Non-Monotonic Reasoning

Classical logic and traditional reasoning systems are 'monotonic' in that the collection of *theorems* (results that are proved) steadily grows as reasoning proceeds, and never shrinks. By contrast, *Non-monotonic reasoning(NMR)* refers to reasoning processes in which the collection of results that have been inferred may grow as well as shrink[4]. In other words, a conclusion drawn at an earlier stage of reasoning may have to be withdrawn, as a result of arrival of new information, so that the set of proved results may shrink with time. A few examples of non-monotonic inference are given below, to illustrate various ways in which this may occur.

Example 2.8 When asked if he has a brother named Jack Niklaus Einstein, the interviewee (Albert) immediately responds "No." This answer is based on *autoepistemic reasoning*: it is presumed that a person knows all about his own family, even though that might not always be the case.

However, the answer would change to "Yes" if Albert's parents were to come forward and inform Albert that they do indeed have another son named Jack Niklaus Einstein about whom Albert had never known before, because they had given up Jack for adoption many years ago.

Even this may not be final: DNA analysis may reveal that Albert was not really the biological child of those he had believed to be his parents. whereupon the answer would again change to "No."

Example 2.9 Most people would hesitate to say "Yes" or "No" when asked whether there is yogurt in a refrigerator that they had not examined before.

---

[4]The phrase Non-monotonic reasoning is used here in a general sense, not to describe a specific system or approach.

But when asked whether there is a cat in the refrigerator, most people would say "No," even though they do not claim to have knowledge about the contents of the refrigerator. This is based on general assumptions about the world, e.g., cats are generally not found in refrigerators. Of course, this assumption may have to be withdrawn when the contents of a specific refrigerator are actually examined.

An even more emphatic "No" may be given as response to the question of whether there is a live cat in the refrigerator, because of the reasonable assumption that any cat in the refrigerator is probably in cat-heaven.

Example 2.10 When asked for information about what time it is, a person may answer "eleven-o-clock" based on cursory examination of a clock or watch. This is a case where the matter is not considered important enough to allocate much effort to determining the correct time, or where giving a quick answer is considered more important than giving an answer that is known to be correct with greater confidence. The answer may be withdrawn if closer observation reveals that the clock had stopped, or a lunch gong strikes (indicating that it is noon), or if the person realizes that he had not reset his watch after flying across an ocean.

Many of these examples of non-monotonic reasoning are characterized by the need to make *defeasible assumptions* in the reasoning process, i.e., assumptions that may have to be withdrawn in the future, even though they appear reasonable until the need to withdraw them. But not all assumptions and conclusions are defeasible in a non-monotonic reasoning system, hence the need to identify clearly the possible sources of non-monotonicity.

Several approaches have been proposed to allow automated reasoning systems to perform non-monotonic reasoning, briefly outlined below; details are omitted in the interest of brevity, and there are similarities in the operational treatment as well as semantics, for many of the following.

Closed-World Assumption[19]: Anything that cannot be derived from the given premises is presumed to be false.

Negation as Failure[4]: General Prolog programs allow non-Horn clauses, e.g., $P : -\neg Q$ (i.e., $\neg Q \supset P$); in executing such a clause, $\neg Q$ is presumed to hold if Q is neither a fact, nor can Q be deduced (by subgoaling or backward chaining). One approach to obtain a clean semantics has been to *stratify* a Prolog program [1] i.e., structure it as a collection of layers so that reasoning with the negated atoms (Q above) is clearly separated from reasoning with such a rule.

Autoepistemic Reasoning[16]:   Anything that does not follow from the beliefs of an ideally rational agent (reflecting on its beliefs) is believed to be false.

Circumscription[15]:   It is assumed that the only objects that satisfy a property P are those that can be shown to satisfy P, by reasoning from the available set of premises. Inferences are carried out by applying the above principle using 'abnormality' as the predicate P; unless an entity (or collection of attributes) can be proved to be abnormal, we assume that it is not abnormal, allowing reasoning to proceed without worrying about various hypothetical situations that may prevent such reasoning.

Default Logic[20]:   Inference rules are qualified with the statement of assumptions under which such rules can be applied; rule application is prevented when these assumptions are violated. We may hold beliefs as reasoned assumptions, because we have no evidence against them. The conclusion may be retracted if the necessary antecedent is shown to be false. In the conventional notation, upper-case letters denote assumed propositions, and 'MX' (read 'consistent X') roughly denotes 'there is no inconsistency in assuming X'. The expression $\frac{S:MY}{Y}$ denotes that we can infer Y from the set of propositions S, if it is consistent to assume Y. For example, an inference rule

> if x is a bird AND it is consistent to believe that x can fly, then conclude that x can fly,

may be represented as

$$\frac{\{Bird(x)\} : M\ Canfly(x)}{Canfly(x)}.$$

Non-monotonicity and defeasibility of rules and conclusions are of practical importance, not mere toys used by theorists to amuse themselves, as illustrated by the following 'practical' example.

Example 2.11 A travel advisory system contains the following rule (written in CLIPS-like notation[5]), intended to be triggered when a traveler is hoping to travel from source city $?S$ to destination city $?D$ budgeting less than $?B$ dollars for the trip.

$$((Source\ ?S)\& \qquad (Destination\ ?D)\&(Budget\ ?B)$$
$$\& \qquad not\ (flight\ ?S\ ?D\ ?\ ?c_0\& : (?c_0 <?B))$$
$$\& \qquad (flight\ ?S\ ?I\ ?f_1\ ?c_1\& : (?c_1 <?B))$$
$$\& \qquad (flight\ ?I\ ?D\ ?f_2\ ?c_2\& : (?c_2 < (?B-?c_1)))$$
$$\Rightarrow \quad (assert(found\_routing\_thru\ ?I\ ?f_1\ ?f_2\ (+\ c_1\ c_2))))$$

Using this rule involves defeasible reasoning, making the assumption that there is no direct flight that meets the budget limitation specified by the traveler. Many kinds of new information can become available, invalidating the conclusion drawn using the above rule, e.g., new flights may be added, old flights removed, and ticket costs may change significantly from day to day. This necessitates non-monotonic reasoning.

The next section describes the implementation of 'Truth Maintenance Systems' that keep track of assumptions made during non-monotonic reasoning, avoiding most of the details found in the technical literature.

2.4 Truth Maintenance

Practical implementations of non-monotonic reasoning must address difficulties not encountered in traditional reasoning. The most important of these is the need to keep track of which assumptions were made to draw which conclusions, possibly *via* long chains of reasoning. When new information becomes available, the system must draw new conclusions and must also examine (and possibly retract) the conclusions drawn earlier, especially if inconsistencies are detected. Systems that implement these mechanisms are known as *Truth Maintenance Systems (TMSs)*. The phrase 'truth maintenance' originates from the detection of inconsistencies followed by changes made to avoid inconsistency; the tasks

---

[5]Data for each flight is assumed to be stored as a fact indicating the source, destination, flight number (e.g., f_1), and ticket cost (e.g., c_0). Variables are prefixed by a question-mark, and '?' by itself matches with any value. Constraints can be specified within a pattern, e.g., $not\ (flight\ ?S\ ?D\ ?\ ?c_0\& : (?c_0 <?B))$ is satisfied if there is no flight from $?S$ to $?D$ with ticket cost $?c_0$ such that $?c_0 <?B$, i.e., if every direct flight from $?S$ to $?D$ exceeds the budget.

accomplished by a truth maintenance system have also been described as *be-lief/reason/opinion maintenance*. The inference process (*problem solver*) can generally be separated from the truth maintenance task, which mainly concerns representing and reasoning about the dependencies between propositions, as well as detecting inconsistency. Truth maintenance systems contain an acyclic *dependency network* that records dependencies among propositions (and design decisions). Truth maintenance systems may also cache inferences made by a problem-solver, and conduct *hypothetical* reasoning.

There are two main flavors of truth maintenance systems that have been developed so far: . Doyle's Truth Maintenance System(TMS) [7] and de Kleer's *Assumption-Based TMS (ATMS)* [6].

Doyle's TMS represents one possible collection of beliefs at a time based on one possible collection of assumptions that may be made (the *environment* or *context*). The TMS keeps track of which assumptions are "in" (accepted) and which are "out" (denied). The problem solver repeatedly applies the inference rules based on the current set of assumptions. If and when the truth main-tenance system discovers an inconsistency (contradiction), the current set of assumptions is modified using a dependency-directed backtracking search pro-cedure. This search procedure modifies the most recent relevant assumption (or hypothesis, or decision) invoked in reaching the failure, where relevance is in terms of the dependency relationships stored in the truth maintenance system. This process, trying to modify another assumption, is attempted in a system-atic manner, searching through the space of collections of assumptions, until a state with no inconsistency is reached. If new facts become available to the system, new inconsistencies may be detected, so that the dependency-directed backtracking process has to be repeated. The search process involves extensive computations if such changes occur frequently, e.g., repeatedly introducing and withdrawing an important fact.

Instead of working with a single context at a time, de Kleer's ATMS main-tains many different contexts, each characterized by a set of assumptions. For each proposition, the ATMS constructs a list of interesting contexts in which the node is true, where each context makes minimal assumptions. Each such context must describe a consistent set of assumptions; background knowledge may rule out certain contexts as impossible. No backtracking is needed, since all that may change are the context lists associated with propositions.

Example 2.12 Let a system contain the formulas

$$A \supset b, \quad C \supset d, \quad A\&C \supset e$$

and the default rules
$$\frac{: MA}{A}, \quad \frac{: MC}{C}.$$

It is consistent to assume A as well as C, hence the corresponding theory (the set of propositions that are consequences of these formulas and defaults) is $\{A, b, C, d, e\}$.

If a new premise, $b \& d \supset false$, is introduced into the system (where $false$ denotes a contradiction), then it is no longer consistent to assume A as well as C.

- Doyle's TMS would then perform dependency-directed backtracking, resulting in the choice of one of the alternative assumptions, say A. If new formulas such as $b \supset g$, $g \& A \supset false$ are then introduced, the current alternative (assumption of A) becomes inconsistent, and the search for a new reasonable set of assumptions is launched again, resulting in changing the current context from the assumption of A to the assumption of C.

- De Kleer's ATMS would instead associate different propositions with the consistent contexts in which they hold:

  - b holds in the context $\{A\}$ (i.e., there is only one minimal set of assumptions under which b holds, the singleton set containing A),

  - d holds in the context $\{C\}$, and

  - e initially holds in the context $\{A, C\}$, but this context disappears when $b \& d \supset false$ is introduced into the system, i.e., e cannot hold in any context.

  If new formulas such as $b \supset g$, $g \& A \supset false$ are then introduced, the context for b disappears (i.e., b no longer holds in any context), but there is no further change to the contexts within which d and e hold.

Truth maintenance systems have been applied to diagnosis problems. We may assume that a certain fault has occurred, and make predictions on this basis, to see if the predictions are backed up by evidence. This method is also useful when the system's task is to generate a configuration that satisfies some criteria.

2.5 Model Based Reasoning

One important reason why humans successfully understand and solve problems is that instead of attempting general-purpose problem-solving, they restrict attention to the domain and construct a model of the domain. Working with a model allows questions and issues to be phrased precisely, and reasoning can be carried out in a systematic manner. Model Based Reasoning systems attempt this task, representing and reasoning with a model of a physical system, mainly for fault diagnosis tasks. The main advantages of MBR are that it can reduce knowledge acquisition effort, and does not require explicit prior listings of everything that might go wrong with a system. Its disadvantages are that this methodology cannot easily manipulate heuristic knowledge nor uncertainty, and the reasoning process becomes difficult when more than one fault may occur at the same time in a system. Also, models or measurements may not be available for some problems.

In the rest of this section, we examine a Model based reasoning system for diagnostic reasoning developed at NASA Kennedy Space Center, called *KATE* (Knowledge-based Autonomous Test Engineer) [22]. KATE analyzes the connectivity and functionality of components in a system, continuously comparing sensor readings to values computed using the model. The model of the system is used to compute each component's *hypothetical value (hv)*, describing its state as implied by available observations. This is computed by inverting the functional representations of the components, and propagating values through the system.

The fault detection process is initiated by KATE when the first ("original") discrepancy (OD) is detected by a sensor. KATE then repeatedly examines various hypotheses regarding one or more failures in various components of the system, to obtain a reasonable explanation of why the OD as well as other detectable errors occur in the system's behavior. Components capable of causing the OD are called "suspects." Initial suspects are the OD sensor and all components structurally preceding it, i.e., those whose malfunctioning may have led to the error detected by the OD sensor.

KATE's diagnoser identifies all the inputs, suspects and *siblings* (other sensors that depend on the same inputs) of the OD sensor, and computes the hypothetical value of each suspect component. Diagnosis involves repeatedly exonerating various suspect components until a small number remain as possible culprits. A suspect X is exonerated if:

1. X controls OD only through components known to be innocent.

2. No hypothetical value for X can be established, because the functional dependency of the OD cannot be inverted.

3. X's hypothetical value agrees with its expected value.

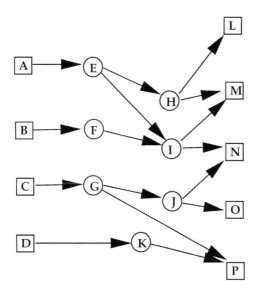

Figure 2.1: Model of a system diagnosed by KATE

4. Assuming X has its hypothetical value causes inconsistency with some sensor values.

For final suspects, hypothetical values should match with actual readings.

Sometimes, "pseudo-objects" are created to bundle some components together or to reason with nonlocal objects (e.g., electric current) or abstractions.

Example 2.13 In the system modeled by Figure 2.1, assume that component N is the OD, and that another discrepancy occurs at component O. Its ancestors (suspects) are E,F,G,I,J.

These are considered by examining sensor values for L,M,O,P.

- I is first exonerated because it doesn't explain the discrepancy at O.

- G is exonerated because P has no discrepancy.

- E and F are exonerated because L and M show no discrepancy.

- J is the last remaining suspect. Hang J.

2.6 Bibliographic Notes

Logic provides the foundations of computer science and artificial intelligence, hence a brief historical note is appropriate. Boole [2] was perhaps the earliest

writer to develop formal mathematical descriptions that can be construed as
rules, in 1854. The first systematic formulation of propositional calculus as
well as the use of quantifiers was by Gottlob Frege in 1879 [9]. Most current
formulations follow the accessible treatment by Russell [23]. Consistency of the
propositional calculus was proved by Post in 1917, and completeness was proved
by Quine in 1938 [18]. An explicit formulation of first order logic was first given
by Hilbert and Ackermann in 1928 [12]. My favorite reference is a little book by
Alonzo Church [3], although there are many more modern and recommendable
presentations, such as the books by Manna and Waldinger [14], and Enderton
[8].

The book by Rescher and Urquhart [21] provides a clear description of
temporal logic. The collection of papers edited by Ginsberg [10] includes many of
the early seminal papers on non-monotonic reasoning, the core of commonsense
reasoning. Model-based reasoning for diagnostic problems is discussed in detail
by Davis [5]. There has also been an attempt to capture commonsense reasoning
by building a large system that includes vast quantities of *general knowledge* [13],
although this approach appears to have had limited success.

Bibliography

[1] K. Apt, H. Blair, and A. Walker, "Towards a theory of declarative knowledge," in *Proc. 1986 Workshop on Foundations of Deductive Databases and Logic Programming*, 1986.

[2] G. Boole, *An Investigation into the Laws of Thought, on Which Are Founded the Mathematical Theories of Logic and Probabilities*, 1854.

[3] A. Church, *Introduction to Mathematical Logic, Part I, (Annals of Mathematics Studies, No. 13)*, Princeton University Press, 1944 (reprinted by Kraus Reprint Corporation, New York, 1965).

[4] K.L. Clark, "Negation as Failure," in H. Gallaire and J. Minker (Eds.), *Logic and Data Bases*, Plenum, New York, 1978, pp.293-322.

[5] R. Davis, "Diagnostic Reasoning Based on Structure and Behavior," *Artificial Intelligence*, 1984, 24(1-3):347-410.

[6] J. de Kleer, "An assumption-based TMS," *Artificial Intelligence*, 1986, 28:127-162.

[7] J. Doyle, "A truth maintenance system," *Artificial Intelligence*, 1979, 12:231-272.

[8] H.B. Enderton, *A Mathematical Introduction to Logic*, Academic Press, New York, 1972.

[9] G. Frege, *Begriffsschrift*, 1879.

[10] M.L. Ginsberg (Ed.), *Readings in Nonmonotonic Reasoning*, Morgan Kaufmann, 1987.

[11] S. Hanks and D. McDermott, "Default Reasoning, Nonmonotonic Logics, and the Frame Problem," in *Proc. AAAI Conf.*, 1986, pp.328-333.

[12] D. Hilbert and Ackermann, *Grundzuge der theoretischen Logik*, 1928.

[13] D.B. Lenat, R.V. Guha, K. Pittman, D. Pratt, and M. Shepherd, "CYC: Toward Programs with Common Sense," *Communications of the ACM*, Aug. 1990, 33(8):30-49.

[14] Z. Manna and R. Waldinger, *The Deductive Foundations of Computer Programming*, Addison-Wesley, 1993.

[15] J. McCarthy, "Circumscription – a form of non-monotonic reasoning," *Artificial Intelligence*, 1980, 13:27-39.

[16] R.C. Moore, "Possible worlds semantics for autoepistemic logic," in *Proc. AAAI Non-Monotonic Reasoning Workshop*, 1984, pp.344-354.

[17] A. Pnueli, "The Temporal Logic of Programs," in *Proc. 18th Symp. on the Foundations of Computer Science*, IEEE, Nov. 1977.

[18] W.V. Quine, "Completeness of the Propositional Calculus," *J. Symbolic Logic*, 1938

[19] R. Reiter, "On closed world data bases," in H. Gallaire and J. Minker (Eds.), *Logic and Data Bases*, Plenum, New York, 1978, pp.119-140.

[20] R. Reiter, "A logic for default reasoning," *Artificial Intelligence*, 1980, 13:81-132.

[21] N. Rescher and A. Urquhart, Temporal Logic, Springer-Verlag, New York, 1971.

[22] E.A. Scarl, J.R. Jamieson, and C.I.Delaune, "Diagnosis and Sensor Validation through Knowledge of Structure and Function," *IEEE Trans. on Systems, Man and Cybernetics*, 1987, SMC-17(3):360-368.

[23] A.N. Whitehead and B. Russell, *Principia Mathematica*, 3 vols, Cambridge: At the University Press, 1910-1913.

2.7 Exercises

1. Derive the following formulas in propositional logic:

   (a) $p \supset (p \supset p)$
   (b) $p \supset ((q \supset p) \supset (q \supset p))$
   (c) $(p \supset (q \supset r)) \supset ((p \& q) \supset r)$

2. Prove the soundness (or unsoundness) and completeness (or incompleteness) of Ethanol Logic and Methanol Logic (from Example 2.5).

3. Express using propositional temporal logic the following natural language sentences, where possible.

   (a) Rule R will be fired infinitely often in the future.
   (b) Whenever rule R_1 is fired, it will lead eventually to R_2 being fired again.
   (c) Every firing of R_1 is eventually followed by R_2, and vice versa.
   (d) Every rule in a set S will be fired eventually.
   (e) Rule R_1 can never be fired after rule R_2 is fired.

4. Discuss whether the solution to the dining philosophers problem can be modified to allow each philosopher (in the eating phase) to put down either chopstick first.

5. The *Nixon diamond* problem consists of reasoning whether Nixon is a pacifist, given the following assertions:

   Nixon is a Quaker.
   Nixon is a Republican.
   Quakers are pacifists.
   Republicans are not pacifists.

   Can this problem be cast into any of the non-monotonic reasoning frameworks discussed in this chapter?

6. What kind of non-monotonic reasoning would be most appropriate for the air travel scheduling problem in Example 2.11?

7. Carry out the computations an ATMS would perform, given the formulas

$$A \supset B, \quad C \supset d, \quad A \& C \supset e, B \& A \supset false$$

and the default rules

$$\frac{:MA}{A}, \quad \frac{:MB}{B} \quad \frac{:MC}{C}.$$

8. How would model-based reasoning be carried out for the system modeled by Figure 2.1, if component O is the OD, and another discrepancy occurs at P?

9. How may KATE be extended to deal with multiple faults in a system?

Chapter 3

Uncertainty

Knowledge is the knowing that we cannot know.
_____ Ralph Waldo Emerson (1850)

Every day of our lives, we make decisions based on rough calculations of the chances that certain events will occur. Examples include estimating the chances that:

- a bus will arrive in the next five minutes;

- there will be a traffic jam on the way to the airport;

- a homework assignment will require x hours of work.

Sometimes, we dismiss events as "improbable" or unlikely enough so that one can ignore the chance of their occurrence, even though these events are not impossible. For instance, there is a chance that a meteorite may strike one's head — however, most people consider the event improbable enough that they take unnecessary risk, not wearing a helmet for protection when walking in the street.

The next section contains a general overview of probability, including the basic axioms and odds. Section 3.2 discusses likelihood ratios, and Section 3.3 presents their use in probabilistic inference networks. Section 3.4 addresses the use of interpolation techniques to compute posterior probabilities in the absence of complete conditional probability information. Methods of combining uncertain evidence are discussed in Section 3.5. Section 3.6 extends this approach to problems where some logical relationships between hypotheses are known. Section 3.7 presents the tricky problems of circular reasoning that can arise with arbitrarily structured probabilistic networks. Section 3.8 presents a well-founded methodology that permits reasoning with a subclass of probabilistic networks. Section 3.9 covers expected-value decision-making, and the utility theory approach to reasoning with subjective preferences. Section 3.10 presents the Dempster-Shafer approach that can be used to express notions of ignorance. Fuzzy systems are briefly discussed in Section 3.11. Section 3.12 presents the popular but much-criticized technique of certainty factors.

3.1   Probability

"Probability" (denoted $\mathcal{P}(\cdot)$) captures notions of uncertainty using numerical measures constrained to lie between 0 and 1, interpreted to mean that $\mathcal{P}(E_1) > \mathcal{P}(E_2)$ when the chances of occurrence are greater for event E_1 than for E_2. Probability is defined to satisfy the following three intuitively reasonable axioms:

1. If an event E cannot occur, then $\mathcal{P}(E) = 0$, i.e., its probability of occurrence is 0.

2. If an event E is certain to occur, then $\mathcal{P}(E) = 1$, i.e., its probability of occurrence is 1.

3. If constituent events E_1 and E_2 are disjoint or *mutually exclusive* (cannot occur simultaneously), then

$$\mathcal{P}(E_1 \cup E_2) = \mathcal{P}(E_1) + \mathcal{P}(E_2), \qquad (3.1)$$

   i.e., probabilities can be summed.

In the notation[1] that we use, $\mathcal{P}(E_1 \cap E_2)$ denotes the probability of the intersection (or conjunction) of E_1 and E_2. Similarly, $\mathcal{P}(E_1 \cup E_2)$ denotes the probability of the union (or disjunction) of E_1 with E_2. We also use $\mathcal{P}(E_1 - E_2)$ to denote the probability that E_1 occurs but not E_2. The use of set-theoretic notation should suggest that a number of simple probability results can be clarified using Venn diagrams.

We are often interested in the probability of an event *given* (assuming) that another event occurs.

Example 3.1 The probability we associate with the delay of an airplane's arrival may be 0.3, but knowing that a snowstorm lies in the path of the airplane may increase the probability to 0.9.

---

[1]The usage $\mathcal{P}(E_1 \& E_2)$ and $\mathcal{P}(E_1, \; E_2)$ instead of $\mathcal{P}(E_1 \cap E_2)$, and $\mathcal{P}(E_1 \vee E_2)$ instead of $\mathcal{P}(E_1 \cup E_2)$, can also be found in the literature.

1. The first quantity is the unconditional probability of the event, also called the *prior probability*, e.g., $P(\text{arrival\_delay}) = 0.3$.

2. The second quantity is the *conditional probability* of the delay *given* the snowstorm information, written $P(\text{arrival\_delay} \mid \text{snowstorm\_in\_path}) = 0.9$.

In general, we write $P(E_2|E_1)$ to denote the probability of the occurrence of E_2 *given* that E_1 is true, often defined using the equation

$$P(E_1 \cap E_2) = P(E_1)P(E_2|E_1). \tag{3.2}$$

In other words, the probability that both of two events occur is obtained by multiplying the prior probability of the first event and the conditional probability of the second, given the first. Note that $P(E_2|E_1)$ is undefined if $P(E_1) = 0$. Once the events denoted after the '|' symbol are known to occur, the conditional probability is the quantity used in subsequent computations, called the *posterior probability* (or *belief*) in the context of the presently available 'evidence'.

Two events E_1, E_2 are said to be *independent* if $P(E_2|E_1) = P(E_2)$, implying that $P(E_1 \cap E_2) = P(E_1)P(E_2)$.

These few simple axioms, definitions and constraints imply the following results.

Complements:

$$P(E \cup \neg E) = P(E) + P(\neg E) = 1,$$

since $E \cup \neg E$ is always true, and since E is disjoint from $\neg E$. Hence $P(\neg E) = 1 - P(E)$.

Disjunction : Equation 3.1 holds only when events are disjoint. The following derivation holds in the general case:

$$\begin{aligned} P(E_1 \cup E_2) &= P(E_1) + P(E_2 - E_1) \\ &= P(E_1) + (P(E_2 - E_1) + P(E_2 \cap E_1)) - P(E_2 \cap E_1) \end{aligned}$$

Since $(E_2 \cap E_1) = (E_1 \cap E_2)$, and E_2 is the union of the disjoint sets $(E_2 - E_1)$ and $(E_2 \cap E_1)$, we conclude:

$$P(E_1 \cup E_2) = P(E_1) + P(E_2) - P(E_1 \cap E_2) \tag{3.3}$$

Calculating Conditional Probabilities:

$$P(E_1)P(E_2|E_1) = P(E_1 \cap E_2) = P(E_2 \cap E_1) = P(E_2)P(E_1|E2),$$

indicating that one conditional probability can be computed from another as follows:

$$P(E_2|E_1) = \frac{P(E_1|E_2)P(E_2)}{P(E_1)} \tag{3.4}$$

Bayes Theorem (also known as *Bayes Law* or *Bayes Rule*): If $E_1, E_2, \ldots, E_n$ are mutually exclusive events of which one must occur, then

$$P(E_i|H) = \frac{P(E_i)P(H|E_i)}{\sum_{j=1}^{n} P(E_j)P(H|E_j)}$$

for each $i \in \{1, 2, \ldots, n\}$.

Multiple Conditionals:

$$P(E_1|E_2 \cap E_3) = \frac{P(E_1 \cap E_2 \cap E_3)}{P(E_2 \cap E_3)}$$
$$= \frac{P(E_1 \cap E_2|E_3)P(E_3)}{P(E_2|E_3)P(E_3)}$$

It follows that

$$P(E_1|E_2 \cap E_3) = \frac{P(E_1 \cap E_2|E_3)}{P(E_2|E_3)}, \tag{3.5}$$

In other words, given E_3, the conditional probabilities of E_1 and E_2 can be manipulated using Equation 3.4.

It is often easier to quantify chance using *odds* (denoted $\mathcal{O}(\cdot)$), defined as the ratio of the probabilities of an event and its negation:

$$\mathcal{O}(E) = \frac{P(E)}{P(\neg E)} = \frac{P(E)}{1 - P(E)}. \tag{3.6}$$

Similarly, the *conditional odds* of H given E are defined as

$$\mathcal{O}(H|E) = \frac{P(H|E)}{P(\neg H|E)} = \frac{P(H|E)}{1 - P(H|E)}. \tag{3.7}$$

Note that the odds of an event are not constrained to lie between 0 and 1.

Example 3.2 If the probability that *QuickSilver* will win a horse race is 0.6, then the odds of the same event are $0.6/(1 - 0.6) = 1.5$, or "3 to 2."

Conversely, probabilities can be calculated from odds: from Equation 3.6,

$$P(E) = \frac{\mathcal{O}(E)}{1 + \mathcal{O}(E)}. \tag{3.8}$$

When probabilities or odds are expressed as ratios of integers, conversions from one to the other are more easily performed as follows:

$$\text{if } \mathcal{O}(E) = a/b, \quad \text{then } \mathcal{P}(E) = a/(a+b);$$
$$\text{and if } \mathcal{P}(E) = c/d, \quad \text{then } \mathcal{O}(E) = c/(d-c).$$

In the context of expert systems, conditional dependencies between events are often represented using *likelihood ratios* indicating the extent to which the odds of a hypothesis are affected by some evidence. The next section defines these ratios and discusses how they constrain each other.

3.2 Likelihoods of Sufficiency and Necessity

A frequently used model in expert systems is that of evidence that accumulates over time, leading to successive updates in the degree of a posteriori belief associated with a hypothesis. Thus, the main question posed is the degree to which the odds of a hypothesis increase (or decrease) as a result of new evidence becoming available. The relevant information is embedded in the the two *likelihood ratios* defined below:

- The *Likelihood of Sufficiency* of H with respect to E, denoted $\mathcal{L}_S(H, E)$, is the factor by which E increases the odds of H, i.e.,

$$\mathcal{L}_S(H, E) = \frac{\mathcal{O}(H|E)}{\mathcal{O}(H)}, \tag{3.9}$$

  assuming $\mathcal{O}(H) \neq 0$. In the literature, $\mathcal{L}_S$ is often denoted by λ or LS.

  The larger the likelihood of sufficiency, the greater the influence of E in increasing the odds of H. Three cases can be examined:

  1. In the extreme case, if E is "sufficient" for H, then $\mathcal{P}(H|E) = 1$, so that $\mathcal{O}(H|E) = \infty$; if H was itself not certain, i.e., if $\mathcal{O}(H) \neq \infty$, then it must be the case that $\mathcal{L}_S(H, E) = \infty$.

  2. In the other extreme, if presence of E makes the odds of H vanishingly small, then $\mathcal{L}_S(H, E) = 0$.

  3. On the other hand, if E is irrelevant for H, then $\mathcal{O}(H|E) = \mathcal{O}(H)$, and $\mathcal{L}_S(H, E) = 1$.

  The likelihood of sufficiency can be expressed directly using probabilities, instead of odds:

$$\mathcal{L}_S(H, E) = \frac{\mathcal{O}(H|E)}{\mathcal{O}(H)} = \frac{\mathcal{P}(H|E)\mathcal{P}(\neg H)}{\mathcal{P}(\neg H|E)\mathcal{P}(H)} = \frac{\mathcal{P}(H|E)/\mathcal{P}(H)}{\mathcal{P}(\neg H|E)/\mathcal{P}(\neg H)}$$

Hence, invoking Bayes law and canceling out common factors,

$$\mathcal{L}_S(H, E) \;=\; \frac{\mathcal{P}(E|H)}{\mathcal{P}(E|\neg H)}. \tag{3.10}$$

Indeed, Equation 3.10 is the relation traditionally used to define the likelihood of sufficiency, following [4].

- The *Likelihood of Necessity* of H with respect to E, denoted $\mathcal{L}_\mathcal{N}(H, E)$, is the same as the likelihood of sufficiency of H with respect to $\neg E$, i.e., the factor by which $\neg E$ increases the odds of H, i.e.,

$$\mathcal{L}_\mathcal{N}(H, E) = \mathcal{L}_S(H, \neg E) = \frac{\mathcal{O}(H|\neg E)}{\mathcal{O}(H)}, \tag{3.11}$$

assuming $\mathcal{O}(H) \neq 0$. Using Equation 3.10,

$$\mathcal{L}_\mathcal{N}(H, E) \;=\; \mathcal{L}_S(H, \neg E) \;=\; \frac{\mathcal{P}(\neg E|H)}{\mathcal{P}(\neg E|\neg H)}. \tag{3.12}$$

In the literature, $\mathcal{L}_\mathcal{N}$ is often denoted by λ' or LN.

$\mathcal{L}_\mathcal{N}(H, E)$ captures the degree to which absence of evidence E influences the odds on the hypothesis H. Once again, we examine three important cases:

1. If E is "necessary" for H, then $\mathcal{O}(H|\neg E) = \mathcal{P}(H|\neg E) = 0$. If H was itself not false to begin with, i.e, if $\mathcal{O}(H) \neq 0$, then this case corresponds to requiring that $\mathcal{L}_\mathcal{N}(H, E) = 0$.

2. In the other extreme, if absence of E makes H certain, then $\mathcal{O}(H|\neg E) = \infty$ and $\mathcal{L}_\mathcal{N}(H, E) = \infty$, assuming that H was not certain *a priori*, i.e., assuming $\mathcal{P}(H) \neq 1$.

3. On the other hand, if the odds of H are unaffected by the absence of E, then $\mathcal{O}(H|\neg E) = \mathcal{O}(H)$, and $\mathcal{L}_\mathcal{N}(H, E) = 1$.

To what extent do $\mathcal{L}_S(H, E)$ and $\mathcal{L}_\mathcal{N}(H, E)$ determine each other? To answer this question, observe that

$$\mathcal{P}(H) = \mathcal{P}(H \cap E) + \mathcal{P}(H \cap \neg E) = \mathcal{P}(H|E)\mathcal{P}(E) + \mathcal{P}(H|\neg E)\mathcal{P}(\neg E). \tag{3.13}$$

If $\mathcal{L}_S(H, E) = 1$, then $\mathcal{P}(H|E) = \mathcal{P}(H)$, hence Equation 3.13 can be written as

$$\mathcal{P}(H) = \mathcal{P}(H)\mathcal{P}(E) + \mathcal{P}(H|\neg E)\mathcal{P}(\neg E),$$

from which we conclude

$$\mathcal{P}(H|\neg E) = \mathcal{P}(H)(1 - \mathcal{P}(E))/\mathcal{P}(\neg E) = \mathcal{P}(H),$$

so that $\mathcal{O}(H|\neg E) = \mathcal{O}(H)$ and $\mathcal{L}_\mathcal{N}(H, E) = 1$. We leave the other cases as exercises (cf. Exercise 1).

Thus, presence or absence of any evidence E will affect the odds of a hypothesis in different ways: either

$$\mathcal{O}(H|\neg E) = \mathcal{O}(H) = \mathcal{O}(H|E)$$

or

$$\mathcal{O}(H|\neg E) > \mathcal{O}(H) > \mathcal{O}(H|E)$$

or

$$\mathcal{O}(H|\neg E) < \mathcal{O}(H) < \mathcal{O}(H|E).$$

The likelihood coefficients are related to each other *via* the conditional probabilities. For example, from Equations 3.10 and 3.12, it follows that

$$\mathcal{L}_\mathcal{N}(H, E) = \frac{1 - \mathcal{L}_\mathcal{S}(H, E)\mathcal{P}(E|\neg H)}{1 - \mathcal{P}(E|\neg H)}. \tag{3.14}$$

Constraints such as Equation 3.14 should be checked as part of the process of verifying the internal consistency of an expert system based on probabilistic inference networks that rely on the use of these likelihood coefficients.

Example 3.3 We examine the consistency of the following set of values:

$$\mathcal{L}_\mathcal{S}(H, E) = 2, \quad \mathcal{L}_\mathcal{N}(H, E) = 0.01, \quad \mathcal{P}(H) = 0.1, \quad \text{and} \quad \mathcal{P}(E) = 0.2.$$

The odds are given by

$$\mathcal{O}(H) = \mathcal{P}(H)/\mathcal{P}(\neg H) = 0.1/0.9 \approx 0.11$$

and

$$\mathcal{O}(E) = \mathcal{P}(E)/\mathcal{P}(\neg E) = 0.2/0.8 \approx 0.25.$$

Using the likelihood coefficients, we compute

$$\mathcal{O}(H|E) = \mathcal{L}_\mathcal{S}(H, E)\mathcal{O}(H) \approx 0.22,$$

and

$$\mathcal{O}(H|\neg E) = \mathcal{L}_\mathcal{N}(H, E)\mathcal{O}(H) \approx 0.0011.$$

From these new odds, we calculate the probabilities:

$$P(H|E) = \mathcal{O}(H|E)/(1 + \mathcal{O}(H|E)) = 0.22/1.22 \approx 0.18,$$

and

$$P(\neg H|E) = \mathcal{O}(\neg H|E)/(1 + \mathcal{O}(\neg H|E)) = 0.0011/1.0011 \approx 0.001.$$

These numbers imply that

$$P(H) = P(H|E)P(E) + P(H|\neg E)P(\neg E) \approx (0.18)(0.2) + (0.001)(0.8) \approx 0.04,$$

which is inconsistent with the original statement that $P(H) = 0.1$.

Thus, the likelihoods of sufficiency and necessity constrain each other but do not determine each other. The next section discusses how these likelihood ratios are used to express the relations between many different hypotheses in a *probabilistic inference network*.

3.3   Probabilistic Inference Networks

A *probabilistic inference network* is a labeled directed graph, in which each node represents a hypothesis or evidence "event." The connection from a node E to a node H is annotated with two numbers: $\mathcal{L}_\mathcal{S}(H, E)$ and $\mathcal{L}_\mathcal{N}(H, E)$, in that order. Each node X is also labeled with its prior probability, $P(X)$. An instance of the simplest of such networks is discussed in the following example.

Example 3.4 Let H represent the disease hypothesis for a patient, and E the symptomatic evidence that suggests the disease. In Figure 3.1, node H is labeled with its prior probability $P(H) = 0.01$. The two numbers annotating the

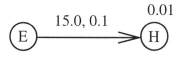

Figure 3.1: A two-node probabilistic inference network

connection between the nodes E and H are $\mathcal{L}_\mathcal{S}(H, E) = 15.0$ and $\mathcal{L}_\mathcal{N}(H, E) = 0.1$, respectively. The arrow indicates directionality: $\mathcal{L}_\mathcal{S}(E, H)$ and $\mathcal{L}_\mathcal{N}(E, H)$ are not given. However, there is no implication that E "causes" H, nor the converse.

- If nothing is known about the presence or absence of E, $\mathcal{P}(H) = 0.01$, hence $\mathcal{O}(H) = 0.01/0.99 \approx 0.0108$. This indicates the level of our "belief" in H.

- If E is known to be present, the new odds of H are

$$\mathcal{O}(H|E) = \mathcal{L}_S(H, E)\mathcal{O}(H) \approx (15.0)(0.0108) = 0.162.$$

Even though the odds of H have increased fifteen-fold, H is by no means certain: $\mathcal{P}(H) \approx 0.162/(1.162) \approx 0.14$.

- If E is known to be absent, the new odds of H are

$$\mathcal{O}(H|\neg E) \approx (0.1)(0.0108) \approx 0.0011,$$

and the posterior probability of H is

$$\mathcal{P}(H|\neg E) \approx 0.0011/1.0011 \approx 0.001.$$

The hypothesis H is still not ruled out, although its probability of occurrence has decreased by a factor of about 10.

This example considered cases when the evidence (E) was *known* with absolute certainty to be true or false. Unfortunately, this is seldom the case in practical situations. For instance, if E corresponds to finding a micro-organism in the patient's blood, the laboratory report concerning the blood test may not be completely reliable: the blood sample may have been tainted, the chemical used for analyzing the blood may have been of the wrong concentration, there may have been a clerical error when the technician was transcribing the results of the test, and so on. To take such scenarios into account, we often distinguish between directly observed evidence and intermediate hypotheses, as illustrated in Example 3.5 below. The posterior odds for the intermediate hypotheses are to be calculated from the direct evidence in the same manner as the odds of the final hypothesis are to be calculated from the intermediate hypotheses.

Example 3.5 Let D denote the directly observable evidence (*e.g.*, the lab. report says the patient has high cholesterol), E the intermediate hypothesis (*e.g.*, the patient does have high cholesterol), and H the final conclusion (*e.g.*, the disease hypothesis), with likelihood ratios and prior probabilities as indicated in Figure 3.2: $\mathcal{P}(H) = 0.01$, $\mathcal{P}(E) = 0.05$, $\mathcal{L}_S(H, E) = 15.0$, $\mathcal{L}_N(H, E) = 0.1$, $\mathcal{L}_S(E, D) = 100.0$, and $\mathcal{L}_N(E, D) = 0.01$. Hence $\mathcal{O}(E) = 0.05/(1 - 0.05) \approx 0.0526$.

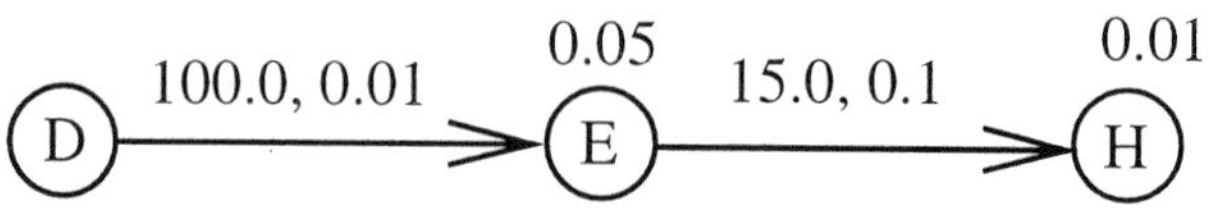

$$
\begin{array}{ccccccc}
& & 0.05 & & & 0.01 & \\
& 100.0,\, 0.01 & & 15.0,\, 0.1 & & & \\
\textcircled{D} & \xrightarrow{\hspace{2cm}} & \textcircled{E} & \xrightarrow{\hspace{2cm}} & \textcircled{H} &
\end{array}
$$

Figure 3.2: A three-node probabilistic inference network with a chain of connections from direct evidence to final conclusion.

- If D is known to be true, the posterior odds of E are given by

$$\mathcal{O}(E|D) \approx (100.0)(0.0526) = 5.26,$$

with $\mathcal{P}(E|D) \approx 5.26/(1 + 5.26) \approx 0.84$.

- Similarly, if D is known to be false, the posterior odds of E are given by

$$\mathcal{O}(E|\neg D) \approx (0.01)(0.0526) = 0.000526,$$

with $\mathcal{P}(E|\neg D) \approx 0.000526/1.000526 \approx 0.0005$.

In both cases mentioned above, E is not known to be true or false with absolute certainty, $\mathcal{O}(H|D)$ is still unknown.

In Example 3.5, the main goal of calculating $\mathcal{O}(H|D)$ remains unsatisfied, even though the indirect relationship between D and H is mediated exclusively by E. To assist in solving this main goal, we use the fact that D is the union of the disjoint sets $D \cap E$ and $D \cap \neg E$:

$$
\begin{aligned}
\mathcal{P}(H \cap D) &= \mathcal{P}(H \cap D \cap E) + \mathcal{P}(H \cap D \cap \neg E) \\
&= \mathcal{P}(H|D \cap E)\mathcal{P}(D \cap E) + \mathcal{P}(H|D \cap \neg E)\mathcal{P}(D \cap \neg E) \\
&= \mathcal{P}(H|D \cap E)\mathcal{P}(E|D)\mathcal{P}(D) + \mathcal{P}(H|D \cap \neg E)\mathcal{P}(\neg E|D)\mathcal{P}(D)
\end{aligned}
$$

Dividing both sides of the equation by $\mathcal{P}(D)$, we conclude

$$\mathcal{P}(H|D) = \mathcal{P}(H|D \cap E)\mathcal{P}(E|D) + \mathcal{P}(H|D \cap \neg E)\mathcal{P}(\neg E|D). \tag{3.15}$$

It is easy to calculate $\mathcal{P}(E|D)$ (as in Example 3.5), interpreted as the *reliability*[2] of D in predicting E, and this quantity is useful in computing $\mathcal{P}(H|D)$ as a weighted average of $P(H|E)$ and $P(H|\neg E)$. However, Equation 3.15 requires knowing $\mathcal{P}(H|D \cap E)$ and $\mathcal{P}(H|D \cap \neg E)$, which are generally unknown. In such cases, reasoning that the only way D can influence H is through E. the following assumption is frequently made.

---

[2] The term 'reliability' is used in a different sense in other literature.

Conditional Independence:

$$P(H|D \cap E) = P(H|E), \text{ and } P(H|D \cap \neg E) = P(H|\neg E),$$

Such *conditional independence* assumptions are sometimes incorrect, and may lead to anomalous results. Where such assumptions are reasonable, the posterior probability for the final conclusion is calculated as

$$P(H|D) = P(H|E)P(E|D) + P(H|\neg E)P(\neg E|D). \tag{3.16}$$

Example 3.5 (continued): We reconsider the conditional probabilities in Example 3.5 and Figure 3.2; as computed earlier, $P(H|E) \approx 0.14$, $P(H|\neg E) \approx 0.001$, $P(E|D) \approx 0.84$, and $P(E|\neg D) \approx 0.0005$.

Making the conditional independence assumptions needed for Equation 3.16 to hold,

$$
\begin{aligned}
P(H|D) &= P(H|E)P(E|D) + P(H|\neg E)P(\neg E|D) \\
&\approx (0.14)(0.84) + (0.001)(1 - 0.84) \\
&\approx 0.12
\end{aligned}
$$

Similarly,

$$
\begin{aligned}
P(H|\neg D) &= P(H|E)P(E|\neg D) + P(H|\neg E)P(\neg E|\neg D) \\
&\approx (0.14)(0.0005) + (0.001)(1 - 0.0005) \\
&\approx 0.001
\end{aligned}
$$

The next section discusses how the conditional independence assumption is used to carry out reasoning in probabilistic inference networks, in the absence of complete conditional probability information.

3.4   Interpolating Conditional Probabilities

Assuming conditional independence, from Equation 3.16, we obtain

$$P(H|D) = P(H|\neg E) + P(E|D)(P(H|E) - P(H|\neg E))$$

since $P(\neg E|D) = 1 - P(E|D)$, so that

$$P(E|D) = \frac{P(H|D) - P(H|\neg E)}{P(H|E) - P(H|\neg E)}. \tag{3.17}$$

We now consider a special case: if D is irrelevant to E, then we should expect that $\mathcal{P}(E|D) = \mathcal{P}(E)$. Also, since the only way D influences H is through E, we should expect that $\mathcal{P}(H|D) = \mathcal{P}(H)$ in this case. Using these equations along with Equation 3.17, we obtain

$$\mathcal{P}(E) \;=\; \frac{\mathcal{P}(H) - \mathcal{P}(H|\neg E)}{\mathcal{P}(H|E) - \mathcal{P}(H|\neg E)} \tag{3.18}$$

whenever the conditional independence assumptions are reasonable. For future reference, we denote the right-hand-side of this equation as $\mathcal{P}_c(E)$, i.e., Equation 3.18 can be written $\mathcal{P}(E) = \mathcal{P}_c(E)$. Unfortunately, the conditional and prior probabilities specified for many problems do not satisfy this constraint.

Several suggestions have been made to overcome such inconsistencies using piecewise linear interpolations for $\mathcal{P}(H|D)$, instead of the linear interpolation in Equation 3.16. Each such modification is constrained so that the prior probabilities $\mathcal{P}(H), \mathcal{P}(E)$ are consistent with each other, for the case when D is irrelevant to E.

Figure 3.3 depicts such a piecewise linear modification, along with the linear interpolation of Equation 3.16. The abscissa (x-axis) of the figure, corresponding to the first coordinate of the points depicted in the figure, describes the reliability $\mathcal{P}(E|D)$. The ordinate (y-axis) of the figure, corresponding to the second coordinate, describes the posterior probability $\mathcal{P}(H|D)$.

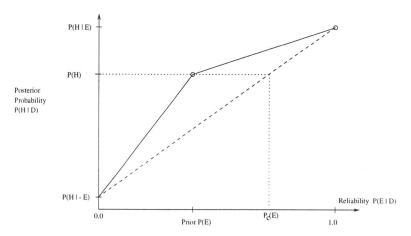

Figure 3.3: Interpolation functions to determine $\mathcal{P}(H|D)$ from $\mathcal{P}(E|D)$.

The simplest piecewise interpolation function consists of two line segments, the first extending from the coordinates $(0, \mathcal{P}(H|\neg E))$ to $(\mathcal{P}(E), \mathcal{P}(H))$, and the second extending from the coordinates $(\mathcal{P}(E), \mathcal{P}(H))$ to $(1, \mathcal{P}(H|E))$. This

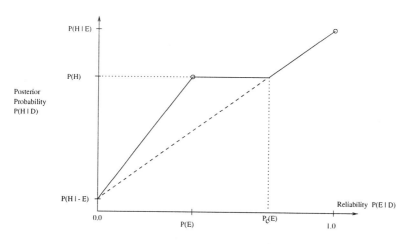

Figure 3.4: Piecewise linear interpolation of $\mathcal{P}(H|D)$, with flat zone between $\mathcal{P}(E)$ and $\mathcal{P}_c(E)$, for the case when $\mathcal{P}(E) < \mathcal{P}_c(E)$.

interpolation is expressed by the following equation:

$$
\mathcal{P}(H|D) = \begin{cases} \dfrac{\mathcal{P}(E|D)(\mathcal{P}(H)-\mathcal{P}(H|\neg E))}{\mathcal{P}(E)} & \text{if } \mathcal{P}(E|D) \leq \mathcal{P}(E) \\[2ex] \mathcal{P}(H) + \dfrac{\mathcal{P}(E|D)(\mathcal{P}(H|E)-\mathcal{P}(H))}{(1-\mathcal{P}(E))} & \text{otherwise.} \end{cases} \tag{3.19}
$$

In the interest of making conservative estimates, it may be argued that the direct evidence D should instead be considered neutral if reliability is intermediate, within the range of values described by[3] $\mathcal{P}(E) \leq \mathcal{P}(E|D) \leq \mathcal{P}_c(E)$, then some piecewise linear interpolation formulas leave the posterior probability of H unchanged from the prior, i.e., $\mathcal{P}(H|D) = \mathcal{P}(H)$ in that range. This approach is expressed using the following formula:

$$
\mathcal{P}(H|D) = \begin{cases} \dfrac{\mathcal{P}(E|D)(\mathcal{P}(H)-\mathcal{P}(H|\neg E))}{\mathcal{P}(E)} & \text{if } \mathcal{P}(E|D) \leq \min(\mathcal{P}(E), \mathcal{P}_c(E)) \\[2ex] \mathcal{P}(H) + \dfrac{\mathcal{P}(E|D)(\mathcal{P}(H|E)-\mathcal{P}(H))}{(1-\mathcal{P}_c(E))} & \text{if } \mathcal{P}(E|D) \geq \max(\mathcal{P}(E), \mathcal{P}_c(E)) \\[2ex] \mathcal{P}(H) & \text{otherwise.} \end{cases}
$$

$$(3.20)$$

This approach treats the region between $\mathcal{P}(E)$ and $\mathcal{P}_c(E)$ as a "no change in $\mathcal{P}(H|D)$" zone, in which the reliability value $\mathcal{P}(E|D)$ is neither high enough nor low enough to warrant any change in posterior probability $\mathcal{P}(H|D)$ from the prior probability $\mathcal{P}(H)$, as indicated in Figure 3.4.

Use of the term "reliability" for $\mathcal{P}(E|D)$ is slightly misleading to humans, especially when a reliability estimate (provided by someone) is small. The intention may not be to say that the direct evidence (D) is to be used against

---

[3]Recall that $\mathcal{P}_c(E)$ was defined as $(\mathcal{P}(H) - \mathcal{P}(H|\neg E))/(\mathcal{P}(H|E) - \mathcal{P}(H|\neg E))$.

the hypothesis (H), which would happen if $\mathcal{P}(E|D) < \mathcal{P}(E)$. This argument leads to another interpolation, described by Equation 3.21. This interpolation is applicable for problems where it is presumed that D can only increase our degree of belief in H if reliability is large enough, but the posterior probability of H remains the same as its prior if reliability is small.

$$\mathcal{P}(H|D) = \begin{cases} \mathcal{P}(H) \text{ if } \mathcal{P}(E|D) \le \max(\mathcal{P}(E), \mathcal{P}_c(E)) \\ \mathcal{P}(H) + \frac{\mathcal{P}(E|D)(\mathcal{P}(H|E) - \mathcal{P}(H))}{(1 - \mathcal{P}(E))} \text{ otherwise.} \end{cases} \quad (3.21)$$

Similar formulas can be constructed for cases where D is only allowed to decrease our degree of belief in H if reliability is large enough.

Cases such as the one in Equation 3.21 correspond naturally to rule-based expert systems (such as MYCIN) in which a rule is constrained to be inactive unless the strength of evidence for the rule's antecedent exceeds a minimal threshold T. In other words, rules can fire only if the conditions in the left-hand-side of the rule are considered strong enough to provoke action. This leads to considerable savings in computational effort, since the weakness of the antecedents spills over to the consequents, so that the facts asserted by the right-hand-side of the rule are also associated with levels of belief or confidence that are too low to warrant making any conclusions from the rule. An implementation of this approach is depicted in Figure 3.5.

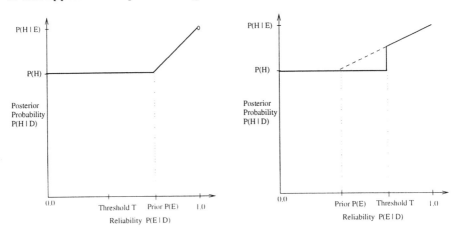

Figure 3.5: Piecewise linear interpolation of $\mathcal{P}(H|D)$, with rules inactive unless reliability exceeds a threshold T; cases when $T \le \mathcal{P}(E)$ and when $T \ge \mathcal{P}(E)$, respectively.

So far, we have addressed 'chains' of reasoning, in networks each of whose nodes has at most one incoming edge. The next section discusses how probabilistic reasoning can be carried out in more general networks, where multiple pieces of evidence must be used to determine the *a posteriori* belief in the same hypothesis.

3.5 Combining Evidence

In the examples considered so far, each probabilistic inference network contained no more than three nodes. In large practical applications such as the mineral exploration expert system PROSPECTOR, the number of nodes is much larger, and additional non-probabilistic logical inference nodes or constraint nodes may also exist. When attention is focused on a small part of the network, the most important issue to be tackled is the method used to combine evidence from different lower level hypotheses to compute the posterior probability of a higher level hypothesis.

In the absence of any evidence to the contrary, conditional independence assumptions are often made in combining probabilities from different hypotheses. For instance, let E_1, E_2, ..., E_n be the evidence nodes bearing on a hypothesis H, as in Figure 3.6. Conditional independence assumptions imply

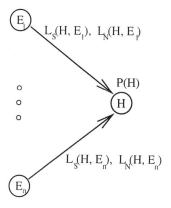

Figure 3.6: Multiple evidence nodes and likelihoods

that

$$P(E_1 \cap \cdots \cap E_n | H) \;=\; P(E_1|H)P(E_2|H) \cdots P(E_n|H) \;=\; \prod_{i=1}^{n} P(E_i|H)$$

and

$$P(E_1 \cap \cdots \cap E_n | \neg H) \;=\; P(E_1|\neg H)P(E_2|\neg H) \cdots P(E_n|\neg H) \;=\; \prod_{i=1}^{n} P(E_i|\neg H).$$

Hence

$$\mathcal{O}(H|E_1 \cap \cdots \cap E_n) = \frac{\mathcal{P}(E_1 \cap \cdots \cap E_n|H)\,\mathcal{P}(H)}{\mathcal{P}(E_1 \cap \cdots \cap E_n|\neg H)\,\mathcal{P}(\neg H)}$$

$$= \frac{\prod_{i=1}^{n}\mathcal{P}(E_i|H)\,\mathcal{P}(H)}{\prod_{i=1}^{n}\mathcal{P}(E_i|\neg H)\,\mathcal{P}(\neg H)}$$

$$= \left[\prod_{i=1}^{n} \mathrm{L}(H, E_i)\right]\mathcal{O}(H) \qquad (3.22)$$

The quantity

$$\prod_{i=1}^{n}\mathrm{L}(H, E_i) = \frac{\mathcal{O}(H|E_1 \cap \cdots \cap E_n)}{\mathcal{O}(H)} \qquad (3.23)$$

is called the *effective likelihood ratio* for H with respect to $E_1, \ldots, E_n$.

Example 3.6 Both John and Joe are witnesses present at a robbery. The prior probability that Tom committed the crime is about 0.6, based on other evidence (e.g., tiremarks left by the getaway car), so that the prior odds are $0.6/0.4 = 1.5$. Assume that Tom would be declared guilty if the posterior probability that he committed the crime exceeds 90%.

John is a little short-sighted, and was not wearing his glasses at the time, so that the following likelihood ratios are reasonable:

$$\mathcal{L}_S(\text{Tom committed the robbery,   John says so}) = 10$$

and

$$\mathcal{L}_S(\text{Tom committed the robbery,   John says otherwise}) = 0.1.$$

Joe's vision is perfect, but he is reputed to be a seedy character and a friend of Tom, leading us to the following likelihood ratios:

$$\mathcal{L}_S(\text{Tom committed the robbery,   Joe says so}) = 100$$

and

$$\mathcal{L}_S(\text{Tom committed the robbery,   Joe says otherwise}) = 0.5.$$

John and Joe are unacquainted with each other, and do not even know that the other was present at the crime scene, so that the conditional independence assumptions are reasonable. Equation 3.22 leads to different answers for the following six separate cases:

1. John says Tom committed the robbery, but Joe says he was not close enough to identify the suspect. In other words, Joe's testimony is useless. Then the posterior odds (that Tom committed the robbery) are

$(10)(1.5) = 15$, so that the posterior probability is $15/16 \approx 0.9375$. This exceeds the threshold that we set (90%), so that Tom would be declared guilty.

2. Joe says Tom committed the robbery, but John says he is not sure. Then the posterior odds $= (100)(1.5) = 150$, so that the posterior probability is $150/151 \approx 0.9933$, and Tom doesn't stand a chance of being declared innocent.

3. Both John and Joe say Tom committed the robbery. Then the posterior odds are $(10)(100)(1.5) = 1500$, so that the posterior probability is $1500/1501 \approx 0.9993$. Once again, Tom will be declared guilty.

4. Both John and Joe say someone else committed the robbery, not Tom. Then the posterior odds $= (0.1)(0.5)(1.5) = 0.075$, so that the posterior probability is $0.075/1.075 \approx 0.0698$, low enough for Tom to be released.

5. John says Tom committed the robbery, whereas Joe says it was someone else. Then the posterior odds are $(10)(0.5)(1.5) = 7.5$, so that the posterior probability is $7.5/8.5 \approx 0.88$. There is reasonable doubt in Tom's guilt; Tom would probably escape criminal conviction but may face penalties based on civil lawsuits.

6. Joe says Tom committed the robbery, whereas John says it was someone else. Then the posterior odds $= (100)(0.1)(1.5) = 15$, so that the posterior probability is $15/16 \approx 0.9375$. As in the first case, this exceeds 0.9, so that Tom would be declared guilty.

Thus, Joe's evidence against Tom is much more damning than John's[4].

The main appeal of this methodology, assuming conditional independence, is that it can be integrated easily into rule-based reasoning systems. The likelihood ratios associated with links in the probabilistic inference network can be conveniently attached to the corresponding rules in the rule-based expert system.

We now apply the above methodology to tree-structured Probabilistic inference networks of the kind used in the PROSPECTOR expert system.

Example 3.7 Figure 3.7 depicts a network with three direct evidence nodes (A,B,D) one intermediate node (C), and a hypothesis node (E) about which

---

[4] *Moral of the story*: A friend can cause much more trouble than a bystander.

final conclusions are to be drawn. For the direct evidence nodes, the labels 1 and 0 indicate whether the associated propositions are true or false. This may be left unspecified when such information is lacking.

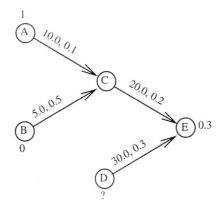

Figure 3.7: A tree-structured probabilistic inference network

The first concern in this example is to compute the posterior probability $\mathcal{P}(C|A \cap \neg B)$. But the given constraints allow us only to compute $\mathcal{P}(C|A)$ and $\mathcal{P}(C|\neg B)$, not $\mathcal{P}(C|A \cap \neg B)$. The problem is underconstrained, and there is no unique value that can be assigned to $\mathcal{P}(C|A \cap \neg B)$. Two extreme cases are discussed below:

Case 1 : One evidence node determines another, e.g., A implies $\neg B$. In this case, $\mathcal{P}(C|A \cap \neg B) = \mathcal{P}(C|A)$, calculated as in Example 3.4.

Case 2 : Evidence nodes are independent, e.g., A and B are independent sources of evidence for C^5. We may then use Equation 3.22, along with the conditional independence assumptions, to obtain

$$
\begin{aligned}
\mathcal{O}(C|A \cap \neg B) &= \mathcal{L}_S(C, A)\mathcal{L}_N(C, B)\mathcal{O}(C) \\
&= (10)(0.5)\frac{(0.1)}{(0.9)} \\
&\approx 0.5556
\end{aligned}
$$

If no information is available regarding the truth or falsity of D, then D can be ignored in calculating the posterior probability of E:

$$\mathcal{P}(E| \text{ all available evidence}) = \mathcal{P}(E|A \cap \neg B),$$

---

[5]Note that this requirement states the conditional independence of C given A and $\neg B$, not the mutual independence of A and B.

calculated as in earlier examples, using the likelihood coefficients $\mathcal{L}_S(E, C)$ and $\mathcal{L}_N(E, C)$. If D is known to be true (or false), then assumptions such as conditional independence can once again be invoked, as done in computing the posterior probability of C.

Conditional independence is frequently assumed, when no other information is available about the problem. One must, however, be careful in invoking conditional independence. For instance, conditional independence does not hold in the seemingly innocent example where A and B are possible symptoms of a disease C: the presence of one symptom may increase the chances that another symptom will occur in patients having the disease. A reasonable instance is described by the numerical quantities in the following example.

Example 3.8 The total number of patients (sample size) is 100, and $|X|$ denotes the number of patients in the sample for whom X is true.

$$|A \cap B \cap C| = 8 \qquad |\neg A \cap B \cap C| = 2$$
$$|A \cap B \cap \neg C| = 12 \qquad |\neg A \cap B \cap \neg C| = 8$$
$$|A \cap \neg B \cap C| = 2 \qquad |\neg A \cap \neg B \cap C| = 0$$
$$|A \cap \neg B \cap \neg C| = 8 \qquad |\neg A \cap \neg B \cap \neg C| = 60$$

Interpreting frequencies (percentages) as probabilities,

$$P(C|A) = \frac{P(A \cap C)}{P(A \cap C) + P(A \cap \neg C)} = \frac{8 + 2}{8 + 12 + 2 + 8} \approx 0.33,$$

since $P(A \cap C) = P(A \cap B \cap C) + P(A \cap \neg B \cap C)$, and $P(A \cap \neg C) = P(A \cap B \cap \neg C) + P(A \cap \neg B \cap \neg C)$.

Similarly, $P(C|\neg B) = (2 + 0)/(8 + 2 + 0 + 60) \approx 0.03$. But $P(C|A \cap \neg B) = 2/(8 + 2) = 0.2$ is different from $P(C|A)P(C|\neg B) \approx 0.33 \times 0.03 \approx 0.01$.

Although there are fortuitous cases for which conditional independence assumptions can give correct results, it is to be emphasized that the assumption is often unjustified and made in desperation as a shortcut when more information about the conditional probability distribution is unavailable.

The next section extends the reasoning process from probabilistic inference networks to networks in which other relationships (embodying logical connectives) exist among nodes.

3.6 Logical Inferences in Probabilistic Networks

Some networks contain nodes labeled with logical connectives such as "AND" and "OR," intended to capture logical relationships between nodes. For instance, the hypothesis H associated with a higher level node may be true only if each of $E_1, E_2, \ldots, E_n$ is true, indicated by an "AND" node whose output goes to the node labeled H, and inputs come from nodes labeled $E_1, E_2, \ldots, E_n$. More generally, the connection from the "AND" node to H may be annotated by likelihood values ($\mathcal{L}_S$ and $\mathcal{L}_N$) used to compute the posterior probability of H.

Interesting cases arise when $E_1, E_2, \ldots, E_n$ are not known to be true or false, and all we have are probabilities associated with each such evidence node. Two approaches are usually employed:

1. The independence assumption leads to the computation

$$P(AND(E_1, E_2)) = \mathcal{P}(E_1 \cap E_2) = \mathcal{P}(E_1)\mathcal{P}(E_2). \qquad (3.24)$$

   Similarly, conditional independence implies

$$P(OR(E_1, E_2)) = \mathcal{P}(E_1 \cup E_2) = \mathcal{P}(E_1) + \mathcal{P}(E_2) - \mathcal{P}(E_1)\mathcal{P}(E_2) \qquad (3.25)$$

   In long chains of reasoning, where the "AND" operator is to be applied repeatedly, repeatedly applying Equation 3.24 yields a very small number, the result of multiplying together many fractions (< 1). The end result may then be far from reasonable. Two supporting pieces of evidence lead to the apparent anomaly that the belief in the hypothesis is less certain than if a single supporting piece of evidence is present.

2. Since $\mathcal{P}(E_1 \cap E_2) = \mathcal{P}(E_1)\mathcal{P}(E_2|E_1)$, and $\mathcal{P}(E_2|E_1) \leq 1$, an obvious constraint is that $\mathcal{P}(E_1 \cap E_2) \leq \mathcal{P}(E_1)$. Symmetrically, $\mathcal{P}(E_1 \cap E_2) \leq \mathcal{P}(E_2)$. Together, these constraints imply $\mathcal{P}(E_1 \cap E_2) \leq \min(\mathcal{P}(E_1), \mathcal{P}(E_2))$. This leads to one approach used when independence assumptions are unreasonable: consider the highest possible value for each probability, i.e., use $\min(\mathcal{P}(E_1), \mathcal{P}(E_2))$ as an estimate for $\mathcal{P}(E_1 \cap E_2)$. This is of course an upper limit, and tends to overestimate the true probability.

   Analogously,

$$\mathcal{P}(E_1 \cup E_2) = \mathcal{P}(E_1) + \mathcal{P}(E_2 - E_1) \geq \mathcal{P}(E_1)$$

   and

$$\mathcal{P}(E_1 \cup E_2) = \mathcal{P}(E_2) + \mathcal{P}(E_1 - E_2) \geq \mathcal{P}(E_2),$$

so that $\mathcal{P}(E_1 \cup E_2) \geq \max(\mathcal{P}(E_1), \mathcal{P}(E_2))$. The lower limit, $\max(\mathcal{P}(E_1), \mathcal{P}(E_2))$, is sometimes used as a surrogate for $\mathcal{P}(E_1 \cup E_2)$.

Much less useful are the lower limit for $\mathcal{P}(E_1 \cap E_2) \geq 0$, and the upper limit for $\mathcal{P}(E_1 \cup E_2) \leq \min(1, \mathcal{P}(E_1) + \mathcal{P}(E_2))$.

NOTE: It is incorrect to justify the use of 'max' and 'min' in probabilistic reasoning by referring to similar operators in fuzzy logic.

Example 3.9 PROSPECTOR is an expert system designed to assist in decision-making in mineral exploration tasks. The goal is to determine the probability of existence of different ore deposits in a given location, based on easily available evidence and geological reasoning. The user provides a list of rocks and minerals observed, matched by the system with its models that contain information about different ore deposit classes; the system analyzes these and then advises the user. Prospector also has a user interface that allows input in simple English sentences.

Figure 3.8 shows the portion of Prospector's inference network published by Duda, Gaschnig and Hart (1979) [3], based on data provided by Marco T. Einaudi. Successively higher levels of the network contain nodes that represent successively higher level hypotheses.

Some of the connections in Prospector's inference network represent logical relations. The "min" (upper limit, for AND) and "max" (lower limit, for OR) functions are used by Prospector when lower level evidence or hypothesis nodes (whose AND/OR is being computed) are not known with certainty to be true or false. [6]

In addition to such logical and probabilistic relations, a Prospector network may also contain "contextual" relations (indicated by dashed lines) that indicate when it makes sense for the system to look for a value associated with some node. If the arrow associated with a dashed line points from node A to node B, then B is the context in which enquiring about A makes sense; B must be known to be true before computations or tests associated with A are performed. For instance, with the network in Figure 3.8, the status of the node "porphyritic texture" will be queried only if "grain size is fine-to-medium;" similarly, it must be known that there are "granitic intrusives in region" before carrying out the computations associated with calculating the posterior probability of "favorable regional environment."

---

[6]Duda, Gaschnig and Hart (1979) [3] mention that they use "the fuzzy-set formulas of Zadeh (1965)" in this context.

The following is an example of the computations carried out with the network in Figure 3.8. Reasoning proceeds bottom-upwards, towards higher level nodes in the network. In what follows, we use abbreviations rather than the full names of hypotheses associated with nodes.

Evidence: $GIR, CVR, FMGS, RCIB$ and RCS are true, PT is false, $OTFSYS, RCAD$ and $RCVP$ are unknown.

- $FMGS \cap PT$ is false.

$$\mathcal{O}(HYPE) = 0.01/0.99 \approx 0.0101$$

$$\mathcal{O}(HYPE|STIR) = (65)(0.01/0.99) \approx 0.6566$$

$$\mathcal{P}(HYPE|STIR) \approx 0.6566/1.6566 \approx 0.3963$$

$$\mathcal{O}(HYPE|\neg STIR) = (0.01)(0.01/0.99) \approx 0.0001$$

$$\mathcal{P}(HYPE|\neg STIR) \approx 0.0001/1.0001 \approx 0.0001$$

$$\mathcal{O}(STIR|FMGS, \neg PT) = 2(0.000001)(0.1/0.9) \approx 2.22 \times 10^{-7}$$

$$\mathcal{P}(STIR|FMGS, \neg PT) \approx 2.22 \times 10^{-7}/(1 + 2.22 \times 10^{-7}) \approx 2.2 \times 10^{-7}$$

By linear interpolation,

$$\mathcal{P}(HYPE|FMGS, \neg PT) \approx 0.0001 + (0.3963 - 0.0001)(2.2 \times 10^{-7}) \approx 0.0001$$

$$\mathcal{O}(HYPE|FMGS, \neg PT) \approx 0.0001/0.9999 \approx 0.0001$$

Thus the first likelihood ratio is

$$\mathrm{L}(HYPE, FMGS \cap \neg PT) \approx 0.0001/0.0101 \approx 0.01$$

- Similar calculations are carried out for the SMIR subtree.

$$\mathcal{O}(HYPE|SMIR) = (300)(0.01/0.99) \approx 3.0303$$

$$\mathcal{P}(HYPE|SMIR) \approx 3.0303/4.0303 \approx 0.7518$$

$$\mathcal{O}(HYPE|\neg SMIR) = (0.0001)(0.01/0.99) \approx 10^{-6}$$
$$\mathcal{P}(HYPE|\neg SMIR) \approx 10^{-6}/(1 + 10^{-6}) \approx 10^{-6}$$

$$\mathcal{O}(SMIR|RCIB, RCS) = 20(300)(0.03/0.97) \approx 185.57$$
$$\mathcal{P}(SMIR|RCIB, RCS) \approx 185.57/186.57 \approx 0.9946$$

By linear interpolation,

$$\mathcal{P}(HYPE|RCIB, RCS) \approx 10^{-6} + (0.7518 - 10^{-6})(0.9946) \approx 0.7478$$

$$\mathcal{O}(HYPE|RCIB, RCS) \approx 0.7478/0.2522 \approx 2.96$$

Thus the second likelihood ratio is

$$L(HYPE, RCIB \cap RCS) \approx 2.96/0.0101 \approx 293$$

- Treating the two subtrees as independent evidence sources,

$$\mathcal{O}(HYPE|(FMGS \cap \neg PT) \cap (RCIB \cap RCS)) \approx (0.01)(293)(0.0101)$$

$$= 0.0293, \text{ and}$$

$$\mathcal{P}(HYPE|(FMGS \cap \neg PT) \cap (RCIB \cap RCS)) \approx 0.0293/0.9707 \approx 0.03.$$

Similar calculations can be used to determine the posterior probability of FLE and FRE, left as an exercise for the reader.

The next section examines whether the inference processes discussed so far can be applied to arbitrary networks with no limitations on the connectivity among nodes.

3.7 Cycles and Multiple Dependencies

When is it reasonable to propagate probabilities in chains of reasoning? Can the approach of Example 3.5 be readily extended to arbitrary networks of hypotheses? Unfortunately, such is not the case; in the well-known process of propagation of rumors in human social life, for instance, each individual increases his/her own belief in some hypothesis, influenced by the opinions of others,

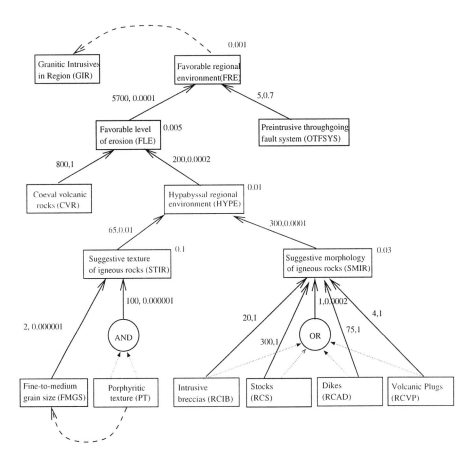

Figure 3.8: Part of Prospector's inference network for porphyry copper deposits (adapted from Duda, Gaschnig and Hart (1979))

whereas such opinions may be far from independent, and may all be traced to a single unreliable "direct" source of evidence. Example 3.10 illustrates how propagation of evidence in networks with cycles can lead to inconsistent results of which it is difficult to make sense.

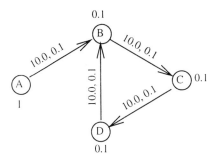

Figure 3.9: A probabilistic inference network with cycles

Example 3.10 Initially, "direct evidence" node A is assumed to be true, and the truth of other hypotheses corresponding to nodes in Figure 3.9 is unknown. The probability of B is updated, multiplying its prior odds $(= 0.1/0.9 \approx 0.1111)$ ten-fold, since $\mathcal{L}_S(B, A) = 10$, yielding $\mathcal{O}(B|A) \approx 1.111$ and

$$P(B|A) \approx 1.111/(1 + 1.111) \approx 0.54.$$

Then $P(C|A)$ is updated using the familiar independence assumption:

$$
\begin{aligned}
P(C|A) &= P(C|B)P(B|A) + P(C|\neg B)P(\neg B|A) \\
&= \left(\frac{(10)\frac{(0.1)}{(0.9)}}{1 + (10)\frac{(0.1)}{(0.9)}} \right)^2 + \left(\frac{(0.1)\frac{(0.9)}{(0.1)}}{1 + (0.1)\frac{(0.9)}{(0.1)}} \right) \left(1 - \frac{(10)\frac{(0.1)}{(0.9)}}{1 + (10)\frac{(0.1)}{(0.9)}} \right) \\
&\approx 0.5.
\end{aligned}
$$

Similarly, $P(D|A) = P(D|C)P(C|A) + P(D|\neg C)P(\neg C|A) \approx 0.5$.

Now D also influences B updating its posterior probability while (erroneously) treating A and D as separate independent sources of evidence. To clarify the reasoning process and notation, imagine a fictitious node B' (instead of B) to which the edge from D is directed. Since $\mathcal{O}(B'|D) = \mathcal{L}_S(B', D)\mathcal{O}(B') = (10)(0.1/0.9) = 10/9$, $P(B'|D) = 10/19$. Similarly, $\mathcal{O}(B'|\neg D) = \mathcal{L}_S(B', \neg D)\mathcal{O}(B') = (0.1)(0.1/0.9) = 1/90$ and $P(B'|\neg D) = 1/91$.

Since $P(D) \neq 0$ and $P(D) \neq 1$, the influence of D on B' is computed using the linear interpolation of Equation 3.16 to be $P(B'|A)$
$= P(B'|D)P(D|A) + P(B'|\neg D)P(\neg D|A) \approx (10/19)(0.5) + (1/91)(0.5) \approx 0.26$.

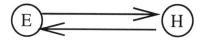

Figure 3.10: Evidence-Hypothesis cycle in inference network

This result is clearly different from the originally calculated value for $\mathcal{P}(B|A) \approx$ 0.54.

If we now attempt to "merge" B' with B, and attempt to estimate the posterior probability of B by treating the information flowing from A and D (to B) as independent, perhaps using a variant of Equation 3.22, the result varies further. Indeed, cyclic computations may proceed without any guarantee that the conclusions will converge to any reasonable value.

Given that cycles cause problems in the propagation of probabilistic inferences in networks, the next section establishes a rigorous approach for carrying out probabilistic computations in certain acyclic networks.

3.8   Reasoning in Acyclic Networks

In the probabilistic networks considered so far, the directions (arrows) associated with edges had no significance other than the desired direction in which inferences were presumed to occur. Unfortunately, confusion can result when inference is allowed to occur in either direction, as determined by an actual user requirement for a specific case. For instance,

1. presence of a symptom (E) in a blood test may increase the likelihood of a disease (H), and

2. knowing that disease H is present may increase the likelihood of the symptom E, prompting a physician to request a test for E if he suspects that a patient is afflicted with H.

This may be represented by a graph with cycles, as in Figure 3.10; but the associated reasoning process is fraught with difficulties as illustrated in Example 3.10.

Such confusion can be avoided by forcing the networks to be acyclic, even if inferences are permitted in all directions. In *causal networks*, this is accomplished by requiring that edges lead from causes to effects, never in the opposite direction. Causal knowledge is considered to be "deep" knowledge, more significant and reliable than the shallow knowledge in production rules where the nature of the relation between the hypotheses (in the *lhs* and *rhs* of a rule) is essentially unknown. Pearl presents the following example to illustrate the confusion that can arise in rule-based systems that invoke shallow knowledge.

Example 3.11 Consider a simple rule-based system that includes the following two rules:

1. *If the ground is wet then the likelihood of rain is increased.*

2. *If the sprinklers are ON, then the ground will be wet.*

If the sprinklers are ON in a given instance of the problem, then we may conclude that the likelihood of rain is increased, as a result of firing these rules! This is clearly contrary to common sense: we should instead consider "sprinklers on" and "rain" as alternative competing hypotheses that can explain "ground wet," so that knowing the sprinklers are on should decrease our belief that it rained. The conditional probability $\mathcal{P}(\text{Rain} \mid \text{GroundWet}, \text{SprinklersON})$ should not be confused with $\mathcal{P}(\text{Rain} \mid \text{GroundWet})$. An appropriate causal representation is shown in Figure 3.11; note that the direction of the causal edge between 'GroundWet' and 'Rain' nodes in the figure is different from the direction of the implication in the first production rule.

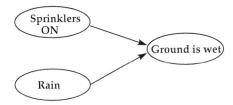

Figure 3.11: A causal network for the sprinkler problem

In some situations, identifying cause and effect may not be straightforward – even the notion of causality is questioned by some philosphers. In constructing these networks, however, it is assumed that one can distinguish causes and effects in the applications of interest to the developer of expert systems. The main issue is to have a simple convention that establishes asymmetric connections between events or hypotheses, and does so in a consistent manner; causality assists us in this respect.

The rest of this section examines the propagation of evidence in probabilistic network models, drawing on the seminal work of Judea Pearl [12], using causal relationships between hypotheses to avoid incorrect reasoning processes such as those in Example 3.11. All nodes in the network are associated with prior probabilities, edges are associated with pairwise conditional probabilities and all causal dependency relationships are shown in the network. Then, independence assumptions can be used to carry out computations with probabilities associated with different nodes.

The crux of the approach is to distinguish clearly between evidential information coming in from 'causes' and 'consequences,' and not confuse these with the belief (posterior probability) associated with any node. Pearl gives the simple analogy of a column (or polytree) of soldiers, where the total count of soldiers can be computed by a soldier using messages arriving from the soldiers in front of him and behind him. Each soldier adds up the numbers coming in from those in front of him, adds one, and passes this number to those behind him. He does a similar operation with the 'messages' coming from behind him. His own count is a sum of the counts in front and behind him, plus one. There should be no reason to confuse his own count with the two counts flowing to him and away from him.

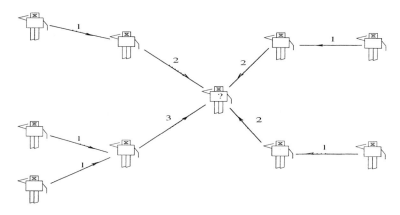

Figure 3.12: Soldier counting: the number above and below each edge indicate the count messages flowing left-to-right and right-to-left, respectively; the count computed by the central soldier (marked '?') is $(2 + 3) + (2 + 2) + 1 = 10$

In the rest of this section, we use graph-theoretic terminology: if there is a directed edge (causal connection) from X to Y, then X is a *parent* of Y, Y is a *child* of X, the *ancestors* of Y consist of its parents and their ancestors (if any exist), and the *descendants* of X consist of its children and their descendants (if any exist).

The discussion in this section is restricted to networks that are 'polytrees,' in which any two nodes are connected by a unique path. Then, each node X_i

separates the graph into its ancestors (referred to as its 'causal support,' denoted E_i^+) and its descendants (referred to as its 'diagnostic support,' denoted E_i^-), as shown in Figure 3.13. Since the only connection between E_i^+ and E_i^- is through X_i, conditional independence assumptions can be invoked, so that the *Belief* (or posterior probability) associated with X_i can be independently updated using evidence coming from E_i^+ and E_i^-, applying a multiplicative law.

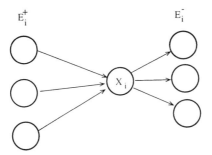

Figure 3.13: Evidence from two directions influencing hypothesis node X_i

In the notation we use, uppercase letters label nodes in the network, and the corresponding lowercase letters refer to the variables associated with nodes. For instance, x_i denotes the variable associated with node X_i, which can take distinct values representing disjoint events; e_i^- and e_i^+ denote variables summarizing evidence in E_i^- and E_i^+, respectively.

Example 3.12 John, Jacob and Jingle Hammerschmidt are the only three suspects in a crime committed by a single person. If node X_i refers to the hypothesis of who committed the crime, then $x_i \in \{$John, Jacob, Jingle$\}$. If a person has committed the crime, then that person's fingerprints are likely to be found on the instrument of crime; so E^- refers to fingerprint evidence collected after the crime. If a person is known to have harbored evil intentions towards the victim of the crime, this increases the probability that he committed the crime, so E^+ refers to information about the motivation of the suspects (e.g., someone may have overheard Jacob discussing his personal animosity towards the victim).

Since $\Pr(x_i = \text{John}) + \Pr(x_i = \text{Jacob}) + \Pr(x_i = \text{Jingle}) = 1$, it is sufficient to keep track of the relative proportions of these three probabilities, from which the probabilities can be calculated. For instance, given that these probabilities are in the proportion 1:1:3, we can conclude that the probabilities are 1/5, 1/5, and 3/5, respectively. We may write $\alpha(1 : 1 : 3)$ to represent these probabilities, using 'α' as a generic symbol that denotes that the numbers need to be normalized to obtain probabilities.

The updated beliefs relating to X_i are computed assuming that E_i^- and E_i^+ are conditionally independent, given X_i. For readability, we use a comma (instead of '$\cap$') to denote conjunction.

$$
\begin{aligned}
\mathcal{P}(x_i|e^-,e^+) &= \mathcal{P}(e_i^-,e_i^+|x_i)\mathcal{P}(x_i)/\mathcal{P}(e_i^-,e_i^+) \\
&= \mathcal{P}(e_i^-|x_i)\mathcal{P}(e_i^+|x_i)\mathcal{P}(x_i)/\mathcal{P}(e_i^-,e_i^+) \\
&= \mathcal{P}(e_i^-|x_i)\mathcal{P}(e_i^+,x_i)/\mathcal{P}(e_i^-,e_i^+) \\
&= k\lambda_i(x_i)\rho_i(x_i)
\end{aligned}
$$

where $k = 1/\mathcal{P}(e_i^-,e_i^+)$, $\lambda_i(x_i) = \mathcal{P}(e_i^-|x_i)$, and $\rho_i(x_i) = \mathcal{P}(e_i^+,x_i)$. Note that $\lambda_i(x_i)$ accounts for evidence coming from the descendants of X_i, and $\rho_i(x_i)$ accounts for evidence coming from the ancestors of X_i. This notation is adopted from Castillo et al. [1]; Pearl [12] uses a slightly different notation.

Case 1 (computing ρ_i): If $U_1, \ldots, U_p$ are the parents of X_i in the graph (with direction connections from each U_j to X_i), we can write e_i^+ as the disjoint combination of evidence associated with nodes in the subtrees containing each U_j, i.e.,

$$
e_i^+ = e_{U_1,X_i}^+, \ldots, e_{U_p,X_i}^+.
$$

Using $(u_1, \ldots, u_p)$ to denote one combination of values for the variables associated with $U_1, \ldots, U_p$, the conditional independence arguments lead to computing

$$
\begin{aligned}
\rho_i(x_i) &= \mathcal{P}(e_i^+,x_i) \\
&= \sum_{(u_1,\ldots,u_p)} \mathcal{P}(x_i|(u_1,\ldots,u_p)\cup e_i^+)\mathcal{P}((u_1,\ldots,u_p)\cup e_i^+) \\
&= \sum_{(u_1,\ldots,u_p)} \mathcal{P}(x_i|(u_1,\ldots,u_p)\cup e_i^+)\mathcal{P}((u_1,\ldots,u_p) \\
&\qquad\qquad \cup e_{U_1,X_i}^+ \cup \ldots \cup e_{U_p,X_i}^+) \\
&= \sum_{(u_1,\ldots,u_p)} \mathcal{P}(x_i|(u_1,\ldots,u_p)\cup e_i^+)\prod_{j=1}^{p}\mathcal{P}(u_j \cup e_{U_j,X_i}^+) \\
&= \sum_{(u_1,\ldots,u_p)} \mathcal{P}(x_i|(u_1,\ldots,u_p)\cup e_i^+)\prod_{j=1}^{p}\rho_{U_j,X_i}(u_j)
\end{aligned}
$$

where the message sent by U_j to X_i is $\rho_{U_j,X_i}(u_j) = \mathcal{P}(u_j \cup e_{U_j,X_i}^+)$, which depends only on the information contained in the subtree containing U_j

but not X_i. This quantity equals 1 or 0 if U_j is a directly observable Boolean hypothesis (depending on whether the evidence for u_j is positive or negative). Otherwise, its computation depends on other nodes in the subtree.

Case 2 (computing λ_i): If $Y_1, \ldots, Y_c$ are the children of X_i in the graph (with direction connections to each Y_j from X_i), we can combine the evidence coming from the subtrees containing each U_j, i.e.,

$$e_i^- = e_{X_i, Y_1}^-, \ldots, e_{X_i, Y_c}^-,$$

and it can be shown that

$$\lambda_i(x_i) = \mathcal{P}(e_i^-|x_i) = \mathcal{P}(e_{X_i, Y_1}^-, \ldots, e_{X_i, Y_c}^-|x_i) = \prod_{j=1}^{c} \lambda_{Y_j, X_i}(x_i)$$

where $\lambda_{Y_j, X_i}(x_i) = \mathcal{P}(e_{X_i, Y_j}^-|X_i)$.

The overall methodology for belief update propagation becomes clear when we view each node as communicating a ρ 'message' to its children and a λ message to its parents in the network. When such messages arrive, the previous beliefs associated with a node are updated; the final belief $\mathcal{P}(x_i|e)$ is proportional to

$$\prod_{j=1}^{c} \lambda_{Y_j, X_i}(x_i) \sum_{(u_1, \ldots, u_p)} \mathcal{P}(x_i|(u_1, \ldots, u_p) \cup e_i^+) \prod_{j=1}^{p} \rho_{U_j, X_i}(u_j).$$

Each node computes the messages it sends to its parents and children from the messages it receives, using the conditional probabilities relating the node to its parents and children. The ρ message to be sent from X_i to Y_j must encompass evidence coming from the parents of X_i (via their ρ messages to X_i) as well as the evidence from the other children of X_i, excluding Y_j, (via their λ messages to X_i). It can be shown that

$$\rho_{X_i Y_j}(x_i) = \mathcal{P}(x_i)\mathcal{P}(e_i^+|x_i)\mathcal{P}\left(\bigcup_{k \neq j} e_{X_i, Y_k}^-|x_i\right)$$

$$\propto \rho_i(x_i) \prod_{k \neq j} \lambda_{Y_k X_i}(x_i). \tag{3.26}$$

Similarly, if $V_1, \ldots, V_q$ are the children of Y_j, it can be shown that

$$\lambda_{Y_j X_i}(x_i) = \sum_{y_j} \lambda_{Y_j}(y_j) \sum_{v_1, \ldots, v_q} \mathcal{P}(y_j|x_i) \prod_{k} \rho_{V_k Y_j}(v_k). \tag{3.27}$$

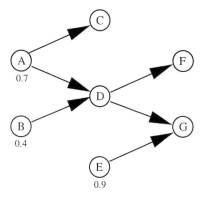

Figure 3.14: Seven node probabilistic network for Example 3.13

Thus, as each node receives ρ and λ messages from its parents and children, it computes and transmits new λ and ρ messages to them. Iterative computations (relaxations) at various nodes spread information from all evidence nodes throughout the network, and final posterior probabilities (belief values) can be calculated for each node.

Example 3.13 (adapted from [1]) The methodology discussed above is applied to a network shown in Figure 3.14, with seven nodes $A, B, \ldots, G$ that denote binary hypotheses that can take on the value 0 (denoting 'false') or 1 (denoting 'true'). Corresponding node variables are $a, b, \ldots, g$.

We assume the prior probabilities

$$\mathcal{P}(A = 1) = 0.7, \quad \mathcal{P}(B = 1) = 0.4, \quad \mathcal{P}(E = 1) = 0.9,$$

and the conditional probabilities

$$\mathcal{P}(C = 1|A = 1) = 0.5, \quad \mathcal{P}(C = 1|A = 0) = 0.75,$$

$$\mathcal{P}(F = 1|D = 1) = 0.7, \quad \mathcal{P}(F = 1|D = 0) = 0.2.$$

Other known relevant conditional probabilities are listed in Table 3.13.

The goal is to calculate the posterior probability of each node, using all currently available evidence. To begin with, no evidence is assumed available.

1. $\lambda = 1$ for nodes C, F, G that do not have children. From the prior probabilities, $\rho_A(0) = \mathcal{P}(A = 0) = 0.3$, and $\rho_A(1) = \mathcal{P}(A = 1) = 0.7$. Similarly, $\rho_B(0) = 0.6$, $\rho_B(1) = 0.4$, $\rho_E(0) = 0.1$, and $\rho_E(1) = 0.9$.

2. Since B has only one child, $\rho_{B,D}(0) = \rho_B(0) = 0.6$ and $\rho_{B,D}(1) = \rho_B(1) = 0.4$, using Equation 3.26.

Table 3.1: Conditional probabilities for Example 3.13

a	0	0	0	0	1	1	1	1
b	0	0	1	1	0	0	1	1
d	0	1	0	1	0	1	0	1
$P(d\|a,b)$	0.40	0.60	0.45	0.55	0.60	0.40	0.30	0.70
d	0	0	0	0	1	1	1	1
e	0	0	1	1	0	0	1	1
g	0	1	0	1	0	1	0	1
$P(g\|d,e)$	0.9	0.1	0.7	0.3	0.25	0.75	0.15	0.85

3. Since A is the only parent of C, Equation 3.27 gives

$$\lambda_{C,A}(0) = \lambda_C(0)P(C = 0|A = 0) + \lambda_C(1)P(C = 1|A = 0) = 1,$$

and similarly

$$\lambda_{C,A}(1) = \lambda_C(0)P(C = 0|A = 1) + \lambda_C(1)P(C = 1|A = 1) = 1.$$

A similar calculation for node F gives $\lambda_{F,D}(0) = 1$ and $\lambda_{F,D}(1) = 1$.

4. Since E has only one child G, $\rho_{E,G}(e) = \rho(e)$, hence $\rho_{E,G}(0) = 0.1$ and $\rho_{E,G}(1) = 0.9$.

5. Equation 3.27 gives $\lambda_{G,D}(d) = \sum_g \lambda_G(g) \sum_e P(g|d, e)\rho_{E,G}(e)$. Substituting known values in the right hand side of this equation, we obtain $\lambda_{G,D}(0) = 1$ and $\lambda_{G,D}(1) = 1$.

6. Using Equation 3.26, $\rho_{A,D}(a) = \rho_A(a)\lambda_{C,A}(a)$, giving $\rho_{A,D}(0) = 0.3$ and $\rho_{A,D}(1) = 0.7$.

7. $\rho_D(d) = \sum_{a,b} P(d|a, b)\rho_{A,D}(a)\rho_{B,D}(b)$, yielding (by substituting appropriate values), $\rho_D(0) = 0.462$ and $\rho_D(1) = 0.538$.

This process continues, leading to the following other computed values:

$$\rho_{D,F}(0) = 0.462, \quad \rho_{D,F}(1) = 0.538,$$

$$\rho_F(0) = 0.531, \quad \rho_F(1) = 0.469,$$

$$\rho_G(0) = 0.419, \quad \rho_G(1) = 0.581,$$

$$\rho_{A,C}(0) = 0.3, \quad \rho_{A,C}(1) = 0.7,$$

and

$$\rho_C(0) = 0.425, \quad \rho_C(1) = 0.575.$$

All λ values remain equal to 1, hence all posterior belief values equal the ρ values for nodes.

We now update the probability computations, assuming that new evidence falsifying D becomes available.

1. For the evidential node, $\rho_D(0) = 1, \rho_D(1) = 0, \lambda_D(0) = 1, \lambda_D(1) = 0$. For nodes A, B, E (without parents), the ρ values are the same as before. For nodes C, F, G (without children), the λ values are the same as before (each equals 1). Calculations of $\rho_{B,D}(b), \lambda_{C,A}(a), \rho_{E,G}(e), \lambda_{F,D}(d), \lambda_{G,D}(d)$, and $\rho_{A,D}(a)$ are also the same as before.

2. $\rho_{D,F}(0) = \rho_D(0)\lambda_{G,D}(0) = 1$, and $\rho_{D,F}(1) = \rho_D(1)\lambda_{G,D}(1) = 0$. Similarly, $\rho_{D,G}(0) = 1$ and $\rho_{D,G}(1) = 0$.

$$\lambda_{D,A}(a) = \sum_d \lambda_D(d) \sum P(d|a, b)\rho_{B,D}(b),$$

yielding $\lambda_{D,A}(0) = 0.42$ and $\lambda_{D,A}(1) = 0.48$. Similarly, $\lambda_{D,B}(0) = 0.54$ and $\lambda_{D,B}(1) = 0.345$.

Computations proceed in this manner, leading to the posterior probabilities (beliefs) $0.727(A)$, $0.299(B)$, $0.432(C)$, $0.0(D)$, $0.9(E)$, $0.2(F)$, and $0.28(G)$, respectively. E is the only hypothesis whose belief is unaffected by evidence $D = 0$, the posterior probabilities of all other nodes decrease significantly.

This methodology gets more complicated when the graph representing relationships between hypotheses is not a simple polytree, and multiple distinct paths exist between nodes. The independence assumptions used earlier cannot then be invoked. The problem is then solved by reworking the network representation, or abstracting it into a form in which the methodology can be applied. This may be done using the *conditioning* or *clustering* methods:

1. In the *conditioning method*, subsets of nodes are instantiated, by techniques such as *evidence absorption* [14], removing variables from the conditional probability distribution.

2. The *clustering methods*, by contrast, collect groups of nodes into clusters, capturing the local structure of the joint probability distribution [7].

So far, our discussions have focused on probability computations. However, practical decision-making is based on combining the probability computations with *costs* (and benefits) associated with the results of making decisions. The next section discusses this issue, showing how monetary as well as subjective costs (in combination with probabilities) can be taken into account in rational decision-making

3.9 Decision Theory and Utilities

Expert systems play an important role in supporting the decision-making process in many applications where decisions must be based on uncertainty as well as cost considerations. This section first describes a commonly-used framework for making such decisions, followed by addressing problems that arise when subjective considerations are involved in evaluating alternative outcomes.

3.9.1 Expected-Value Decision-Making

The overall approach begins by constructing a tree whose nodes represent events or hypotheses relevant to the problem, as well as decisions that may have to be made. Each subtree below a node corresponds to one possible case (true/false) associated with the node. A leaf node represents a conjunction of Boolean values associated with its ancestor nodes. For example, if we adopt the convention that the left branch and subtree below a node refer to the 'True' (or 'Yes') case and the right branch and subtree refer to the 'False' (or 'No') case, the rightmost leaf node denotes the case when all hypotheses (associated with its ancestor nodes) are false.

The next important step is the association of a 'payoff' [7] with each leaf node in the tree, followed by computation of payoffs for intermediate nodes in the tree as well. In the simplest cases, *expected-value decision-making* is to be carried out using measures of real money (e.g., dollars), where *expected value* is defined as $\sum_{B_i \in S} P(B_i) payoff(B_i)$, where S is a partition over the collection of combinations of events, i.e., $\bigcup_i B_i = S$ and each B_i is an event combination disjoint from B_j for each $j \neq i$. Calculation of probabilities and expected payoffs proceeds using Bayes rule and other elementary probability manipulation rules discussed in Section 3.1. The payoff for a higher level node is computed from

---

[7] *Payoff* is a term used to describe a quantification of the combination of the cost and benefit associated with an event, possibly non-monetary. Payoff < 0 implies that the cost exceeds the benefit, assuming these can be directly combined into a single measure.

those of its children, using the associated probabilities. For instance, if node A has children B and C, as in Figure 3.15, where the branch to B corresponds to the hypothesis associated with A being false, and this occurs with probability p, then the expected payoff associated with node A is

$$p \times payoff\,(B) + (1 - p) \times payoff\,(C).$$

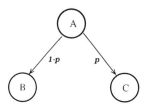

Figure 3.15: Payoff computation: $payoff\,(A) = p \times payoff\,(B) + (1 - p) \times payoff\,(C)$.

Example 3.14 Figure 3.16 depicts a small tree relevant to the decisions of an oil company, which often performs a seismic survey, followed by initial test drilling in promising sites, and then by full scale drilling. The main decisions to be made concern whether to carry out test drilling, and (if yes) whether to carry out full scale drilling.

The seismic survey provides the context for all decision-making. Let O refer to finding a sufficient quantity of oil at a reasonable depth, given the results of the seismic survey. Let $\mathcal{P}(O) = 0.6$ in a specific location.

Let D refer to positive results from the test drilling. Let $\mathcal{P}(O|D) = 0.9$, and $\mathcal{P}(O|\neg D) = 0.3$. Hence $\mathcal{P}(\neg O|D) = 0.1$, and $\mathcal{P}(\neg O|\neg D) = 0.7$. The following results can then be obtained:

$$\mathcal{P}(O) = \mathcal{P}(O \cap D) + \mathcal{P}(O \cap \neg D) = \mathcal{P}(O|D)\mathcal{P}(D) + \mathcal{P}(O|\neg D)(1 - \mathcal{P}(D)),$$

hence $\mathcal{P}(D) = (0.6 - 0.3)/(0.9 - 0.3) = 0.5$,
$\mathcal{P}(O \cap D) = \mathcal{P}(O|D)\mathcal{P}(D) = 0.9 \times 0.5 = 0.45$ and
$\mathcal{P}(O \cap \neg D) = \mathcal{P}(O|\neg D)\mathcal{P}(\neg D) = 0.3 \times 0.5 = 0.15$.

Now we assume specific monetary cost and benefit values, to allow payoff computation. Suppose the expense associated with the test drilling is $20,000, and the cost of full scale drilling is $180,000. If oil is really found, we assume that the expected monetary benefit is $1,000,000. The decision-making process requires examining payoffs associated with various nodes, as follows.

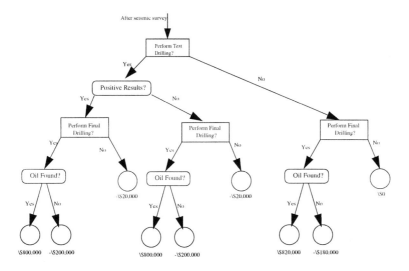

Figure 3.16: A simple decision tree

1. If neither test drilling nor full scale drilling is carried out, the net payoff is zero, irrespective of whether oil is present at the site.

2. If test drilling is not carried out but full scale drilling is carried out, the expected payoff is $((0.6) \times (\$1,000,000) - \$180,000) = \$420,000$.

3. If test drilling is carried out and the test results are positive, there is one more decision to be made:

   (a) If full scale drilling is then carried out, the net payoff is $(0.9 \times \$1000,000) - (\$20,000 + \$180,000) = \$700,000$.

   (b) If full scale drilling is not conducted, the net payoff is $-\$20,000$.

   Clearly, the second option can be pruned from the decision tree, omitted from future considerations.

4. If test drilling is carried out and the test results are negative, there is again a decision to be made:

   (a) If full scale drilling is then carried out, the net payoff is $(0.3 \times \$1000,000) - (\$20,000 + \$180,000) = \$120,000$.

   (b) If full scale drilling is not conducted, the net payoff is $-\$20,000$.

   In this case, the second option is pruned from the decision tree, i.e., full scale drilling should be carried out even if test drilling results are negative!

This strange result may be traced to the fact that $P(O|\neg D)$ is as high as 0.3 in this example.

5. Using the payoffs calculated above, an expected payoff can also be associated with the node that represents test drilling being carried out. This payoff is estimated to be $(0.5 \times \$700,000) + (0.5 \times \$120,000) = \$410,000$, since $P(D) = 0.5$, as calculated above, and assuming that full scale drilling is carried out irrespective of whether test drilling results are positive.

In this example, since $\$410,000 < \$420,000$, the probabilities and payoff values are such that full scale drilling should be carried out without test drilling at all! For a medical analogy, if the initial examination of a patient leads a physician to believe strongly in a disease hypothesis, treatment may begin without further testing.

On the other hand, if we had specified that $P(O|\neg D) = 0.01$, we would conclude $P(D) \approx 0.67$. In this case, if test results are negative, the payoff associated with full scale drilling is $(0.01 \times \$1000,000) - (\$20,000 + \$180,000) = -\$190,000$, which is less than the alternative of not full scale drilling (with payoff of $-\$20,000$). Choosing the latter alternative, the payoff if test drilling is carried out $\approx (0.67 \times \$700,000) + (0.33 \times -\$20,000) = \$460,000$, implying that it is better to carry out test drilling before deciding about full scale drilling.

3.9.2 Utility Theory

There are two major difficulties with the procedure illustrated in Example 3.14:

1. It may not be possible to evaluate outcomes in monetary terms. For instance, alternative outcomes may involve balancing between considerations of cost and loss of life, goodwill, or reputation. One such example involves deciding whether to administer a drug to a patient, considering probabilities of various side-effects (some of which may be serious) as well as the probability that the patient will get well.

2. Real life decision makers are often *not* expected-value decision makers, and make decisions contrary to what an objective analysis might reveal to be optimal. In a classic example [10], a group of Stanford University students was asked how much they were willing to pay to participate in a gamble in which they had a 50% chance of winning $100 (and 50% chance of not winning anything). Surprisingly, students were only willing to put up about $27 (on average) instead of the optimal expected value of $50.

Both of these concerns are addressed by using a *utility function* to evaluate outcomes, instead of monetary values. A utility function maps outcomes to an interval of real numbers, attempting to capture a human decision-maker's subjective evaluations of outcomes and non-monetary payoffs. The first step is to determine the utility function by examining the relative preferences of the decision-maker for various outcomes. Thereafter, the procedure is exactly the same as discussed in Example 3.14, with the only difference that we use the utility function values instead of monetary amounts. In the rest of this section, the term *lottery* refers to an event with disjoint outcomes that occur with different probabilities; we use $(p_1, E_1;\ p_2, E_2;\ \ldots;\ p_n, E_n)$, such that $\sum_{i=1}^n p_i = 1$, to denote a lottery in which each outcome E_i occurs with probability p_i.

For the utility function approach to be applicable, the following assumptions must hold:

1. There is a transitive 'preference' relation that can be used to compare any two outcomes.

2. Preferences can be assigned to lotteries, not just to outcomes. If A is preferred to B, then A should also be preferable to any lottery $(p, A;\ 1 - p, B)$ in which A is obtained with probability p and B is obtained with probability $(1 - p)$, where $0 \leq p < 1$. This extends to lotteries as well: if $0 \leq p < q \leq 1$, then the lottery $(q, A;\ 1 - q, B)$ is preferable to the lottery $(p, A;\ 1 - p, B)$.

3. There is no intrinsic reward in lotteries: preferences should not be affected by the exact manner in which uncertainty is resolved. This assumes that a decision-maker will not gamble for the sake of gambling, and that the manner in which the lottery is conducted is irrelevant to decision-making. The only important aspect of the lottery is in the probability associated with the outcomes. For instance, there should be no preference between:
   (i) tossing a coin resulting in *heads*,
   (ii) tossing a die resulting in an even number, and
   (iii) tossing two dice resulting in the sum being even.

4. Outcomes of intermediate preference can be considered equivalent to some lottery of extreme preference values. If A is preferred to B, and B is preferred to C, then there exists a probabilty p such that the decision maker is indifferent to choosing between B and the lottery $(p, A;\ 1-p, C)$.

These assumptions lead directly to the formulation of four axioms of utility; we use the notation $A \succ B$ to denote that A is preferred to B, and $A \sim B$ to

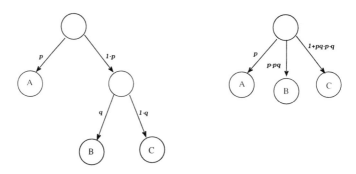

Figure 3.17: A composite lottery equivalent to a single lottery

denote indifference between A and B (neither $A \succ B$ nor $B \succ A$), where A, B are outcomes or lotteries [8]

1. (Transitivity:) If $A \succ B$ and $B \succ C$, then $A \succ C$.
   Similarly, if $A \sim B$ and $B \sim C$, then $A \sim C$.

2. Let $A \succ B$, $0 \le p \le 1$ and $0 \le q \le 1$.
   Then $(p, A; \ 1 - p, B) \succ (q, A; \ 1 - q, B)$ if and only if $p > q$.

3. Let $0 \le p \le 1$ and $0 \le q \le 1$.
   Then $(p, A; \ 1 - p, (q, B; \ 1 - q, C)) \ \sim \ (p, A; \ p - pq, B; \ 1 + pq - p - q, C)$, where the left-hand-side of the relation denotes a succession of two lotteries, as illustrated in Figure 3.17.

4. Let $A \succ B$ and $B \succ C$.
   Then there exists p such that $0 < p < 1$ and $C \sim (p, A; \ 1 - p, B)$.

If the assumptions stated above are satisfied, then a decision-maker's preferences can be consistently described using a utility function u that assigns a number to each lottery or outcome, such that $u(A) > u(B)$ if and only if $A \succ B$, and such that the utility of a lottery is the mathematical expectation of the utility of the outcomes, i.e.,

$$u(C) = p \times u(A) + (1 - p) \times u(B) \quad \text{if} \ \ C \sim (p, A; \ 1 - p, B).$$

The latter property suggests the following simple procedure for constructing a utility function. We begin with two extreme 'reference' outcomes and assign them utilities of 0 and 1 respectively; precise choices are not important

---

[8]The preference relation '$\succ$' should not be confused with the numerical comparison '$>$'.

as long as we ensure that the outcome more preferred by the decision-maker receives a higher utility value. Utilities for any other outcome may be estimated by asking questions that attempt to find an equivalent lottery between the reference outcomes. For instance, if the reference outcomes are A and B, then we ask what choice of p is such that a new outcome $C \sim (p, A; 1 - p, B)$. Then $u(C) = p \times u(A) + (1 - p) \times u(B) = 1 - p$.

To minimize inconsistencies, the decision-maker may be asked to evaluate the utility of new outcomes with respect to the closest outcomes for which utility values have already been determined. For example, if we have just determined $u(C)$ based on evaluating C with respect to reference outcomes A and B, with $B \succ C \succ A$, then for a new outcome D we would first ask whether $C \succ D$ or $D \succ C$. If $C \succ D \succ A$. then $u(D)$ should be assigned by determining the appropriate lottery between C and A, i.e., the choice of p such $D \sim (p, C; 1 - p, A)$. If $B \succ D \succ C$, then $u(D)$ should instead be assigned by determining the appropriate lottery between C and B. Such a process is continued with other outcomes; for example, if $C \succ E \succ D$, we ask for the choice of p such $E \sim (p, C; 1 - p, D)$.

Example 3.15 Consider the problem of modeling the preferences of students who are non-expected-value decision-makers.

1. We may ask how much one would be willing to pay to participate in a lottery in which they had a 50% chance of winning $100, and 50% chance of not winning anything. An answer of $27 would mean that the decision-maker is indifferent between $27 and the lottery. Using reference outcomes $u(\$0) = 0$, $u(\$100) = 1$, we obtain

$$u(\$27) = 0.5u(\$0) + 0.5u(\$100) = 0.5.$$

2. We may instead attempt to determine the value of p such that the decision-maker has no preference between the lottery $(p, \$100; 1 - p, \$0)$ and a specified amount. For instance, if the decision-maker is willing to pay $50 when $p = 0.8$, we conclude $\$50 \sim (0.8, \$100, 0.2, \$0)$, hence $u(\$50) = 0.8 \times u(\$100) + 0.2 \times u(\$0) = 0.8$.

One of the problems with the utility function approach is that human experts tend to be inconsistent in the utility values they generate. Best results may be obtained by asking multiple questions and bringing inconsistencies to the attention of the expert, forcing a clear resolution rather than risk errors.

Since each subjective decision-maker may have his own preference structure, the utility function only models one decision-maker. The approach is 'descriptive,' not 'prescriptive,' and does not dictate what a new decision-maker ought to do in a given situation, unless it is necessary to mimic the decisions of a specific decision-maker.

3.10 Dempster-Shafer Calculus

So far, we have followed the approach of 'traditional' probabilistic analysis. Such an approach is often criticized on account of its need for complete information regarding all possible conditional probabilities. In practical problems, complete information may be unavailable, or may require excessive amounts of computation. This difficulty has been addressed by Dempster's theory of evidence, subsequently elaborated by Shafer into a form that is known as the Dempster-Shafer Calculus, discussed in this section. Many practitioners have used the Dempster-Shafer approach [15] to model uncertainty in problems involving the combination of multiple sources of evidence, and where attempts are made to represent partial or total ignorance about hypotheses.

3.10.1 Belief Mass

In this approach, each hypothesis is associated with a belief interval $\subseteq [0,1]$, specified by a lower bound called the *belief* (in the hypothesis) and an upper bound called the *plausibility* (of the hypothesis). Unlike probability, the belief in a hypothesis and the belief in its complement need not add to 1. But the belief in a hypothesis and the plausibility of its complement must add to 1. These values are calculated using a *belief mass* (or *basic probability mass*) function, referred to as *mass* in the rest of this section.

For a given problem, the *universe of discourse* is a collection of disjoint hypotheses. A total mass of 1 is divided up among nonempty subsets of this universe. Allocation of mass to non-singleton sets represents partial ignorance regarding the hypotheses in question. Each set represents a disjunction of the hypotheses it contains. The belief in a set S, denoted $Bel(S)$, is defined as the sum of masses allotted to its subsets.

Example 3.16 For the crime problem referred to in Example 3.12, let the universe of discourse $U = \{N, B, E\}$, consisting of the three hypotheses regarding who committed the crime. One possible mass distribution is as follows:

$$m_1(\{N\}) = 0.3, \ m_1(\{B\}) = 0.2, \ m_1(\{E\}) = 0.1,$$

$$m_1(\{N, B\}) = 0.1, \ m_1(\{B, E\}) = 0.1, \ m_1(\{N, E\}) = 0.05,$$

expressing partial ignorance, and

$$m_1(U) = m_1(\{N, B, E\}) = 0.15,$$

expressing complete ignorance. By definition, the belief in each singleton set is the corresponding mass, and the belief in the universal set is 1 (as can be verified by adding up all the mass values). In addition,

$$Bel(\{N, B\}) = m_1(\{N\}) + m_1(\{B\}) + m_1(\{N, B\}) = 0.3 + 0.2 + 0.1 = 0.6,$$

and similarly $Bel(\{B, E\}) = 0.4$ and $Bel(\{N, E\}) = 0.45$.

Since the complement of $\{N\}$ is $\{B, E\}$, the plausibility of $\{N\}$ is given by

$$Pl(\{N\}) = 1 - Bel(\{B, E\}) = 1 - 0.4 = 0.6.$$

Thus the belief interval associated with $\{N\}$ is

$$Int(\{N\}) = [Bel(\{N\}), \ Pl(\{N\})] = [0.3, \ 0.6].$$

Similarly, the belief intervals associated with the other singleton sets are

$$Int(\{B\}) = [0.2, \ 0.55], \ \text{and} \ Int(\{E\}) = [0.1, \ 0.4].$$

3.10.2 Combining Evidence

Evidence coming in from multiple sources can be represented using different mass functions.

If m_1 and m_2 are two mass functions for the same universe of discourse, Dempster-Shafer calculus provides a simple rule combining them into a single mass function $m_1 \oplus m_2$. For each $X \subset U$, the combined mass function is defined as

$$(m_1 \oplus m_2)(X) = k \sum_{A \cap B = X} m_1(A) m_2(B), \tag{3.28}$$

where $k = 1 / \left(\sum_{A \cap B \neq \{\}} m_1(A) m_2(B) \right)$, normalizing the mass function to ensure that $\sum_{X \subseteq U} (m_1 \oplus m_2)(X) = 1$.

Example 3.17 Consider again the crime problem in Example 3.16, with the universe of discourse $U = \{N, B, E\}$. One witness suggests the mass function m_1 of Example 3.16, whereas another witness independently suggests a different mass function m_2, described as:

$$m_2(\{N\}) = 0.3, m_2(\{B\}) = 0.5, m_2(\{E\}) = 0.1, m_2(\{N, E\} = 0.1,$$

with zero mass allocated to other subsets of U. Combining evidence from the two witnesses, using k to denote the normalizing constant, we obtain

$$(m_1 \oplus m_2)(\{N,\ E\}) = k\,(m_1(\{N,\ E\})m_2(\{N,\ E\}))$$

$$+m_1(\{N,\ E\})m_2(\{N,\ E,\ B\}) + m_2(\{N,\ E\})m_1(\{N,\ E,\ B\}))$$

$$= k\,((0.05)(0.1) + (0.05)(0) + (0.15)(0.1)) = 0.02k.$$

Similarly, $(m_1 \oplus m_2)(\{N\}) = 0.22k$, $(m_1 \oplus m_2)(\{B\}) = 0.275k$, and $(m_1 \oplus m_2)(\{E\}) = 0.06k$, with other sets being allotted a combined mass of 0. Adding the terms obtained above, $0.02k + 0.22k + 0.275k + 0.06k = 0.575k$ must equal 1, hence $k \approx 1.74$, so that the normalized masses above equal 0.035, 0.383, 0.478, and 0.104, respectively.

The amount of computation required to combine evidence is much less when the universe of discourse is binary, e.g., $U = \{D, \neg D\}$.

The Dempster-Shafer approach provide a simple evidence-combination rule intended to be used in the absence of a complete probabilistic model, when some parameters such as prior or conditional probabilities are missing. However, this approach ignores dependence relationships between hypotheses (even when available), and may hence lead to erroneous conclusions.

Example 3.18 The belief associated with the statement "Tweety can fly" needs to be estimated, based upon the statements "Tweety is a penguin," "Penguins are birds," "Penguins normally do not fly," and "Birds normally fly."

Let mass $m_1 = \epsilon_1 \approx 0$, corresponding to the evidence that Tweety is a penguin and penguins do not normally fly. Let mass $m_2 = 1 - \epsilon_2 \approx 1$, corresponding to the evidence that Tweety is a bird and birds normally fly. Using Equation 3.28, the Dempster-Shafer approach combines m_1 and m_2, resulting in a combined belief of ≈ 0.5 if $\epsilon_1 \approx \epsilon_2$, instead of concluding that Tweety should not be expected to fly. The evidence that Tweety is a bird has affected the conclusion, although knowing that Tweety is a penguin should make m_2 useless for the commonsense reasoning process. In probabilistic terms, Tweety's being a bird depends on its being a penguin and penguins being birds; hence

$$\mathcal{P}(\text{Tweety can fly} \mid \text{Tweety is a penguin AND Tweety is a bird})$$

should equal $\mathcal{P}(\text{Tweety can fly} \mid \text{Tweety is a penguin})$. Ignoring the conditional dependence relations leads to an anomalous answer.

Pearl [13] suggests that the Dempster-Shafer approach does not "provide full answers to probabilistic queries but rather resigns itelf to providing partial answers" and "estimates how close the evidence is to forcing the truth of the hypothesis, instead of estimating how close the hypothesis is to being true."

3.11 Fuzzy Systems

The preceding sections have addressed the issue of carrying out computations in the context of uncertainty associated with various events. This section addresses a related (though different) issue, i.e., *imprecision* associated with describing events and their occurrence, especially when natural language descriptions must be translated to numerical terms that allow computations to be carried out.

In some contexts, the primary question to be answered is not the probability or belief in a hypothesis, but the degree of truth that can be associated with a hypothesis, or the degree to which an element belongs to a 'fuzzy' set. For instance, a yes/no answer may be useless for the question of whether the sky is cloudy: instead, it may be more helpful to answer how cloudy is a given sky, with answers such as "30% cloudy" being reasonable and meaningful. Such a statement should not be confused with an assertion that the "sky is cloudy with probability 30%," wherein the understanding is that there are only two possibilities ("cloudy" vs. "not cloudy"), of which the former is believed to occur with 30% probability. Similarly, a statement that one has parked a car "90% in the driveway" implies that 10% of the car is sticking out into the road (or garage), not that the probability of the car being parked in the driveway is 90%.

Fuzzy systems address such non-probabilistic issues, including natural language statements that express imprecision, e.g., "the car is *mostly* parked in the driveway" and "the sky is *not very* cloudy" [18]. For such statements, a precise quantitative interpretation is not possible, and reasoning with such statements involves mechanisms unlike classical logic, and unlike probabilistic reasoning.

Fuzzy logic draws upon an infinite-valued logic proposed by Lukasiewicz in the 1920s[8], allowing statements whose truth value is intermediate between classical extremes. For instance, a statement with truth value 0.7 is 'more true' than a statement with truth value 0.5, while neither is absolutely true (1.0) nor absolutely false (0.0).

Fuzzy sets allow partial membership of elements in sets, e.g., $F = \{A : 0.7, B : 0.6, C : 1.0, D : 0.0\}$ describes[9] a fuzzy set F in which A belongs to the degree 0.7, B belongs to the degree 0.6, and C belongs to the degree 1.0. The symbol μ, subscripted by the name of the fuzzy set, is often used to denote the membership function, e.g., the fuzzy set F may be described by specifying $\mu_F(A) = 0.7$, $\mu_F(B) = 0.6$, $\mu_F(C) = 1.0$, and $\mu_F(D) = 0$. Elements completely

---

[9]Many authors use the symbol '/' instead of ':' to separate an element from its membership value, a notation not preferred here, to minimize confusion with the division operator, since numbers may be the elements of the fuzzy set being considered.

absent from a set need not be mentioned, e.g., D could have been omitted from the above description of F.

We may attach a numerical meaning to natural language expressions and sentences that allow a fuzzy interpretation.

Example 3.19 Let $F = \{A : 0.7,\ B : 0.6,\ C : 1.0,\ D : 0.0\}$ as before. Although $\mu_F(A) \neq \mu_F(B)$, a fuzzy interpretation would consider these membership values to be *approximately equal*. So "belong equally in" may be considered a fuzzy predicate or relation, defined as follows:

$$BEI(F, X, Y) = \begin{cases} 0.0 \text{ if } |\mu_F(X) - \mu_F(Y)| > 0.3; \\ 1.0 \text{ if } \mu_F(X) = \mu_F(Y); \\ 1 - (|\mu_F(X) - \mu_F(Y)|/0.3) \text{ otherwise.} \end{cases}$$

Then $BEI(F, A, B) = 2/3$, whereas $BEI(F, B, C) = 0$.

The choice of such functions depends significantly on the problem domain. A person whose height equals $160cm$. may be considered to be tall if the domain is that of jockeys who ride race horses, but not if the domain is that of basketball players.

In the context of expert systems, the fuzzy approach suggests a way of combining evidence that differs from the probabilistic and the Dempster-Shafer approaches. Logical operators are associated with specific mathematical operators applied to truth values or membership degrees; the earliest treatment is to use max for disjunctions and min for conjunctions, although several other mathematical functions are currently in use. For example, if $tv(x) \in [0, 1]$ denotes the truth value of x, alternative computation rules are

$$tv(a \text{ OR } b) = tv(a) + tv(b) - tv(a)tv(b), \quad tv(a \text{ AND } b) = tv(a)tv(b).$$

The choice of the computation rule is generally justified by what appears appropriate for the specific application being considered.

Such computation rules are extended to the problem of assessing the conclusions of multiple production rules with the same consequent, given the fuzzy truth values or degrees of imprecision associated with each hypothesis as well as each production rule. A collection of rules that separately lead to the same conclusion may be treated as a disjunction of their respective antecedents, so that computations may be carried out by applying the 'min' function to elements conjoined in the antecedents of each rule, and applying the 'max' function to the results.[10]

---

[10]This rule is often expressed in terms of matrix multiplication, using 'min' instead of product and 'min' instead of product.

Example 3.20 Consider a rule based system that contains two rules $P_1\&Q_1 \Rightarrow R$ and $P_2\&Q_2 \Rightarrow R$, with the same rhs but different lhss. For instance, P_1 may denote the proposition "it is snowing nearby in the east," Q_1 denotes "there is a strong wind from the eastward direction," P_2 and Q_2 denote similar propositions for the westward direction, and R denotes the proposition that "it will soon snow in this town." It can be argued that the rules are not probabilistic:

- The definition of 'nearby' is fuzzy, e.g., with a fuzzy membership function μ_{nearby} defined as $\max(0, 1-(\text{Distance in miles})/100)$.

- 'The east' is fuzzy since a reasonable interpretation includes directions ranging from northeast to southeast, e.g., with a fuzzy membership function μ_E defined as $\max(0, 1-(\text{Difference in orientation in degrees})/45)$.

What can we conclude about R if the various predicates in the rules are only partially true in a given state of the working memory? For example, let $tv(P_1) = 0.5$, $tv(P_2) = 0.7$, $tv(Q_1) = 0.8$, and $tv(Q_2) = 0.6$. The existence of two rules with the same consequent may be interpreted as equivalent to a single rule $(P_1\&Q_1)$ OR $(P_2\&Q_2)$ $\Rightarrow$ R, whose antecedent is the disjunction of the antecedents of the two rules. Using the 'min' function for conjunctions, and 'max' for disjunctions, the truth value of the antecedent of the combined rule is computed to be $\max(\min(0.5, 0.8), \min(0.6, 0.7)) = 0.6$. The consequent R is hence associated with the truth value 0.6.

Classical logicians object to the fuzzy approach on the grounds that the inference rules and the meanings attached are excessively intertwined, so that one cannot reason about whether the reasoning process is reasonable. By contrast, in classical logic, soundness and completeness results establish the connection between "what can be proved" and "what is true" (in every possible interpretation).

Concluding this section, it is re-emphasized that fuzziness addresses *imprecision*, to be distinguished from *uncertainty*. The choice of a fuzzy or probabilistic methodology depends on a careful interpretation of the problem to determine whether there are variables whose values can vary within a range, or whether there are categorical variables that take discrete values with different probabilities.

3.12 Certainty Factors

For completeness, this section briefly discusses another popular approach for representing uncertainty, called *certainty factors*. Although the justifiability of this approach is questionable, understanding its mechanics is important since many past and current expert systems do utilize certainty factors.

In this approach, an expert is asked to articulate a *Measure of Belief (MB)* as well as a *Measure of Disbelief (MD)* in a hypothesis. These measures are intended to capture the strength of evidence for and against the hypothesis, as subjectively evaluated by the expert. The goal is that an expert uses $MB(H, E)$ to express the extent to which the evidence E leads to an increase in the belief in the hypothesis H. Similarly, the expert uses $MD(H, E)$ to express the decrease in the belief in H. These values are constrained to lie in the $[0, 1]$ real interval; values from other intervals can be mapped to $[0, 1]$ using a simple linear transformation.

MB and MD are combined into a single measure, the *certainty factor* associated with the hypothesis H according to the expert X, as follows:

$$CF(H, E) = \frac{MB(H, E) - MD(H, E)}{1 - \min(MB(H, E), MD(H, E))}$$

This formula was first used in 1977, in the MYCIN expert system. Note that $-1 \leq CF(H, E) \leq 1$.

Since there may be several experts involved, we use a subscript to specify the expert, whenever appropriate. Given the certainty factors independently obtained using two experts X and Y, beliefs of different experts are combined using the following rule, where, for brevity, c_x denotes $CF_X(H, E)$ and c_y denotes $CF_Y(H, E)$:

$$CF_{X,Y}(H, E) = \begin{cases} c_x + c_y(1 - c_x) & \text{if } c_x > 0 \text{ and } c_y > 0 \\ c_x + c_y(1 + c_x) & \text{if } c_x < 0 \text{ and } c_y < 0 \\ \frac{c_x + c_y}{1 - \min(|c_x|, |c_y|)} & \text{otherwise} \end{cases} \qquad (3.29)$$

This approach can lead to counterintuitive results, primarily since the certainty factors approach ignores prior probabilities as well as the dependence relationships among evidence sources and hypotheses. The problem is not just a question of precise choice of numerical values, it occurs even when we attempt to answer qualitatively whether one hypothesis is more likely than another competing hypothesis. For instance, if the prior probability of a hypothesis H_1 is significantly higher than another hypothesis H_2, availability of evidence may increase belief in H_1 less than the corresponding increase in belief in H_2; so the certainty factor associated with H_2 may be higher than for H_1, although the posterior probability is lower for H_2 than for H_1.

Hence, despite ease of use and popularity, practitioners are warned to avoid this approach.

3.13   Bibliographic Notes

We have discussed notions of probability, odds, and likelihood coefficients, focusing on their use in expert systems that use probabilistic inference networks. This topic gained prominence due to its early use in expert systems such as PROSPECTOR and Mycin, discussed by Duda, Hart and Nilsson (1976) and Shortliffe (1976)[17], respectively.

Due to our focus on expert systems, we have ignored many interesting issues associated with calculating, using, thinking about, and reasoning with probabilities, best dealt with in textbooks on probability such as those by Feller (1950) [5]. and Fine (1973) [6].

Probabilistic reasoning in causal networks and related models is well described in the books of Pearl [12] and Castillo, Gutierrez and Hadi [1], which contain detailed derivations of the results mentioned in Section 3.8.

North's article [10] is a nice summary of Decision Theory, discussed in greater detail in books such as [11]. Decision Theory is closely connected with Game Theory, for which a classic reference is [9].

Several articles addressing Dempster-Shafer calculus occur in [16]. A large amount of literature exists on fuzzy logic, fuzzy sets, and their applications; a useful collection of many important papers on these topics is [2].

Bibliography

[1] E. Castillo, J.M. Gutierrez, and A.S. Hadi, *Expert Systems and Probabilistic Network Models,* Springer, New York, 1997.

[2] D. Dubois, H. Prade, and R.R. Yager (Eds.), *Readings in Fuzzy Sets for Intelligent Systems,* Morgan Kaufmann, 1993.

[3] R. Duda, J. Gaschnig and P. Hart, "Model Design in the Prospector Consultant System for Mineral Exploration," in D. Michie (ed.), *Expert Systems in the Microelectronic Age,* Edinburgh Univ. Press, 1979, pp.153-167.

[4] R. Duda, P. Hart, and N. Nilsson, "Subjective Bayesian methods for rule-based inference systems," in *Proc. National Computer Conference (AFIPS),* vol. 15, 1976. Also in G. Shafer and J. Pearl (Eds.), *Readings in Uncertain Reasoning,* San Mateo: Morgan-Kaufmann, 1990, pp.274-281.

[5] W. Feller, *An introduction to probability theory and applications, vol. 1* (3rd edition 1968), New York: Wiley, 1950.

[6] T. E. Fine, *Theories of Probability,* New York: Academic Press, 1973.

[7] S.L. Lauritzen and D.J. Spiegelhalter, "Local computation with probabilities in graphical structures and their application to expert systems," *Journal of the Royal Statistical Society B,* 1988, 50(2):157-224.

[8] J. Lukasiewicz, "Many-valued systems of propositional logic" (originally published in 1930), in S. McCall (Ed.), *Polish Logic 1920-1939,* Oxford University Press, 1967.

[9] J. von Neumann and O. Morgenstern, *Theory of Games and Economic Behavior,* Princeton, 1968.

[10] W. North, "A Tutorial Introduction to Decision Theory," in G. Shafer and J. Pearl (Eds.), *Readings in Uncertain Reasoning*, Morgan Kaufmann, 1990, pp.68-78.

[11] H. Raiffa, *Decision Analysis,* Addison-Wesley, 1968.

[12] J. Pearl, *Probabilistic Reasoning in Intelligent Systems: Networks of Plausible Inference,* Morgan Kaufmann, San Mateo (CA), 1988.

[13] J. Pearl, "Bayesian and Belief-Functions Formalisms for Evidential Reasoning: A Conceptual Analysis," in G. Shafer and J. Pearl (Eds.), *Readings in Uncertain Reasoning*, Morgan Kaufmann, pp.540-574, 1990.

[14] R.D. Shachter, "Evidence Absorption and Propagation Through Evidence Reversals," in M. Henrion, R.D. Shachter, L.N. Kanal, and J.F. Lemmer (Eds.), *Uncertainty in Artificial Intelligence 5,* North Holland, Amsterdam (The Netherlands), 173-190.

[15] G. Shafer, *A Mathematical Theory of Evidence,* Princeton Univ. Press, 1976.

[16] G. Shafer and J. Pearl (Eds.), *Readings in Uncertain Reasoning*, Morgan Kaufmann, pp.540-574, 1990.

[17] E.H. Shortliffe, *Computer-based Medical Consultations: MYCIN*, New York: American Elsevier, 1976.

[18] L.A. Zadeh, "Fuzzy Sets," *Information and Control,* 1965, pp. 338-353.

3.14 Exercises

1. Show that the following relationships hold among likelihood ratios:

   (a) If $\mathcal{L_S}(H, E) > 1$, then $\mathcal{L_N}(H, E) < 1$.

   (b) If $\mathcal{L_S}(H, E) < 1$, then $\mathcal{L_N}(H, E) > 1$.

   (c) If $\mathcal{L_S}(H, E) = 0$, then $\mathcal{L_N}(H, E) = 1/\mathcal{P}(\neg E | \neg H)$.

   (d) If $\mathcal{L_N}(H, E) = 0$, then $\mathcal{L_S}(H, E) = 1/\mathcal{P}(E | \neg H)$.

2. Draw a card at random from a well-shuffled deck of 52 distinct cards, where each card is identified by a suit (Spades, Hearts, Clubs, or Diamonds) and a card-value $\in$ {Ace, King, Queen, Jack, 2, 3, 4, 5, 6, 7, 8, 9, 10}. Let E_1 denote the event that the card drawn is the Ace of Spades, E_2 that the card drawn is a Spade, E_3 that the card is a Heart, and E_4 that the card remaining on the top of the rest of the deck of cards is a Spade.

   - Which of these events are mutually exclusive (considered pairwise)?
   - Which of these events are independent (considered pairwise)?
   - Evaluate $P(E_4 \cup E_1 | E_2 \cup E_3)$.

3. Is it possible for two events A, B to be independent, but not so in the context of a third event C? In other words, does $\mathcal{P}(A \cap B) = \mathcal{P}(A)\mathcal{P}(B)$ imply $\mathcal{P}(A \cap B | C) = \mathcal{P}(A|C)\mathcal{P}(B|C)$? Prove the result or give a counterexample.

4. An event A does not affect the probability of a hypothesis H. Similarly, another event B also does not by itself affect the probability of H. Is it possible that the combination of A and B affects the probability of H? In other words, do $\mathcal{P}(H|A) = \mathcal{P}(H)$ and $\mathcal{P}(H|B) = \mathcal{P}(H)$ imply $\mathcal{P}(H|A \cap B) = \mathcal{P}(H)$? Prove the result or give a counterexample.

5. If A, B are two pieces of evidence supporting a hypothesis C, then is it true that $\mathcal{P}(C|A \cap B) = \mathcal{P}(C|A)\mathcal{P}(C|B)$? Prove the result or give a counterexample.

6. A and B are two events such that $\mathcal{L_S}(A, B) = 5$ and $\mathcal{L_N}(A, B) = 0.1$. Is this information sufficient to calculate $\mathcal{L_S}(B, A)$? If not, what additional information is minimally needed to calculate $\mathcal{L_S}(B, A)$?

7. For the Prospector inference network given in Figure 3.8, compute the posterior probability of FRE, given that FMGS is false, RCIB is true, RCVP is true, CVR is true, and other evidence is unknown.

8. Figure 3.18 gives distances (d, in miles) from Syracuse to some neighboring towns.

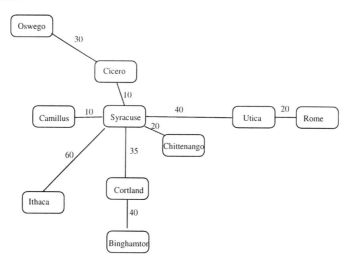

Figure 3.18: A rough distance map, Syracuse area

In each of these towns, the number of days it snows in the twelve months (Jan.-Dec.) are approximately 15, 20, 15, 10, 1, 0, 0, 0, 0, 1, 5, 10, respectively. Odds of snowing are not influenced by weather in towns that are at least 100 miles away. If it is snowing in town X and $d(X,Y) < 100$, assume that the odds that it also snows the same day in town Y are increased by a factor of $(101 - d(X,Y))$. If it is not snowing in town X, and if $d(X,Y) < 100$, the odds that it snows the same day in town Y change by a factor of $1/(101 - d(X,Y))$. There is one caveat, however: if a town Y lies roughly in between X and Z, and information is available about whether it is snowing in Y, then Z can be ignored in estimating the probability that it is snows the same day in X.

(a) Develop a probabilistic inference network to estimate the probability that it is snowing in Syracuse on February 15, based on information about whether it is snowing in neighboring towns.

(b) What is the probability that it snows in Syracuse on February 15, given that it is snowing on that day in Rome, Cortland, Oswego, and Chittenango, but not in Utica, nor in Binghamton?

(c) What is the probability that it snows in Syracuse on April 15, given the same information about neighboring towns as in part (b) above?

(d) Would your answer change if the same question was asked regarding April 30?

9. In the 'truel' problem [11], each of three players (A, B, C) is provided a small number of turns throwing a ball (say 3 per player). A throws first, followed by B (if left in the game), followed by C (if left in the game), and the cycle continues until all bullets are exhausted or only one player is left in the game. Each player may aim at himself or either of the other players, or at the ground. A player who aims at himself is guaranteed to eliminate himself, and a player who shoots at the ground is guaranteed not to eliminate anyone. A player who aims at another player succeeds in eliminating him with some probability; assume this probability is 0.5 for A, 0.6 for B, and 0.7 for C. A player wins if he is the only one left in the game. Nobody wins if more than one player is left in the game.

(a) Where should A aim? Where should the next player aim?

(b) How would your answer change if every eliminated player pays a dollar to each of the players left in the game when the game is over? (Now the winners are all the players left in the game at the end of maximum 3 turns with each ball.)

(c) How would your answers change if there is no upper bound on the number of turns allowed per player, i.e., the game continues to be played until only one player is left in the game?

10. In a popular television game, contestants may risk some amount (equal to potential gain) and attempt to answer questions pertaining to various subjects. An answer increases or decreases a contestant's current 'score' (a monetary quantity) by the amount risked, depending on whether the answer is correct. In the final stage of the game, each contestant gets to answer the question, but must state the amount he is willing to risk (not to exceed his current score), knowing the category but not the precise question. The player with the highest score wins (that amount), the other two players get nothing. Discuss whether a player's decision (regarding how much to risk) can be made using the methodology in Section 3.9; assume that there are only two players.

11. Formalize the decision-making process you would use to select one offer of employment from several offers (received at about the same time). Identify the relevant criteria and their relative importance, then construct an

---

[11] Modified from a feudal and violent version mentioned by Ray Smullyan.

example to show how decision-making would be carried out, given that each offer is better than the others in some respect.

12. Model using a probabilistic inference network and carry out the ρ and λ computations, given the following evidence relevant to a crime scenario, where a, b, c denote the three suspects, respectively. We presume the prior probabilities are equal for all three suspects.

- The lab. report says the fingerprints are likely to be those of a, b, c in the ratio $7 : 2 : 1$, i.e., with probabilities 70%, 20% and 10%, respectively. The reliability of the lab. reports is not perfect, and perhaps we may assume that they are 95% accurate, with

$$\mathcal{P}(\text{fingerprints belong to X} \mid \text{lab. report says so}) = 0.95.$$

- The witness says the person seen running from the scene was about as tall as a or b, but not as tall as c, placing the relevant probabilities in the proportion $4 : 4 : 1$.

- Regarding motive, suspect a is reported to have evinced lack of affection towards the victim of the crime, whereas suspects b and c have possible financial gain from the crime. Weighing these motives differently, the proportions of associated probabilities (that each suspect had motives strong enough to attack the victim) may be placed at $1 : 3 : 3$.

- A friend of a claims that he was present with her around the time the crime is believed to have been committed, but this testimony is not completely reliable since the exact time of the crime has not been clearly established. No such alibi exists for b and c, placing the alibi-related probability proportions (that each suspect was present elsewhere when the crime occurred) at $10 : 1 : 1$.

Determine the relative belief in the guilt of a, b, c, assuming that no other evidential information becomes available.

13. How would the results of Example 3.17 change if yet another witness were to come forward, with mass function m_3 defined as in each of the following cases:

(a) m_3 identical to m_2

(b) $m_3(\{N, E, B\}) = 1.0$

(c) $m_3(\{N\}) = m_3(\{E\}) = m_3(\{B\}) = 1/3$

(d) $m_3(\{N, E\}) = m_3(\{E, B\}) = m_3(\{B, N\}) = 1/3$

14. In the above exercises, would different results be obtained if the three witnesses came forward in a different sequence, e.g., is $m_1 \oplus (m_3 \oplus m_2) = m_2 \oplus (m_3 \oplus m_1)$?

15. Can the fuzzy combination rules (e.g., max and min) be used to combine posterior probabilities computed using different pieces of evidence, i.e., to compute $P(H|(E_1 \cap E_2))$ from $P(H|E_1)$ and $P(H|E_2)$?

16. Discuss whether probabilistic reasoning can be used to solve the non-monotonic reasoning problems of Section 2.3. The suggestion is that the truth of every statement be qualified by a probability. Hypotheses routinely assumed in commonsense reasoning can be considered to be those that hold with high prior probability; given new evidence, we have to consider the posterior probability of such hypotheses, updated conditional to the available evidence.

Chapter 4

Rule Based Programming

Cause and effect, means and ends, seed and fruit, cannot be severed;
for the effect already blooms in the cause, the end pre-exists in the
means, the fruit in the seed. ———— Ralph Waldo Emerson, 1841

This chapter addresses the most important and widely used paradigm of expert systems: rule-based programming. Some practitioners identify rule-based systems with expert systems, because the most visible industrial successes of expert systems (and artificial intelligence) involve rule-based systems.

The primary motivation for rule-based systems is their modularity. The standard recipe for solving complex problems is to decompose it into many little parts, solve each part separately, and put the results together. When rule-based systems are used to solve difficult problems, each rule represents a small chunk of knowledge, whose applicability is easy to determine, essentially ignoring other parts of the system.

Before discussing rule-based programming, we discuss its precursors, *viz.*, grammar rules in Section 4.1 and rewrite rules in Section 4.2. Section 4.3 discusses the issue of partially or totally ordering (sequencing) rules, with implications for rule interpreters. In Section 4.4, we examine the *backward chaining* model of working with rules, exploited in the programming language Prolog. *Production rules*[1] of the kind most commonly used in expert systems are discussed in Section 4.5. Commonly used inference engines that process production rules are discussed in Section 4.6. The matching process, perhaps the most expensive computational step in rule-based system execution, is addressed in

---

[1] Use of the phrase "production rules" is restricted in this book to rules that occur in rule-based expert systems, wherein the right-hand-side of a rule specifies an action to occur when the rule is executed.

Section 4.7. Section 4.8 discusses how an inference engine may select one out
of many possible rule instances for execution. Finally, Section 4.9 addresses
possible approaches to specifying and verifying rule-based expert systems.

4.1   Grammar Rules

The syntactic structure of natural languages as well as artificial programming
languages is most often described using rules of a context-free grammar. Each
such grammar consists of a set of *terminals* (words or atomic symbols acceptable
in the language), a set of *nonterminals* (special symbols used to denote categories
of word-groups or symbol-groups), a special *Start* symbol (usually denoted S),
and a set of rules. In context-free grammars, the left-hand-side (lhs) of each rule
consists of a single nonterminal, and the right-hand-side (rhs) of each rule is a
sequence that may contain terminals and nonterminals. A *sentence* is a legal
sequence of terminals, recognized by repeated application of grammar rules, a
process that also reveals the structure of the sentence, constructing a *parse tree*.
A parse tree is an ordered tree whose leaves are terminals, and root is the start
symbol, such that if $x_1, \ldots, x_n$ is the ordered sequence of children of X, then
the grammar contains a rule $X \rightarrow x_1 \ldots x_n$. A sequence of terminals (leaves
of a parse tree) is *recognized* by the grammar if one can apply the rules of the
grammar (beginning from S), repeatedly replacing some nonterminal in the lhs
of a rule by the corresponding rhs, until the sequence of leaves is obtained.

Example 4.1 Consider the grammar with nonterminals S, N, V, A, and P, of
which S is the distinguished start symbol, the terminals are the English words
Tarzan, eats, spicy, tofu, and the rules are:

$$S \rightarrow P\ V \qquad\qquad S \rightarrow P\ V\ P$$
$$P \rightarrow N \qquad\qquad P \rightarrow A\ P$$
$$N \rightarrow Tarzan \qquad\qquad N \rightarrow tofu$$
$$V \rightarrow eats \qquad\qquad A \rightarrow spicy$$

The same symbol may be used several times within the same parse tree,
each time with different children. This grammar also recognizes several less
meaningful sentences, e.g., *tofu eats spicy Tarzan*, but that is not our present
concern. Syntactic analysis (using grammar rules) merely identifies acceptable
word sequences; attaching meaning to them is the task of semantic analysis.

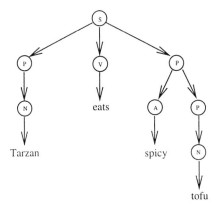

Figure 4.1: Parse tree for the sentence *Tarzan eats spicy tofu*

4.2 Rewrite Rules

Rewrite systems [3] use rules for computation in yet another manner. Perhaps the oldest such models are Post's string rewriting systems dating from 1943 [14]. In these systems, the global state consists of one string (sequence of characters or symbols) modified by the *firing* (execution) of each rule. Any rule may be fired at any time, if its *lhs* matches with some part of the string. As a result, the matching part of the string would be replaced by the corresponding instance of the *rhs* of the rule. The part of the string that matches with the *lhs* of a rule is deleted in the process. Unlike rules in a grammar, rewrite rules may contain variables.

A variable that occurs on the *rhs* of the rule must also occur on the *lhs*. This variable is local to the rule, and is analogous to a formal parameter in a procedure or function in traditional programming languages. The matching process associates each variable with some symbol (element of the string). There is no specific order in which rules are fired, and no specific order in which different parts of the string are matched with the *lhs* of a rule. Example 4.2 illustrates these notions.

Example 4.2 Given the two rules

$$XaY \implies YaX$$

$$aa \implies b$$

where a, b are constants and X, Y are variables, the input string *baaba* may be modified in three possible ways:

1. The occurrence of *aa* may be replaced by *b*, using the second rule, yielding *bbba*. No further rule can then be applied to the resulting string.

2. The substring *baa* may be replaced by *aab*, using the first rule, thereby modifying *baaba* to *aabba*. Either rule can now be applied to the resulting string.

3. The substring *aab* may be replaced by *baa*, using the first rule, thereby modifying *baaba* to *bbaaa*. Again, either rule can now be applied.

Such systems have been extended to *term rewriting* and *graph rewriting* systems. In string rewriting, the *lhs* of the string rewrite rule must match with a sequence of symbols (substring) in the input string; in term rewriting, the *lhs* of the term rewrite rule is a term that must match with some subterm of the input term. Similarly, in graph rewriting, the *lhs* of the graph rewrite rule is a graph that must match with some subgraph of the input graph. The notion of using more structure is invoked in production-rule based expert systems, which often perform rewriting on structures called frames (cf. Section 1.4).

4.2.1   Petri Nets

A *Petri net* is a special kind of rewrite rule system popular in system modeling, thanks to a convenient pictorial depiction scheme. Petri nets have been used in modeling communication protocols, distributed systems, and nondeterministic computation systems, and also for reasoning about production systems.

In a Petri net, the global state (or *marking*) is a *multiset*[2] of elements of the vocabulary. If the vocabulary consists of elements U, V, W, X, Y, Z (called *places*), then the multiset with two occurrences of U and three occurrences of X (and none of the other elements) can be succinctly written as $\{U : 2, X : 3\}$. The number of occurrences of each element is referred to as the number of *tokens* of that element.

The *lhs* and *rhs* of each *transition* (or rule) are also multisets of elements. Execution of a Petri net rule involves deleting (from the global state) the tokens corresponding to the *lhs* of the rule, and inserting (into the global state) tokens corresponding to the *rhs* of the rule. However, note that the *lhs* and *rhs* are unordered; in this respect they differ from string rewrite rules.

---

[2]In a *multiset* (or 'bag'), each element can occur any number of times, and there is no implicit sequence or order of the elements.

Example 4.3 Consider the Petri net depicted in Figure 4.2, with vocabulary $\{U, V, W, X, Y, Z\}$, initial global state $\{U : 2, X : 3\}$, and the following rules:

$$\langle U, X \rangle \rightarrow \langle V, W \rangle$$

$$\langle U, V \rangle \rightarrow \langle X, W \rangle$$

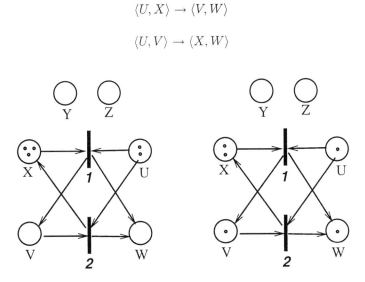

Figure 4.2: Petri net with six places and two transitions; an initial marking is shown, followed by the marking after the first rule is fired

To begin with, the first rule can be applied, leading to the global state $\{U : 1, V : 1, W : 1, X : 2\}$. We can then apply the first rule, obtaining $\{V : 2, W : 2, X : 1\}$, or the second rule, obtaining $\{W : 2, X : 3\}$. In either case, execution terminates since rules cannot be applied any more.

4.3 Ordering the rules

In contrast to complete nondeterminism in rule execution, Markov[3] [8] suggested imposing a total order on rules, and applying them in a strict sequence to the input string. In Example 4.2, for instance, the first rule may be considered to be of greater priority than the second, in which case the substring *baa* must first be replaced by *aab* modifying *baaba* to *aabba*. Indeed, we would repeatedly apply the first rule to the initial three-element substring, so that this 'program' would not terminate.

---

[3]This Markov is not to be confused with his father, the mathematician renowned for his formulation of "Markov chains".

The modern equivalent of Markov's approach is to label each rule with a distinct number called *priority* or *salience*. We can compare the priorities of different rules. At any given time, the rule with the highest possible priority is to be fired. By contrast, Post's string rewrite systems presume equal priorities for all rules. Post's system is highly modular and easy to modify, but it is harder to enforce a specific control strategy. Markov's approach compromises modularity, since changing any rule in the system would require us to examine closely whether the behavior of other rules in the system would be affected. Current practice for modern expert systems lies between these extremes, using a small number (1-10) of priority levels for rules, which are thus partially ordered.

Instead of completely ordering the rules, a *discrimination tree* organizes rules as a hierarchy. Each node in the hierarchy is associated with a test, and has two subtrees. One subtree is activated if the test yields an affirmative result, and the other subtree is activated if that test yields a negative result.

Example 4.4 Consider the task of printing the roman numeral representation of a number between 1 and 999 (e.g., Romanize(847) → 'DCCCLVII'). Here is a simple sequence of rules to solve this problem:

```
Romanize(N):
 If N>899, print 'CM' and Romanize(N-900)
else if N>499, print 'D' and Romanize(N-500)
  else if N>399, print 'CD' and Romanize(N-400)
    else if N>99, print 'C' and Romanize(N-100)
      else if N>89, print 'XC' and Romanize(N-90)
        else if N>49, print 'L' and Romanize(N-50)
          else if N>39, print 'XL' and Romanize(N-40)
            else if N>9, print 'X' and Romanize(N-10)
              else if N>8, print 'IX'
                else if N>4, print 'V' and Romanize(N-5)
                  else if N>3, print 'IV'
                    else if N>0, print 'I' and Romanize(N-1)
                    else EXIT
```

When this totally ordered sequence of rules is applied, the conditions of all rules need to be tested when N=0. The maximum number of tests (amount of computation) to be performed in the worst case can be reduced from $|RuleSet|$ to $\lceil \log_2 |RuleSet| \rceil$ by using a discrimination tree, reducing the maximum distance between the root and leaves of the tree.

```
Romanize(N):
 IF N>9,
   If N>99,
     if N>499,
       if N>899, print 'CM' and Romanize(N-900)
       else print 'D' and Romanize(N-500)
     else if N>399, print 'CD' and Romanize(N-400)
         else print 'C' and Romanize(N-100)
   Else  if N>49,
         if N>89, print 'XC' and Romanize(N-90)
         else print 'L' and Romanize(N-50)
       else  if N>39, print 'XL' and Romanize(N-40)
           else  print 'X' and Romanize(N-10)
  ELSE If N>4,
        if N>8, print 'IX'
        else  print 'V' and Romanize(N-5)
      Else if N>0,
            if N>3, print 'IV'
            else  print 'I' and Romanize(N-1)
          else EXIT
```

The rigid structure of such trees makes them difficult to modify, although this structure is very efficient from the viewpoint of computational effort. Ideally, a programmer should be able to work with a more modular, easily modifiable program, which may be compiled by the system into an efficient format such as a discrimination network.

4.4 Backward ho!

The execution models of rule systems, described so far, may be characterized as *forward chaining*: rules are applied in their 'natural' form, from left to right, as indicated by the direction of the arrow that separates the *lhs* and *rhs*. Another important execution model invokes *backward chaining*: rules are to be applied right to left.

In applying grammar rules, both forward and backward rule application procedures are common. The left-to-right procedure is referred to as *top-down* parsing, since we move 'down' from the root of the tree towards the leaves; the right-to-left procedure is *bottom-up* parsing, since we then move 'up' from the leaves of the tree towards the root[4].

Backward chaining may also be used when rules are treated as logical implications, with the *lhs* implying the *rhs*. Forward chaining may then be viewed as asking:

What are the consequences of the initial set of premises?

In contrast, backward chaining asks:

What premises can lead to the final goal to be proved?

Computation can terminate if this set (required to prove the goal) is indeed found to be a subset of the actual set of premises for the problem.

Multiple sets of premises may lead to the same goal (consequence). Hence, given a goal, the search for a single such set (of premises) may fail, and computation would have to continue with searching for other sets of premises that may instead lead to the goal. This necessitates a 'backtracking' search procedure, storing information that allows systematic search for premises that imply the goal.

Prolog is a goal-directed backward chaining language that uses such a backtracking search procedure. In Prolog, assuming the negation symbol does not occur in any l_i nor in any r_j,

$$l_1 \& \ldots \& l_n \supset r_1 \& \ldots \& r_m$$

is written as the collection of the following *Horn clauses* (disjunctions in which only one literal appears un-negated):

$$r_1 :\text{-} l_1, \ldots, l_n.$$

$$r_2 :\text{-} l_1, \ldots, l_n.$$

$$\ldots \ldots \ldots \ldots$$

$$r_m :\text{-} l_1, \ldots, l_n.$$

A *fact* (premise) f is written 'f.' with the period indicating that f requires no further proof.

The current state consists of a set of goals and subgoals to be proved, in addition to book-keeping information to keep track of how the search process has progressed so far. If the goal r_i is part of the current state, then it may be

---

[4]The 'top-down' and 'bottom-up' terminology is an artifact of the common (unnatural) practice of depicting trees with the root shown above the leaves.

replaced by the *subgoals* $l_1, \ldots, l_n$ that correspond to the part of the rule to the right of ':-' symbol (i.e., to the left of the '$\supset$' symbol in non-Prolog notation). There are three possible cases to consider:

- If l_1 is found as a fact ('l_1.'), it is removed from the set of goals.

- Instead, if there exists a rule of the form

$$l_1 :\text{-} l_{1,1}, \ldots, l_{1,k}.$$

  then l_1 is removed from the current state and replaced by its new subgoals $l_{1,1}, \ldots, l_{1,k}$.

- This search path fails if the system contains no fact 'l_1.' and no rule 'l_1 :- ....' We must instead look for other rules that may lead to the earlier goal g. If there is no way of satisfying g, then we have to examine other possible ways of satisfying its 'parent' in the goal tree, i.e., the formula for which g was generated as subgoal.

The focus of this section was on backward chaining, and the process of solving goals via successive generation of subgoals. Prolog may be studied from other perspectives, not explored here.

4.5 Production Rules

Each rule-based program consists of many *production rules*, where each rule is a subroutine whose form is that of a conditional "if C then X," where C is a sequence of expressions whose values depend on the global state, and X is a sequence of actions that may modify the global state. A rule "if C then X" may be *fired* when the sequence of elements in C is satisfied. Firing this rule results in the execution of actions in X.

Rule-based programming differs from other programming paradigms in its 'execution engine' that dictates how components of the program are processed when the program is executed. Procedural programming languages (such as C) have an implicit sequencing of statements: if the main program contains the phrase 'S_1; S_2' then we understand that the statement S_1 is first executed, followed by the execution of S_2, assuming no unexpected failures occur in the execution of S_1.

Rule-based programming does not adhere to this sequential approach. Within the body of a rule, something analogous to sequential processing does occur. Instead of executing a sequence of statements (or evaluating a sequence of expressions), the execution engine for a rule-based program picks *some* rule whose execution may be permitted. The programmer should not make any assumption about which rule may be fired when.

Example 4.5 The following is a set of three rules related to traffic signals:

$Rule_1$:   Light is green $\longrightarrow$ Drive through the intersection

$Rule_2$:   Light is red $\longrightarrow$ Don't drive through

$Rule_3$: Color of light unchanged for 2 minutes $\longrightarrow$ Change color

The state information associated with this system may indicate whether the light is currently red or green, when the light last changed color, and information regarding the present time. Although this system appears to be reasonable, a few simple questions highlight its flaws:

1. Who updates the clock?

2. What is to be done if the light is neither green nor red?

3. What is to be done if the light is both green and red?

4. If more than two colors are possible, then to which color should the light be changed by $Rule_3$?

5. If the light has been green for two minutes, should we drive through or change light color?

6. Suppose I am ready to drive through the intersection because the light is green; the light then turns red due to $Rule_3$. Can I still drive through?

The first and fourth questions illustrate that *ad hoc* rule-based specifications are often incomplete, and it is easy to overlook essential components. The second question addresses the possibility that no rules may be applicable, another aspect of the incompleteness of the specification. The third question indicates that there are certain logical relationships which may be obvious to the human (a single light cannot be both red and green), but may stump an automated system unless explicitly stated. The fifth question raises a genuine "conflict" situation: when either of two rules can be fired, which one takes precedence? The relevance of this issue is raised by the sixth question: the most reasonable interpretation is that if the light turns red due to $Rule_3$, even a rule that was previously ready to fire should not be fired: I have to wait until the light turns green again, especially if I am not driving in New York city.

Table 4.1: Terminology used in production rule-based expert systems

Phrase	Meaning
Knowledge base, Production memory	The set of rules in the program
Rule	A two-tuple of the form *if C then X*, possibly annotated with a priority (salience) value
Condition elements	Elements of the left hand side of a rule
Patterns	Simple condition elements to be matched directly with facts; these do not contain logical/arithmetic connectives, nor predicates
Actions	Elements of the right hand side of a rule
Facts	Elements of global state, possibly frame structured
Fact template	The structure associated with a class of facts
Working memory	Collection of facts present at a given time
Matching	Comparing rule patterns with the global state (elements of the working memory)
Agenda	Set of rule instances that have been successfully matched and are ready to fire
Rule activation	Placing a rule instance on the agenda
Rule deactivation	Removing a rule instance from the agenda (because some other rule was fired, and its actions resulted in violating some pattern for this rule)
Rule firing	Executing actions in a rule instance on the agenda when all of its condition elements are satisfied
Inference engine	Control mechanism that determines which rule fires

The terminology of production rule-based systems is explained in Table 4.1. The following features distinguish such systems from other formalisms that use rules.

1. The *rhs* of a rule is a sequence of *actions* to be performed when the *lhs* is satisfied.

2. These actions may modify any part of the working memory (system state), e.g., any element in a large database. Often, the working memory has some structure, and the *lhs* of the rule identifies specific components of the working memory that are modified by the *rhs*. Elements of the *lhs* are referred to as *Condition Elements* (CEs); the term *patterns* describes

simple CEs that do not contain logical or relational connectives.

3. Actions may include *asserting* new *facts* (elements in the database), as well as modifying or *retracting* (removing) existing facts identified by the *lhs* of the rule.

4. Each rule may be annotated with

   (a) control information, such as the relevant phase of system execution during which the rule may be executed,

   (b) the name of a module within which the rule is intended to be wholly contained, and

   (c) priority (salience) information describing the partial order of rules for execution purposes.

5. Components of a rule are evaluated and executed in left to right sequence.

6. Components of the *lhs* of a rule may describe the presence or absence of an element (of the working memory) that matches some (partial) description.

7. More than one element of the working memory may match a component of the *lhs* of a rule.

In executing a rule, we invoke the *frame assumption*[5]: the rule only modifies what is specified in the actions; everything else is believed to remain unchanged (cf. Chapter 2).

The process of developing a rule-based system involves identification of the tasks to be performed, determination of working memory parameters, development of rules (which may require interaction with experts), and finally their evaluation. Such an exercise is carried out in Example 4.6 which develops a rule-based system for traffic control.

Example 4.6 The task addressed by this rule-based system is to change the color of the traffic light and manipulate the pedestrian signal at a traffic intersection in New York city, where 42nd street meets 5th avenue. We assume that the working memory consists of the following variables:

1. *Street_light*, constrained to be red, yellow or green, and associated with the *clock_value* when the *Street_light* last changed color.

---

[5]The 'frame assumption' (or 'frame axiom') should not be confused with the knowledge representation mechanism of frames.

2. *Avenue_light*, constrained to be red, yellow or green, also associated with a *clock_value*.

3. *Street_walk_signal*, constrained to be "walk," "don't_walk" or "caution", also associated with a *clock_value*.

4. *Avenue_walk_signal*, constrained to be "walk," "don't_walk" or "caution", also associated with a *clock_value*.

5. *Global_clock*, indicating the current time in seconds, constrained to be an integer between 0 and 3599.

The following are candidate rules for the system; the first rule addresses global clock updates, the next three concern modifying the street light, and the next three are relevant to the walk signal.

1. At the lowest priority level, a rule represents periodic updates of the *Global_clock*. Its *lhs* is empty, and its *rhs* adds 1 (modulo 3600) to *Global_clock*. Such a rule would not be needed in a system that can access an external clock.

2. The next rule governs changing *Street_light* from red to green. Its *lhs* contains the following condition elements:

   - *Street_light* is red
   - (*Global_clock* > *Street_light_changed_time* + 120) OR
     (*Global_clock* < *Street_light_changed_time* < *Global_clock* + 3600 − 120)
   - *Street_walk_signal* is don't_walk
   - *Avenue_light* is red

   Its *rhs* contains the following actions:

   - Change *Street_light* to green
   - Change *Street_light_changed_time* to *Global_clock*

3. The next rule governs changing the *Street_light* from green to yellow. Its *lhs* contains the following patterns:

   - *Street_light* is green
   - (*Global_clock* > *Street_light_changed_time* + 120) OR
     (*Global_clock* < *Street_light_changed_time* < *Global_clock* + 3600 − 120)

Its *rhs* contains the following actions:

- Change *Street_light* to yellow
- Change *Street_light_changed_time* to *Global_clock*

4. The next rule governs changing the *Street_light* from yellow to red. Its *lhs* contains the following patterns:

   - *Street_light* is yellow
   - (*Global_clock* > *Street_light_changed_time* + 10) OR
     (*Global_clock* < *Street_light_changed_time* < *Global_clock* +3600−10)

   Its *rhs* contains the following actions:

   - Change *Street_light* to red
   - Change *Street_light_changed_time* to *Global_clock*

5. The next rule governs changing the *Street_walk_signal* from don't_walk to walk. Its *lhs* contains the following patterns:

   - *Street_walk_signal* is don't_walk
   - *Street_light* is red

   Its *rhs* contains the following actions:

   - Change *Street_walk_signal* to walk
   - Change *Street_walk_sig_change_time* to *Global_clock*

6. The next rule governs changing the *Street_walk_signal* from walk to caution. Its *lhs* contains the following patterns:

   - *Street_walk_signal* is walk
   - (*Global_clock* > *Street_walk_sig_change_time* + 30) OR
     (*Global_clock* < *Street_walk_sig_change_time* < *Global_clock* +3600-30)

   Its *rhs* contains the following actions:

   - Change *Street_walk_signal* to caution
   - Change *Street_walk_sig_change_time* to *Global_clock*

7. The next rule governs changing the *Street_walk_signal* from caution to don't_walk. Its *lhs* contains the following patterns:

- *Street_walk_signal* is caution
- ($Global\_clock > Street\_walk\_sig\_change\_time + 10$) OR
  ($Global\_clock < Street\_walk\_sig\_change\_time < Global\_clock + 3600 - 10$)

Its *rhs* contains the following actions:

- Change *Street_walk_signal* to don't_walk
- Change *Street_walk_sig_change_time* to *Global_clock*

Similar rules can be written to modify *Avenue_walk_signal* and *Avenue_light*.

4.6 Inference Engine

In this section, we state more precisely how a rule-based system executes rules. The classic execution cycle, followed in languages such as CLIPS, is described in the algorithm given below.

Rule-based Inference Algorithm:

- Determine which instances of which rules can be activated, and place these on the *agenda*;

- **while** the agenda is non-empty, **do**:

  1. Select one rule-instance from the agenda;
  2. Fire this rule-instance, executing its actions;
  3. Modify the agenda, adding or removing rule-instances, as dictated by the changes in working memory effected by the rule that has been fired;

  end while.

The initial step (before the while loop) involves significant computation, since the inference engine must exhaustively compare all the facts in the working memory with all the patterns of all rules. Note that each rule may be fired using different sets of facts to match its patterns. Hence we refer to the firing of *rule-instances*, that associate rules with information identifying which specific facts match which patterns. Since the same rule can be activated with several different instances or facts, the system must also explicitly store which facts matched with which patterns, for each possible activation. The agenda stores rule instances, not just rules.

This algorithm incurs some extra initial computational expense because some of the early rule activations may be unnecessary (since other rule firings may deactivate these rule instances). But the extra effort is more than compensated for by the significant reduction in the computational effort in subsequent steps. In each iteration of the while-loop, we only examine the possible changes to the agenda that may arise because of the most recently fired rule, and not repeatedly compare all possible facts with patterns in various rules.

In addition to determining all possible instances of all rules that can be activated and placed on the agenda, the inference engines of modern rule-based languages also compute and store *partial matches* in the initialization phase. Partial matches correspond to cases where only some of the patterns in the *lhs* of the rule match successfully with existing facts. If partial matches can be stored initially, then iterations of the while loop examine the remainder of the patterns in the *lhs* of the rule instances, determining whether the rule can be fired, without having to recompute the previously stored partial match information. Computational effort (in space and time) is reduced if the number of partial matches is limited, e.g., by placing highly specific or constraining patterns early in the rule.

Example 4.7 Given a rule $(P_1 \& P_2 \& \ldots \& P_9) \longrightarrow A$, if current facts in the system match $P_1, \ldots, P_7$ but not P_8, then this information would be stored by the inference engine. When some rule instance (on the agenda) fires, we determine if the changes to the working memory (facts in the database) affect any of the previously matched patterns $(P_1, \ldots, P_7)$. If the matches corresponding to $P_1, \ldots, P_4$ are unaffected but the one for P_5 no longer holds, then the system now stores only the matching information for $P_1, \ldots, P_4$. On the other hand, if none of the matches for $P_1, \ldots, P_7$ are affected, and if P_8 can also now be matched, then the system now stores the matching information for $P_1, \ldots, P_8$. In addition, if P_9 can also be matched, the corresponding rule instance can be placed on the agenda.

4.7   Matching

Empirical observations show that about 90% of the computational effort spent by an expert system is in the *matching* process, comparing facts in the database to condition elements in the *lhs* of each possible rule. Indeed, the strongest reason to use an expert systems shell or specialized language such as CLIPS is that the matching process is carefully implemented to optimize the match computation process, whereas this is likely to be much less efficient if the programmer attempts to code it from scratch in a general-purpose programming language. In this section, we examine the matching process closely to determine what is involved.

1. *Presence of facts*: The simplest case is when the system must determine if the database contains any fact whose specified attribute matches with a specific symbolic or numeric value in the *lhs* of a rule. For instance, if the system contains the rule

   (student's grade is 'possible-A') $\Rightarrow$ (modify student's grade to 'A'),

   the matching process involves examining all the student records to determine if there is any record in which the student's grade is 'possible-A'. Matching succeeds for all such student records.

   Matching a single condition element or pattern can involve several steps.

   Example 4.8 Using CLIPS syntax to denote variables by symbols prefixed by a question-mark, if the first conditional element in a rule is

   (C_0 (length ?any) (color red) (breadth ?any)),

   intended to match frames with the three attributes mentioned (and perhaps some other attributes not mentioned in the pattern), the matching process involves:

   (a) identifying that the relevant frame-name is C_0;

   (b) among existing facts in the working memory with that frame-name, using the color attribute to filter out any that are not red; and

   (c) of red C_0 instances, testing that the breadth attribute has the same value as the length attribute.

   Note that no matching computation was involved directly with the length attribute, it merely binds the value of the length attribute to a variable.

2. *Absence of facts*: Some rules are to be fired if there is no fact that matches a specified pattern. For instance, if the system contains the rule

   $\neg$ (student's grade is 'F') $\longrightarrow$ ...

   then the matching process examines the grade attribute of every student record. The rule is to be fired only if there is no case where the student's grade is 'F'. A clearer expression of the rule would be

$\neg$ exists (student's grade is 'F') $\longrightarrow$ ...

3. *Logical conditions in pattern elements*: Some rules are to be fired if a fact satisfies a logical expression, containing connectives *AND, OR, NOT*.

   For instance, if the system contains the rule
   (student's grade is not F) $\Rightarrow$ (modify student's status to 'Passed'),
   then the matching process examines the grade attribute of every student record, and the rule is to be fired for each case such that the student's grade is not 'F'. Note the difference between this rule and the previous one that tested for the absence of facts.

4. *Arithmetic constraints*: Numeric values and expressions may be compared.

5. *Other predicates*: System-defined or user-defined predicates may occur.

6. *Variable repetitions*: With the exception of variables matched against 'NOT'-conditional elements, the scope of each variable extends over the rule. In general, the value of a variable is bound by matching its first occurrence in the rule, and subsequent occurrences are constrained by this value. In other words, the rule may be thought of as a nested expression: a sequence $ABCD$ is interpreted as $(A(B(C(D))))$.

Modern rule-based inference engines attempt to minimize the computational effort in matching, by sharing as much information as possible between different rules. Although the programmer writes and sees independent rules, the inference engine "compiles" them into an internal implementation called the *Rete network* [4] with as few nodes as possible. The first part of the Rete network is the *pattern network*, sharing common nodes among patterns that involve the same matching computations.

Example 4.9 Given the two rules

$$C_0 \& C_1 \& C_2 \& C_4 \Rightarrow A_1$$

$$C_0 \& C_1 \& C_3 \& C_2 \Rightarrow A_2$$

partial match information for C_0 and C_1 can be shared between the rules. However, since matching occurs in a strict left-to-right sequence for each rule, partial match information about C_2 is not shared between the two rules, since C_3 intervenes in the second rule between C_1 and C_2. The resulting network will have one node representing C_0, with one child representing C_1, which has two children (representing C_2 and C_3), each of which has one more child.

If a variable has multiple occurrences in a pattern, compatibility of variable bindings is tested as the pattern is being matched. But a little more work is involved when the same variable occurs in multiple patterns, since matching a single pattern does not involve comparing variable bindings with other patterns that are matched. Hence the Rete network contains another part called the *join network*, containing *join* nodes at which consistency is enforced for bindings of variables that occur in multiple patterns.

Example 4.10 Given the rule

$$(C_0 \text{ (length ?x) (breadth ?x)) } (C_1 \text{ (length ?x) (height ?y)) } \Rightarrow A,$$

the comparison between length and breadth values for C_0 is done within the pattern network, but the comparison between bindings of the variable ?x in C_0 and C_1 is accomplished at a join node. Figure 4.3 illustrates the complete Rete network for a system containing the above rule as well another rule

$$(C_0 \text{ (length ?y) (breadth ?y)) } (C_1 \text{ (length ?x) (height ?x)) } \Rightarrow B,$$

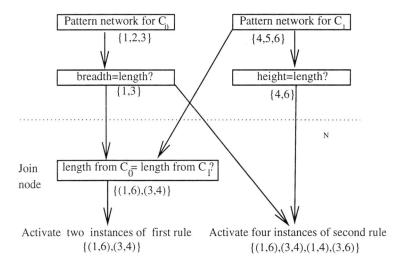

Figure 4.3: Rete network for the two rules of Example 4.10; each node is associated with facts passed from its parent nodes that satisfy the matching criterion at that node

Suppose the working memory contains the following facts:

1. $(C_0 \text{ (length 10) (breadth 10))}$

2. $(C_0$ (length 20) (breadth 10))

3. $(C_0$ (length 20) (breadth 20))

4. $(C_1$ (length 20) (height 20))

5. $(C_1$ (length 20) (height 15))

6. $(C_1$ (length 10) (height 10))

Then two instances of the first rule and four instances of the second rule are placed on the agenda. Information about which facts have already matched is stored in the network. If a new fact such as

7. $(C_1$ (length 20) (height 30))

is introduced into the working memory, perhaps as a result of firing a rule, then new partial matches are created, with new firing activations. On the other hand, if firing a rule retracts some of the existing facts in the working memory, that change would also be registered in the partial match information stored in the network, and previously activated rule instances may have to be removed from the agenda.

4.8   Conflict Resolution

The sequential execution assumed in most computer implementations presents the famous *von Neumann bottleneck*, witnessed in the examples presented above. Matching may have been successful for many instances of many rules, but only one rule-instance can be fired at a time, unless a parallel execution model is invoked. The inference engine must repeatedly make decisions regarding which one of the present instances of rules on the agenda can be fired. This is referred to as the *Conflict Resolution* task.

The following are some of the conflict resolution strategies in use:

1. *Refractoriness*: Each rule-instance is fired exactly once. However, if a fact matching a pattern (in a rule) is removed and reintroduced into the working memory, then that rule may be fired again.

2. *Specificity*: A rule with more specific *lhs* (condition elements) is fired before a less specific one. For example, if a system contains the rules

$$Bird(x) \Rightarrow CanFly(x)$$

and

$$Bird(x)\&Pigeon(x) \Rightarrow CannotFly(x),$$

the latter rule is more specific and is fired first by the specificity strategy, although this does not prevent the former rule from being fired later.

3. *Salience (Priorities)*: Each rule is associated with a number indicating its relative importance, called *salience* or *priority*. If not explicitly specified, each rule has a default salience value assigned by the system. Rule instances (on the agenda) with the highest salience are chosen for firing. This strategy does not specify what is to be done if the agenda contains multiple rule instances with the same salience value.

4. *LIFO* (last-in-first-out) *on rules*: A rule supplied later to the rule base is fired preferentially. LIFO implies a *depth-first* search strategy.

5. *FIFO* (first-in-first-out) *on rules*: A rule supplied earlier to the rule base is fired preferentially. FIFO implies a *breadth-first* search strategy.

6. *LIFO on facts*: The system fires a rule instantiated by the facts most recently introduced into the database.

7. *FIFO on facts*: The system fires a rule instantiated by the facts least recently introduced into the database.

8. *Focusing*: Modularity is an essential principle of modern software engineering: any reasonable software system should be decomposable into several modules, with interactions between modules being minimal and clearly defined. This principle can also be applied to expert systems, rule-based or not. Thus, a large rule-based expert system may consist of several subsystems, each of which is explicitly invoked by some other subsystem: under normal circumstances, only the rules in this subsystem will continue to execute until some explicit control transfer instructions are executed. The system maintains a *focus stack* of expert system modules, pushed and popped by the user. The only rules considered for firing are those in the module on top of the focus stack.

9. *Pattern Ordering*: OPS5 and descendant languages provide the option of a strategy called *MEA (means ends analysis)*, which assumes a partial order $\prec$ among patterns in rules. Given two rules

$$P_1 \& P_2 \& \ldots \& P_p \quad \Rightarrow \quad R$$

and

$$Q_1 \& Q_2 \& \ldots \& Q_q \quad \Rightarrow \quad S$$

the MEA strategy fires the first rule preferentially over the second if there is some $i > 0$ such that $Q_i \prec P_i$, and for no $j < i$ does it happen that $P_j \prec Q_j$. Rule firing then depends on the arrangement of patterns in a rule.

Refractoriness is always adopted, and salience is also used in many expert systems; the other strategies are less standard. Some systems and tools adopt combinations of these strategies, e.g., Prolog uses FIFO on rules and LIFO on facts.

The LIFO and salience strategies are inherently not *fair*: certain activated rules may never be fired, just as a Prolog program may execute indefinitely without finding a solution that could have been discovered quickly by breadth-first search.

The process of developing an expert system is least complicated if the user makes few assumptions about the sequence in which the system may fire rule instances on the agenda. Otherwise, the system can be difficult to build, understand and maintain.

The *Soar* model of rule-based execution [7] is distinguished from traditional rule-based systems in avoiding conflict resolution: all possible productions fire in parallel until no further rule firings can occur. Soar also adopts a goal-based execution procedure, and uses a two-phase execution cycle in attempting to satisfy goals maintained in a stack. Another major difference is that Soar uses a mechanism called *chunking* to create new production rules from the traces of previous rule execution sequences which result in special 'impasse' situations.

4.9   Specifying and Verifying Rules

The task of verifying rule-based systems is generally crippled by the absence of clear specifications, so that reliance is placed on the unreliable subjective opinions of human experts, rather than on comparing an expert system implementation with a specification. Often, the 'specifications' themselves are written as production rules, or in other non-declarative manner, serving more as preliminary design rather than as a specification.

Two kinds of properties are of general interest in evaluating a system:

- "Good things will happen," e.g., if certain facts are present in the working memory, the system will eventually generate the appropriate answer.

- "Bad things will not happen," e.g., the system will not loop forever in an undesirable cycle of rule firings.

For an arbitrary rule-based system, proving termination is undecidable, and there is no guarantee that a desirable rule will be executed. In other words, one cannot say for certain whether either kind of property holds for a system. The fact that rules are written separately does not mean that their behavior can be understood without reference to other rules in the system and the inference engine. Therefore, emphasis should be on specifying and designing a system whose properties can be reasoned about, rather than attempting to prove properties of arbitrary systems.

If a specification is already written as a collection of rules, it is straightforward to check whether these rules have been correctly implemented. More work is required if the specification contains other structures such as state transition diagrams. It may be possible to establish a direct correspondence between components of the specification and fragments of the implemented expert system, if the 'specification' is itself described in operational terms or a quasi-procedural language.

Current attempts to verify rule-based expert systems focus on the common concerns of *Conflict* and *Incompleteness*. The first concern is that errors may arise when rules have premises that may hold at the same time, possibly with conflicting consequences. The second concern is the possibility that none among a desired set of rules can fire. Most work focuses on surface-level examination of rules, e.g.,to test whether the disjunction of antecedents of all rules implies a tautology.

Proving such properties can be easier if one utilizes results on proving such properties for conditional term rewriting systems and inductive theorem proving (e.g., [9]). Where consequents of rules are also examined, these approaches are largely restricted to cases where the consequents are treated as propositions rather than actions. Some tools are available to help in V&V: these exhaustively compare components of rules, or apply graphical simulation models such as Petri Nets.

There are four major sources of difficulty in specifying and reasoning with rule-based expert systems:

1. Actions occur, and the state of the system changes with time.

2. Many rule-based programs are written with the intention of behaving correctly irrespective of the conflict resolution strategy, i.e., no deterministic execution policy can be assumed.

3. Patterns and actions contain variables quantified in the rule.

4. Rules may be prioritized.

The rest of this section addresses these problems and sketches directions along which potential solutions may be found.

4.9.1   Reasoning about actions

The *rhs* of a production rule specifies an action to be executed, not a hypothesis nor a proposition. For example, a production system that contains the rule

$$P \Rightarrow retract(P)$$

should not be understood to mean the logical implication

$$P \supset \neg P.$$

A similar problem has been studied by researchers in commonsense reasoning and nonmonotonic logic, in reasoning about actions, as discussed in Chapter 2. Any reasonable logic for understanding rule-based expert systems must recognize that the *rhs* of a rule specifies an action, and that consequences of the action hold after rule firing, whereas the antecedent of the rule holds before rule firing. In other words, explicit modeling of time is needed, e.g., using the temporal logic defined in Chapter 2.

4.9.2   Nondeterminism

In any expert system with modular structure and nondeterministic execution, verifying that a desired action occurs may require examining a large number of components in the expert system, since various components may cause modification of system state, influencing the existence of conditions that allow the desired action to occur. For instance, in most rule-based expert systems, any rule may be fired at any moment, complicating the verification task. It is necessary to demonstrate not just that the relevant rules may fire, but also that other rules that may influence the behavior of the desired rules do not fire. Requisite verification work involves showing for different collections of rules that implicit nondeterminism in the inference engine of the rule-based system will not be detrimental to the desired behavior. It must be shown that if rule r_i is enabled (ready to fire), and if the specification requires that such a rule must be fired under the appropriate conditions, then this rule will eventually fire, e.g., it will not be deactivated as a side effect of the firing of other rules.

This calls for a branching time interpretation, and also requires that all rules be taken into account when describing the possible effects of each rule.

The following example illustrates how nondeterministic execution may be represented using temporal logic.

Consider a simple rule-based system with rules

$$\phi_1 \Rightarrow \alpha\psi_1$$
$$\phi_2 \Rightarrow \alpha\psi_2$$
$$\vdots \quad \vdots \quad \vdots$$
$$\phi_n \Rightarrow \alpha\psi_n$$

where '$\alpha\psi_j$' indicates that ψ_j is asserted by the *rhs* of the jth rule. Condition elements in the *lhs* of each rule are assumed to be used to detect the presence of facts in the working memory. By a minor abuse of notation, a fact and the proposition denoting its existence are being denoted by the same symbol.

For any set $S \subseteq \{1, \dots, n\}$, we define Φ_S to be the conjunction of conditions $\{\phi_s | s \in S\}$, Φ'_S to be the conjunction of negated conditions $\{\neg\phi_s | s \notin S\}$, and Ψ_S to be the disjunction of *rhs* elements $\{\psi_s | s \in S\}$.

Then the behavior of the given set of rules is partially described by the collection of formulas

$$\{(\Phi_S \& \Phi'_S \supset \circ\Psi_S) \mid S \subseteq \{1, \dots, n\}\}.$$

Special cases arise when S is a singleton set, and when $S = \{1, \dots, n\}$. When n is large, the corresponding collection of formulas increases drastically, but one simplifying approach is to specify a set of dependencies or constraints in describing the properties of the expert system that is to be built. For instance, we may specify or be able to prove that $\phi_1 \& \phi_2 \supset \neg\phi_3$, so that the large collection of formulas containing $\phi_1 \& \phi_2 \& \phi_3$ need not be generated, i.e., the cases when $\{1, 2, 3\} \subseteq S$ can be ignored.

If the expert system specification requires that $\phi_j \supset \circ\Psi_j$, then one must ensure that $\phi_j \supset \neg\phi_i$ for each $i \neq j$. We may ensure $\phi_j \supset \Diamond\Psi_j$, by requiring termination of execution of other rules whose execution is not ruled out in this manner, assuming a fair conflict resolution policy, and a *non-interference criterion*: none of the other rules that can be executed should result in implying $\neg\phi_j$. Reasoning is simplified if condition elements are positive, and facts are not frequently retracted in the *rhs*s of rules, but this is an excessively constraining restriction for practical systems.

4.9.3 Variables

The theory developed for conditional term rewriting systems with logical variables and negation [11] may be adapted for the purpose of interpreting production rules of the form

$$(P_1 \& P_2 \& \ldots \& P_p) \& (\neg N_1 \& \neg N_2 \& \ldots \& \neg N_n) \Rightarrow \alpha Z, \tag{4.1}$$

where each P_i, N_j and Z is an atom.

Let $\boldsymbol{v}_P$ denote the collection of variables that occur in $(P_1 \& \ldots \& P_p)$, let $\boldsymbol{v}_N$ denote the collection of variables that occur in $(\neg N_1 \& \ldots \& \neg N_n)$, and let $\boldsymbol{v}_Z$ denote the collection of variables that occur in Z. Note that $\boldsymbol{v}_Z \subseteq \boldsymbol{v}_P$, since the only facts that can be asserted are those whose variables have been bound to values. Using '\' to denote removal of elements of a set from another, let $\boldsymbol{x} = \boldsymbol{v}_P \setminus \boldsymbol{v}_Z$ (i.e., variables in the positive part of the antecedent but not in the *rhs* of the rule), and $\boldsymbol{y} = \boldsymbol{v}_N \setminus \boldsymbol{v}_P$ (i.e., variables that occur only in the negated condition elements). Then, a reasonable interpretation for rule (4.1) is the temporal logic formula

$$\forall \boldsymbol{x}. \left[((P_1 \& \ldots \& P_p) \ \& \ \forall \boldsymbol{y}(\neg N_1 \& \ldots \& N_n)) \supset \circ Z \right]. \tag{4.2}$$

This is under the assumption that the rule is isolated; otherwise, the formulas become more elaborate, as discussed in Section 4.9.2. When multiple rules are considered, such formulas should be constructed only after renaming variables such that different rules use different variable names.

4.9.4 Priorities

Priorities embed hidden control since we can reason about the possibility of a rule execution only after considering the possible execution of all other rules with higher priority. Reasoning about prioritized rule-based expert systems can again benefit from results obtained for prioritized term rewriting systems, e.g., [10]. For instance, in developing declarative descriptions of possible rule execution, as in the preceding sections, we may augment the antecedent of each rule by the conjunction of negated antecedents of all rules that have higher priority.

Example 4.11 Let $\{p_1 \Rightarrow \alpha r_1, \ldots, p_n \Rightarrow \alpha r_n\}$ be the set of rules of no lower priority than $p \Rightarrow \alpha r$. Then the possible firing of the latter rule can be expressed by the temporal logic formula

$$p \& \neg p_1 \& \neg p_2 \& \ldots \& \neg p_n \supset \circ r.$$

4.10 Bibliographic Notes

The earliest work on grammatical rules is that of Panini (520BC-460BC, est.), who formulated formal production rules and definitions to describe Sanskrit grammar [13, 6]; his approach resembles the "Backus-Naur Form (BNF)" [1, 12] currently used to describe the syntax of programming languages, using context-free grammars introduced by Chomsky in 1956 [2]. A comprehensive survey of rewrite systems is contained in the paper by Dershowitz and Jouannaud [3].

Rule-based programming is the core of expert systems development, and is covered in considerable detail in most books on Expert Systems, mentioned in the bibliographic note following Chapter 1. In particular, the book by Giarratano and Riley [5] presents a comprehensive description of rule-based programming in CLIPS. CLIPS source code and documentation can be accessed on the internet from the CMU repository at

www.cs.cmu.edu/afs/cs.cmu.edu/project/ai-repository/ai/areas/expert/systems/clips
It is strongly recommended that newcomers to the field of expert systems obtain some practice in rule-based programming using CLIPS or Prolog.

A useful internet-accessible volume, focusing on the verification and validation of expert systems, has been developed by Wentworth, Knaus and Aougab [15].

Bibliography

[1] J. Backus, "The syntax and semantics of the proposed international algebraic language of the Zurich ACM-GAMM conference," *Proc. International Conf. on Information Processing*, pp. 125-132, 1959.

[2] N. Chomsky, "Three models for the description of languages," *IRE Trans. on Information Theory,* 2:113-124.

[3] N. Dershowitz and J.P. Jouannaud, "Rewrite Systems," in J. van Leeuwen (Ed.), *Handbook of Theoretical Computer Science (Vol. B: Formal Models and Semantics)*, North-Holland, 1990.

[4] C. Forgy, "Rete: A Fast Algorithm for the Many Pattern/Many Object Pattern Match Problem," *Artificial Intelligence*, 1985, 19:17-37.

[5] J. Giarratano and G. Riley, *Expert systems: principles and programming*, third edition, PWS Pub. Co., Boston (MA), 1998.

[6] P. Z. Ingerman, "Panini-Backus form," *Communications of the ACM* 10 (3): 137, 1967.

[7] J.E. Laird, A. Newell, and P.S. Rosenbloom, "Soar: An architecture for general intelligence," *Artificial Intelligence*, 1987, 33(1):1-64.

[8] A.A. Markov, *Theory of Algorithms* (translated by Jacques J. Schorr-Kon in 1962, Israel Program for Scientific Translations, Jerusalem), Russian original *Teoriya algorifmov*, Izdatel'stvo Akademii Nauk SSSR, Moskva-Leningrad, 1954.

[9] C.K. Mohan, *Negation in Equational Reasoning and Conditional Specifications*, Ph.D. dissertation, Computer Science Dept., State University of New York at Stony Brook, Dec. 1988.

[10] C.K. Mohan, "Priority Rewriting: Semantics, Confluence and Conditionals," in *Proc. 3rd Conf. on Rewriting Techniques and Applications (RTA)*, Chapel Hill (N.C.), Springer-Verlag LNCS 355, April 1989, pp. 278-291.

[11] C.K. Mohan and M.K.Srivas, "Negation with Logical Variables in Conditional Rewriting," in *Proc. 3rd Conf. on Rewriting Techniques and Applications (RTA)*, Chapel Hill (NC), Springer-Verlag LNCS 355, April 1989, pp. 292-310.

[12] P. Naur (ed.), "Revised Report on the Algorithmic Language ALGOL 60," *Communications of the ACM*, May 1960, 3(5):299-314.

[13] Panini, *Ashtadhyayi* (Sanskrit Grammar), 5th century BC, est.

[14] E. Post, Formal reductions of the general combinatorial decision problem, *American J. of Math.*, 65:197-215, 1943.

[15] J.A. Wentworth, R. Knaus, and H. Aougab, *Verification, Validation and Evaluation of Expert Systems: An FHWA Handbook, Volume 1*, Turner-Fairbank Highway Research Center, McLean VA (http://www.tfhrc.gov/advanc/vve/cover.htm).

4.11 Exercises

1. Discuss whether the number of partial matches (generated by a rule-based inference engine) is affected by the use of salience values.

2. Generate a set of rules to illustrate how the number of partial matches (generated by a rule-based inference engine) is affected by the sequence of condition elements in the *lhs* of a rule.

3. Under what circumstances would the initial computations of partial matches (performed by an inference engine) be wasteful?

4. In some expert systems, it is necessary for execution to go through a sequence of phases:

$$phase_1 \rightarrow phase_2 \rightarrow \ldots \rightarrow phase_n$$

   (a) How can such a system be implemented using a rule-based system *with* priorities?

   (b) How can such a system be implemented using a rule-based system *without* priorities?

   (c) Compare the above two alternatives, from the viewpoint of computational efficiency.

   (d) Implement a simple expert system for a task such as medical diagnosis, with the following four phases:

   Initialization $\rightarrow$ Preprocessing $\rightarrow$ Analysis $\rightarrow$ Presentationofresults

   (e) What would be the appropriate phases for a task such as generation of student grades (A-F) from raw scores (for quizzes, assignments and tests) in a course?

5. Develop a reasonable set of rules for assigning grades to students. Execute your program on facts in the system including the following student records:

   - (student (Name: John Doe) (Score: 93) (Grade: unknown) (id.no.: 777))

   - (student (Name: Jane Doe) (Score: 95) (Grade: unknown) (id.no.: 555))

- (student (Name: Sour Doe) (Score: 97) (Grade: unknown) (id.no.: 333))

- (student (Name: Elmun Doe) (Score: 91) (Grade: unknown) (id.no.: 222))

- (student (Name: Perdi Doe) (Score: 21) (Grade: unknown) (id.no.: 111))

What rules fire, and with what results?

6. In some expert systems, execution must cycle repeatedly through various phases, e.g.,

$$phase_1 \rightarrow phase_2 \rightarrow phase_3 \rightarrow phase_1 \rightarrow phase_2 \ldots$$

   (a) How can such a system be implemented using a rule-based system?

   (b) Implement a rule-based travel planning advisory system that cycles through the following phases:

   $$\text{User Input} \rightarrow \text{Compute Possible Answer}$$

   $$\rightarrow \text{Generate One Answer} \rightarrow \text{User Input} \ldots$$

   In successive cycles, the user may refine or modify his request, so that results of recent computations should not be thrown away.

7. How can non-determinism be introduced in the choice of phases, for a rule-based expert system that cycles through various phases (e.g., $phase_1$ may be followed by either $phase_A$ or $phase_B$, followed by $phase_1$ again)? Construct an example to illustrate your answer.

8. Develop a rule-based expert system that captures the desired behavior of the software controlling a multi-car elevator system that must direct elevator cars to the floors as requested by passengers in cars and others waiting at various floors of a large building.

9. With prognosis problems, a projection over time is needed, e.g., regarding the future course of a disease. How may such timing information may be introduced into a rule-based system? Are any changes to the inference engine required (to handle such temporal reasoning tasks)?

10. Discuss the relative difficulty of developing rule-based expert systems for the following kinds of problems:

    (a) Classification

    (b) Prediction

    (c) Configuration

    (d) Planning

11. How would you evaluate expert systems designed for the following tasks?

    (a) Disease diagnosis

    (b) Fault detection in an electronic circuit

    (c) Configuring machines on a factory floor

    (d) Ordering supplies for a grocery store (based on a database that tracks inventory levels of different items)

12. Develop a rule-based system to assist the player of a card game (such as Bridge) in evaluating the cards held by the player.

13. Develop a rule-based system to help a Chess player select one out of a number of possible moves, based on static evaluation of the resulting states.

14. Develop a rule-based system to serve as a student's 'quick-and-dirty' recipe book with a small number of generic recipes.

15. In an election 'primary,' one from among several candidates (from the same party) must be chosen. Their opinions tend not to vary drastically, and simple decision criteria may not be available to select a candidate. Develop a rule-based system to assist a voter in deciding for whom to vote in a primary. Facts in the working memory express the voter's opinions on various issues, possibly with some indication of relative importance. Candidates' opinions are also given as facts. Rules should be used to determine the overall assessment of each candidate, from the voter's viewpoint, resulting in a final choice of one candidate.

Chapter 5

Evolving Classifiers

Each animal or vegetable form remembers the next inferior and predicts the next higher. —————— Ralph Waldo Emerson, 1876

The literature on machine learning describes a *classifier* as a system that produces a decision for each permissible input set [38]. Given a classifier model whose parameters need to be determined for a specific application, a *learning system* uses example data from which features have been extracted, and produces an application-specific classifier. When compared to the traditional expert system development model, mechanizing the learning process has the major advantage of not requiring an expensive and unreliable knowledge acquisition phase. In this chapter, we focus on a learning approach based on *evolutionary computation*.

The fundamental principles of biological evolution have been applied recently with great success to a large number of difficult optimization problems, in applications such as scheduling, design, and pattern recognition [16, 13, 29, 30]. Evolutionary computation techniques have been found to be useful even for problems traditionally solved using rule-based expert systems. Such rule-based systems, in which the rules are evolved using evolutionary algorithms, have come to be referred to as *Learning Classifier Systems* (LCS), a phrase often shortened to 'classifier systems'.

In such systems, a population of rules evolves on the basis of intermittently given stimuli and reinforcement from the environment, learning which responses are appropriate when a stimulus is presented. The earliest such system applied to a practical problem was Goldberg's [12] classifier system to control the flow of natural gas through a pipeline, detecting leaks and optimizing profit in the face of seasonal and daily fluctuations in demand. Other examples include the design of optimal structures [11, 22], optimizing shape contours in the flow vectoring of supersonic exhaust nozzles [24], strength and stiffness optimization of laminates [7] optimum weld design [10], path planning of mobile transporters [2], airplane engine design [1], VLSI cell placement [25], air-injected hydrocyclone design [23], and design of composite material structures [31].

Section 5.1 describes the overall architecture of classifier systems, whose details are given in subsequent sections. Representation issues are addressed in Section 5.2, rule execution is discussed in Section 5.3, credit allocation policies are discussed in Section 5.4. The rule discovery component of a classifier system, and its use of a genetic algorithm, are described in Section 5.5. Rule grouping techniques are covered in Section 5.6. Section 5.7 presents a few example problems to which classifier systems have been applied.

5.1 Learning Classifier Systems

A classifier system contains a collection of rules called *classifiers* that evolve through time, generally using the principles of evolutionary computation (described in Section 5.5). For clarity, the discussion in this chapter uses the term 'rule' whereas researchers in the field prefer the term 'classifier.' These rules receive external inputs and generate actions or outputs applied to the environment. The results of these actions can then be evaluated, generating the feedback necessary to apply selection pressure to the rules.

At a high level, if firing some rules results in actions that enable the system to do well in the environment, then these rules are considered desirable, and persist in the system. On the other hand, if rule-firing leads to poor performance (in the context of the current environment), then such rules are likely to disappear from the population, or at least be applied with considerably reduced frequency in the future.

Such selection pressure is generally exerted by associating each rule with a "strength" that indicates its relative quality. However, the behavior of the entire system is to be distinguished from that of a rule in the system. High quality rules may exist in a poorly performing system, and conversely. The external input to the system may only estimate the quality of the system with considerable environmental noise and randomness. The difficult task is to determine how to apply system level feedback to individual components. Credit allocation strategies address this issue, and are discussed in Section 5.4.

The classical *Learning Classifier System* (LCS) proposed by Holland [16]

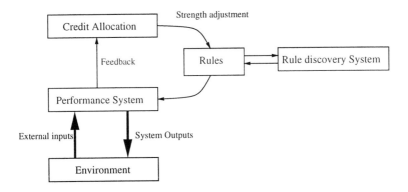

Figure 5.1: Architecture of Holland's 'Learning Classifier System'

has the following three main components, illustrated in Figure 5.1.

1. *Performance System:* This executes rules, possibly in parallel. Rule-firing may result in direct interaction with the environment, or the generation of *messages* (components of the working memory of the system) that lead to the firing of other rules. The basic execution cycle is similar to rule-based expert systems with some parallelism.

2. *Credit Assignment:* This is a mechanism to evaluate rules and adjust their strengths depending on system performance. Algorithms such as the "bucket-brigade" are frequently used, discussed in Section 5.4.

3. *Rule Discovery System:* Evolutionary algorithms are used, with simple representations of rules evolved using mixing operators (mutation and crossover) that operate along with selection mechanisms.

In Holland's classifier system, and in many others that followed, the conditions of rules were represented as strings over the alphabet {1, 0, # }; other representations have been suggested in more recent work, discussed in Section 5.2.

Performance is often improved by grouping together rules in some manner, just as modularization is helpful with traditional rule-based systems. Grouping can reflect interdependencies and close connections between rules. Subsets of rules may be collectively evaluated and rewarded or punished, an issue addressed in Section 5.6. At one extreme, in 'Pittsburgh-style' classifier systems [33], a complete solution (a collection of many rules) is evaluated and rewarded or punished, rather than a single rule or small group of rules. By contrast, Holland's classifier systems and its descendants are referred to as the 'Michigan-style' systems, characterized by the fact that individual rules need to be rewarded or punished.

5.2   Representation

Most classifier systems use a simple language in which the right hand side is a bit string indicating which actions are to occur and which 'messages' are to be posted (added to the working memory), and the left hand side is a string with elements drawn from the alphabet $\{1, 0, \# \}$, where the '$\#$' symbol represents *don't-care* cases, when the value of the corresponding attribute is irrelevant to the rule.

Each position in the left-hand-side of the rule represents a specific condition. The right hand side of each rule is treated as identifying which messages are posted to the working memory when a rule is fired. Posting messages is analogous to asserting facts in the working memory of a rule-based system. These messages may match with the left hand side of another rule, leading to its activation and possible firing. However, this process does not occur in *stimulus-response* classifier systems, in which every rule interacts directly with the environment.

Holland's formulation also allows for the left hand side of a rule to contain any number of ternary strings, and also allows negation. For instance, the rule

$$0\#1\#, \quad \#\#00, \quad \neg 11\#\# \quad \longrightarrow \quad 10$$

can be fired if two messages matching $0\#1\#$ and $\#\#00$ are present, AND if there is no message matching $11\#\#$.

Language restrictions arise as a result of a tradeoff of descriptive power for adaptive efficiency: simpler rules are easier to learn. Using a more general language also complicates the matching algorithms required to determine rule activations.

Booker [4, 5] has shown that the ternary alphabet used (in classifier systems) is not as restrictive as might appear at first sight. Intervals, negation, and disjunction can all be expressed using *feature manifolds* suggested by Hayes-Roth [14]. For instance, *ordinal feature manifolds* permit comparisons of numeric, continuous or noisy data.

Example 5.1 Let X be a variable whose range is the continuous interval $[0.0, 10.0]$. An 11-bit representation may be chosen, with each bit representing an interval of diameter 3.0 centered at an integer, e.g., the third bit represents the interval $[0.5, 3.5]$. A specific value $\in [0.0, 10.0]$ is represented by identifying the intervals to which it belongs, e.g., the value 2.9 is represented by the bit-string 00111000000 since 2.9 is contained in each of the intervals $[0.5, 3.5]$, $[1.5, 4.5]$, and $[2.5, 5.5]$. Similarly, the value 5.2 is represented by the bit-string 00001110000. A bitwise logical product (conjunction) of these bit-strings yields 00001000000, indicating that $[2.5, 5.5]$ is the only subinterval that contains both values. The most specific ternary string matching both values is 00##1##0000, representing the interval $[0.5, 5.5]$.

Representations of desired degree of accuracy can be obtained using a hierarchical ordinal manifold, with lower levels of the hierarchy representing greater precision or refinement. In the rule generation procedure discussed in Section 5.5, newly generated rules can also be interpreted as intervals if obtained using restricted mating or mutation operators applied only to classifiers that have some overlap (cf. 'niching' in Section 5.6).

Disjunction may be represented using bits that represent negated values, as in the following example.

Example 5.2 Let 'color' be an attribute with five possible values: red, blue, green, orange, yellow. A 6-bit representation may be adopted, with the first bit representing the presence of some (at least one) color, and each of the remaining bits representing the absence of a specific color. Thus, the color orange may be represented as 111011, interpreted as $orange \equiv \neg red\ \&\neg blue\ \&\neg green\ \&\neg yellow$. Then 1##11# denotes a logical expression such as $red\ OR\ blue\ OR\ yellow$; the first bit must equal 1 to prohibit the possibility of each # being instantiated to 1.

A few generalizations of the bit-string representation are enumerated below.

1. Real valued representations: Elements in a rule may describe real-valued parameters of a problem, possibly using a bit string to encode a number or an interval. *Gray coding* is often used to preserve distance relationships between adjacent values [8]. Traditional binary representations of integers in the range 0-15 would use '1000' to represent eight, maximally distant from '0111' (the representation of seven) and minimally distant from '0000' (the representation of zero), whereas Gray coding would ensure that the representations for eight and seven differ very little.

2. Messy representations: A rule's left hand side may be described using a multiset of arbitrary size, where each element of the multiset is a two-tuple identifying an attribute and a value [28]. For instance, the messy representation $\{[3,0],[4,1],[7,1],[4,0]\}$ determines values for the third and seventh attributes of the condition, is overspecified for the fourth (in which case the first occurrence $[4,1]$ takes precedence), and is underspecified with respect to the remaining elements.

3. S-Expressions[1]: As in *Genetic Programming* [27], the components of a rule may express symbolic expressions in a well-defined format, amenable to matching. For instance, the condition of a rule may be represented as

$$AND(OR(x_3, x_4),\ OR(x_5, \neg x_1)),$$

to be matched by message strings (with components $x_1, x_2, \ldots$) that satisfy the specified logical conditions.

4. Fuzzy representations: Expressions which stand for fuzzy sets (such as 'long' and 'tall') may be used in rules, possibly with linguistic variables and modifiers (e.g., *very long tail and somewhat heavy* $\Rightarrow$ *Dinosaur of type XYZ*).

5.3   Rule Firing

In a traditional rule-based expert system, facts may persist in the system well after they have led to rule firing. In classifier systems, messages are much more transient, and rule firing in most classifier systems results in the removal of messages and their wholesale replacement by new ones.

As in any rule-based system (cf. Chapter 4), the left hand sides of rules (classifiers) must be examined to determine whether a rule can be activated and possibly fired. Matching becomes very efficient with the use of a simple representation scheme, e.g., with components in the left hand side of a rule restricted to $\{0, 1, \#\}$.

However, the main problem is not the matching effort but rather the collection of rules for which matching is to be done. Unlike traditional rule-based systems, rules are being evolved during the application of the classifier system,

---

[1] An 'S-Expression' is a data structure in Lisp programming, constructed using matching sets of parentheses that enclose any number of atomic expressions (such as numbers) or other S-Expressions.

hence there is no assurance that satisfactory rules exist that correctly and exactly match the present conditions.

Booker [4] proposed the solution of allowing 'near-matches,' i.e., rules may be activated even if not all their conditions are met. Various fuzzy matching algorithms can also be used [21]. Booker and other authors use the following notation:

- **Population [P]**: the current set of rules

- **Match set [M]**: the set of rules currently activated since the conditions in their antecedents have been matched by the messages present, or by the environment

- **Action set [A]**: rules in [M] that advocate the same action as the rule selected for execution

- **Previous Action set $[A]_{-1}$**: action set of the previous time step

A conflict resolution phase ensues if a parallel firing regime is not assumed, or if the message list is limited in size. In addition to rule strength, another major consideration in conflict resolution is the *specificity* of rules. Relative rule specificity may vary, and one rule may have a left hand side that is a special case of the left hand side of another rule in the population. Since the rules in a classifier system are not hand-tailored by an expert, a population may contain very general rules as well as very specific rules that are activated by a given set of conditions. Allowing the more general rule to fire (and be rewarded) has the possible side-effect that more general rules persist and slowly gain in strength, coming to dominate the population even though they may not be the most appropriate rules for many situations. Specialized or exception rules should instead be allowed to persist and override more general or default rules. Specificity is often quantified and normalized to lie in the interval $[0, 1]$, with the value 0 corresponding to a most general rule (that matches every condition) and the value 1 corresponding to a most specific rule (that matches under exactly one set of conditions).

Conflict resolution is based on the *bid* of a rule, a non-decreasing function of rule strength and specificity, e.g., for a rule r,

$$Bid(r) = c_1 * \text{Strength}(r) * (1 + c_2(\text{Specificity}(r))_3^c)$$

where c_1, c_2 and c_3 are non-negative constants. The case $c_2 = 0$ corresponds to ignoring specificity information, while larger values imply greater relative emphasis on specificity.

The simplest strategy is to conduct an *auction*, selecting for execution the rule with greatest bid. An alternative is to select rules with probability proportional to the bid.

Some classifier systems report success even with small population sizes, thanks to the use of adaptive *default hierarchies* [19] in which nodes that represent more general 'default' rules have more specific 'exception' rules as children in the hierarchy, resembling the indexing methodology used in case based reasoning systems (cf. Chapter 7). For systems with an adaptive default hierarchy, performance is improved by the use of a *necessity auction* in which the amount paid out by a winning classifier equals the bid of its nearest competitors, whenever there are multiple bidders [34]. It has also been suggested that in addition to a measure of rule strength in terms of the expected reward, a separate *priority factor* must be maintained with each rule, updated (for a winning rule) by a multiple of the difference between the actual reward and the nearest competitor's reward estimate.

When a rule is executed, the credit allocation mechanism (described in Section 5.4) may be activated, with effects on the strengths of rules and hence on the results of future auctions.

5.4   Credit Allocation

The problem of credit allocation or assignment involves deciding how to reward or punish rules, given that some rules may not have direct interaction with the external environment that provides reinforcement or feedback. To avoid this problem, the simplest classifier systems (referred to as *stimulus-response systems*) require that every rule interacts directly with the environment, i.e., every rule is activated as a result of external inputs and performs actions that directly influence the environment, possibly through the use of 'effectors' that modify the environment. More general classifier systems use a number of strategies for credit assignment, outlined in this section.

If an auction is conducted to determine the rule to be fired, then the winning rule's strength is diminished by its bid value, and also increased (or decreased) by a quantity corresponding to the reward (or penalty) associated with this rule as a result of environmental consequences. The magnitude of change in rule strength as a result of a single such interaction may be constant or may vary with the quality of the outcome.

If a succession of rules must be fired before an observable interaction of the classifier system with the environment, then the strengths of all the fired

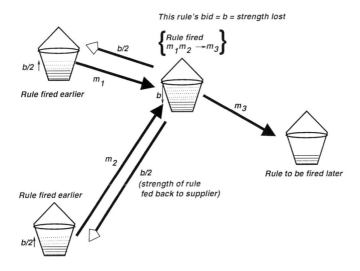

Figure 5.2: Bucket Brigade Algorithm

rules must be modified upon evaluating the results of such an interaction. This may occur through a process such as the *Bucket Brigade Algorithm* (BBA) [18], illustrated in Figure 5.2. In the bucket brigade algorithm, the "bid" of a fired rule r is subtracted from its strength and distributed to other rules whose firing had activated r, i.e., rules that placed messages matched by the left-hand-side of r. Thus, positive reward received from the environment is indirectly distributed among all the rules whose firing led to the reward, and strengthens the chaining of the rules responsible. Negative reinforcement from the environment weakens the final rule in the chain, so that competing rules eventually become the winners of the auction, leading to the disintegration of the old rule chain and the formation of new rule chains.

In principle, any other reinforcement learning algorithm may be used instead of the bucket brigade algorithm. The *Q-learning* algorithm [37] has received much attention in this regard, and it has been claimed that variations of this algorithm lead to improved performance of classifier systems [40]. Here, the strength of a rule r is increased by an amount that depends on the external reward as well as a fraction of the strengths of rules fired following r. In principle, every rule that fires is affected by every reward received in future, though the effect of each successive reward is reduced by a constant factor. When external reinforcement is received, it affects the strength of the most recently fired rule, as well as the rules fired earlier, in reverse time sequence, weakened by an attenuation factor at every step backwards in time.

In some classifier systems, a *bid tax* (proportional to the bid value) is imposed on rules that bid in an auction, decreasing their strength; this has the effect of discouraging very general rules that bid often but win rarely due to low specificity. In some classifier systems, a *life tax* (proportional to current strength) is additionally imposed on all rules, decreasing the strength of each rule so that persistently inactive rules can fade away from the population. The life tax should be chosen such that rules that have remained inactive (for a small period) by chance are not excessively weakened too soon for their utility to be demonstrated.

As mentioned earlier, each rule is associated with a strength measure intended to capture its relative quality (*a la* 'fitness' in evolutionary algorithms). Researchers currently distinguish between the effectiveness of firing a rule in a specific environment, the confidence associated with how well a rule is expected to perform in a specific environment, and the contribution of a rule towards accomplishment of a long range goal.

Wilson's XCS [42], for instance, distinguishes between three quantities associated with each rule, updated in the following sequence:

1. *prediction error*, measuring the average magnitude of the difference in a rule's payoff prediction and actual payoff, normalized to be in the range [0, 1] (dividing by the difference between maximum and minimum payoff values);

2. *payoff prediction* (strength), used in determining which rule is to be fired, obtained by averaging past performance of the rule; and

3. *fitness* or prediction accuracy, inversely correlated with prediction error.

In XCS, the reward or penalty for a rule depends on the accuracy of its prediction (not the correctness of the answer).

Classifier systems such as XCS have addressed the issue of completeness of rules for a problem: the presence of 'good' rules in a classifier system should not preclude a search for other good rules that cover cases not covered so far. If this issue is satisfactorily addressed, a good quality rule of limited scope of applicability may be dormant for most of the system's life, and be awakened into action in very specific circumstances for which it is well suited, without adversely affecting the long term goals of the classifier system. Kovacs [26] has formulated an empirically supported *optimality hypothesis* for XCS, paraphrased as follows: *XCS will succeed in evolving an optimal population of complete maximally general rules.*

5.5   Rule Discovery

Genetic algorithms are frequently used to modify the collection of rules constituting a classifier population. In the Michigan approach, i.e., learning classifier systems as proposed by Holland, a straightforward application of this methodology follows three steps:

1. Probabilistically select rules based on strength.

2. Apply genetic operators to the selected rules.

3. Merge the previous rules with the newly generated rules, possibly deleting some of the former (to limit growth of the population of rules).

   Changes in the population may be massive or incremental:

1. In the "generational" variant of an evolutionary algorithm, the number of offspring produced is the same as the population size, and decisions are then made to determine which offspring go into the next "generation."

2. In the "steady-state" variant, more frequently adopted in classifier systems, the population is changed only a small amount at a time: one evolutionary operator is applied, and the resulting offspring may immediately move into the population, but most of the population remains unchanged when this occurs.

Selection pressure, driving the increase in quality of solutions present in the population, may be implemented in several ways:

1. Allocate chances of reproduction to individuals based on their fitness, so that better quality individuals (in the current population) are expected to generate more offspring. Two common ways of implementing such a "reproductive selection" strategy are:

   (a) For each offspring generation step, select participating individuals (parents) with probability proportional to fitness.

   (b) For each offspring generation step, select participating individuals (parents) with probability a linear function of "rank," where the rank of an individual X is defined as the number of individuals in the current population whose fitness is not lower than that of X.

2. Parents may be chosen randomly with equal probability, but the decision of whether to include offspring in the next generation depends on offspring fitness, in one of the following ways:

(a) Offspring may replace the least fitness individuals in the current population.

(b) A *deterministic tournament* may be carried out between the offspring and their parents (or other individuals chosen at random from the current population), allowing the ones with higher fitness to continue into the new population.

(c) A *nondeterministic tournament* may be carried out between the offspring and their parents (or other extant randomly chosen individuals), selecting individuals for the next population with a probability proportional to fitness.

(d) Offspring replace the weakest element from a randomly chosen 'crowding subpopulation' consisting of substantially similar individuals.

3. Many evolutionary algorithms allow a small number of the best individuals from the population to continue unchanged into the next population.

The following operators are most frequently used to generate offspring from currently existing (parent) individuals.

1. *Mutation* performs a small random change in an individual.

2. *Local Improvement* operators (whose variants are referred to as hill-climbing or gradient-descent) consider small changes in an individual, accepting such changes only if they result in improved fitness.

3. *One Point Crossover (1PTX)* splits two parents at a randomly chosen position and splices together the pieces from different parents, generating two offspring. This is the genetic operator most often used in classifier systems.

4. *Two Point Crossover (2PTX)* picks two positions in two parents, and exchanges the middle segments (between these randomly chosen positions) of the parents, generating two offspring.

5. *Uniform Crossover (UX)* selects each component of the offspring from either parent with equal probability. "HUX" is a variant of UX that ensures that equally many components are inherited from each parent.

6. *Evolution Strategies* used for real-valued parameter optimization use *recombination* operators that obtain offspring components by arithmetic operations on the parent components, such as computing a weighted average using parent fitness values as weights.

Multi-parent variations of these operators exist, with more than two parents participating in each offspring generation step. A number of problem-specific operators have also been proposed in the literature.

Offspring are assigned the average strength of their parents. Although most researchers apply crossover only to the left hand sides of rules, Wilson[42] argues that it is helpful to apply crossover to the right hand sides of rules as well.

When none of the currently existing rules in the population satisfactorily matches a set of conditions, i.e., the match set [M] is empty, some classifier systems invoke a specialized *Triggered Cover Detector Operator (TCDO)* that generates a new rule whose left hand side exactly matches the current set of conditions, and whose right hand side is randomly generated. Such a rule is then assigned a strength that is the average strength of all rules in the current population.

5.6 Grouping Rules

In Holland's classifier system, concepts are represented by groups of rules. The structure of a concept is modeled by the organization, variability and distribution of strength among the rules, which compete to become active. In addition to module-formation, where groups of related rules constitute each module, other explicit rule groupings are also helpful, improving efficiency in the rule activation phase.

In human reasoning, the methodology followed by a 'novice expert' (e.g., a physician who has just graduated from a medical school) may involve reasoning from first principles, whereas a 'seasoned expert' carries out the reasoning much faster, relying on inferential shortcuts established through years of experience or exposure to the topic. Chains of reasoning, if frequently encountered, are succinctly stored by remembering the head and tail of the chain. For instance, when the chain of rules

$$A \longrightarrow B, \ B \longrightarrow C, \ \ldots, \ Y \longrightarrow Z$$

is executed a few times, the expert "learns" the redundant rule

$$A \longrightarrow Z$$

that allows inferring Z directly from A, instead of going through the various steps in the original chain of reasoning [2]. The new rule does not add to the knowledge of the expert, but improves efficiency of inference when a new (relevant) case is encountered, matching A. Such a learning mechanism is most useful when physical muscular movements need to be coordinated: in situations of imminent danger, an animal cannot afford to go through the elaborate reasoning process that connects the appearance of a predator to the appropriate actions (flight or fight) necessary for survival.

A similar mechanism can be applied in classifier systems. In this context, groups of rules can be chained together to form a "corporation." In a *Corporate Classifier System* [35, 36], rules are clustered, forming "corporations" of arbitrary size. Each corporation is treated as a collective unit by the other major components of the classifier system. Each rule has the same fitness as the average strength of all rules in the corporation to which it belongs. Entire corporations may be deleted or selected for reproduction, with crossover on two corporations yielding a new offspring corporation with some rules from each parent corporation. Representing each corporation as a doubly linked list (chain) of rules permits easy application of one-point crossover. Each corporation encapsulates temporal chains of inference, selecting candidates from successive match sets [M] using roulette wheel selection based on rule strengths; this enables the easy solution of multi-step tasks in which several such rules need to be executed in sequence. If a rule in a corporation is selected for execution by the performance system, then the rules in that corporation continue to be executed as long as possible, or until external reward or punishment is received, after which a new rule or corporation may be chosen for execution.

Rule groups are also used in some classifier systems in yet another manner, within the evolutionary algorithm, invoking a "niching" approach. Niching suggests that evolutionary operators such as crossover should be applied only (or mostly) to individuals that are considerably similar to one another. This allows different peaks in the fitness landscape to be focused on, rather than mating individuals substantially different from each other. In classifier systems, crossover can be limited to rules whose conditions match the same set of stimuli, so that each offspring also responds to the same stimuli with a composite of the actions associated with the parent rules. This mechanism was analyzed by Wilson [39] and found to be helpful, and is also employed by his XCS system.

---

[2]It may be argued that "aptitude" for a subject consists of the ease with which a person learns such inferential shortcuts.

5.7 Examples of Classifier Systems

A task frequently addressed by classifier systems is the development and evolution of simulated creatures in artificial environments [4, 6]. Models described in the literature include cases where such creatures must learn to run away from predators, travel towards food, avoid obstacles, and avoid going around in circles. In addition to their relevance to artificial life research, such systems are potentially useful in problems such as robot navigation and path planning.

Example 5.3 Booker, Goldberg and Holland [6] present a classifier system intended to represent the behavior of a simple simulated organism capable of moving through an environment, with the broad goals of acquiring certain objects (e.g., prey) and avoiding others (e.g., predators).

A two-bit tag may be used to identify the source of a message, e.g., '00' to represent that a message is being supplied by the environment or sensors, and '01' to indicate that the message is being generated by a rule. Longer tags may be used to implement elaborate rule-chaining mechanisms.

Sensors provide visual information, including the nature and relative position of an object within the visual field, e.g., the last six bits of a message, in right-to-left sequence, encode whether the object is moving, left of center (with respect to the classifier system's visual field), right of center, adjacent to the classifier system, large, or striped. Other bits are allocated to determine attributes such as the system's direction of motion.

The right hand side of a rule describes actions such as rotating (changing the direction of motion), moving forwards or backwards, and setting speeds of movement (fast, cruise, slow or stop).

Using these conventions, for instance, a rule intended to specify that the organism should move rapidly towards a small moving nonstriped object is represented as

$$00\#\#\#\#\#\#\#000001 \longrightarrow 0100000000000000, \text{ALIGN, FAST}$$

where the last part of the rule describes the effector actions modifying the state of the organism.

The detection of a 'T'-shaped object may involve two steps, chaining two rules. The first rule detects an object that is large, has a long axis, and is moving along the direction of that long axis. The second rule is triggered if such an object had just previously been observed AND if there is currently a centered object at the appropriate location that is large, with a long axis, and moving perpendicular to that axis. To achieve this, the seventh and eighth bits

```
. . . . . . . . . . . . . .      . . . . . . . .0. . . . . .
.OOF. .OOF. .OOF. .      .OFO. . .F. . . . .
.OOO. .OOO. .OOO. .      . . . . . . . .0. . . . .
.OOO. .OOO. .OOO. .      . . . . . . . . . . . . .
. . . . . . . . . . . . . .      . . .F. . .OFO. . .
. . . . . . . . . . . . . .      . . .OO. . . . . . . .
.OOF. .OOF. .OOF. .      . . . . . .OO. . . . .
.OOO. .OOO. .OOO. .      .OFO. . .F. . . . .
.OOO. .OOO. .OOO. .      . . . . . . . . . . . . .
```

Figure 5.3: Fragments of Woods1 and Woods7 enviroments; 'O' denotes an obstacle, 'F' represents food, and '.' denotes an empty square

of messages are devoted to determining if the object in the field of vision is moving in the direction of its long axis, or perpendicular to the same. The resulting rules are:

$$00\#\#\#\#\#\#01\#1\#001 \longrightarrow 0100000000000001, \text{V-FORWARD}$$

$$0100000000000001, 00\#\#\#\#\#\#10\#1\#001 \longrightarrow 0100000000000010$$

As seen in these rules, each rule may contain multiple components in the left hand side as well as the right hand side.

Example 5.4 Wilson [40] describes a sequence of successively more difficult environments (*Woods1, Woods2, . . . , Woods7*), each consisting of a two-dimensional grid; objects are placed in repeating patterns along the grid, as shown in Figure 5.3. Among these, the nature of the pattern is most difficult to learn in the case of *Woods7*, where the system must keep track of its recent history.

Each object is coded using bit-strings, e.g., '11' codes for food, '10' codes for a rock, and '00' codes for a blank cell. An animat (artificial organism) is in an empty cell, and can sense its eight surrounding cells, whose description thus consists of a 16-bit string, with pairs of bits arranged in predetermined order (e.g., clockwise beginning from the north). The animat must evolve rules whose left hand side matches such strings, and right hand side determines the next desirable position for the animat. Moving to a cell with food implies that such food is then eaten, providing positive reinforcement.

Example 5.5 Wilson's XCS [41] has been shown to reliably evolve optimal solutions for Boolean multiplexer functions of size 6 and 11 [26]. Here, the goal is to evolve classifiers whose left hand sides represent possible input combinations and right hand sides correspond to multiplexer outputs for those inputs. For a 6-multiplexer, for instance, the first two bits identify the 'address', indexing into the remaining four bits of the input string, and the output value (another bit) is the chosen one among the latter four bits. For example, the input string 100010 must lead to the generation of the output 1, since the address ('10') points to the third member of the bit string '0010'. The rules that should ideally be 'learnt' resemble those in Figure 5.4.

$$
\begin{array}{ccc}
000\#\#\# & \longrightarrow & 0 \\
001\#\#\# & \longrightarrow & 1 \\
01\#0\#\# & \longrightarrow & 0 \\
01\#1\#\# & \longrightarrow & 1 \\
10\#\#0\# & \longrightarrow & 0 \\
10\#\#1\# & \longrightarrow & 1 \\
11\#\#\#0 & \longrightarrow & 0 \\
11\#\#\#1 & \longrightarrow & 1
\end{array}
$$

Figure 5.4: Rules for 6-multiplexer

Example 5.6 Goldberg [12] developed a system to simulate the induction of expert knowledge, regulating the transmission of natural gas in a pipeline. The gas storage and transmission problem is further complicated by the possibility of leaks that cannot be detected directly, but whose presence must be inferred from readings of gauges. In this classifier system, a 16-bit message was obtained every hour from the input interface, describing the readings of various gauges (e.g., inflow, outflow, inlet pressure, outlet pressure, pressure change rate), detectors (e.g., current temperature) and external information (e.g., season). The ranges of continuous parameters such as pipeline flow are coarsely partitioned into intervals represented by components of input messages. Season (winter/summer) is represented by a single binary component.

The output of the classifier system controlled the settings for the pipeline flow. The quality of this output (payoff) was estimated by comparing the demand with the actual pressure delivered, as well as by the ability of the system to detect leaks and take appropriate actions. Goldberg's system contained sixty rules, and the message list could hold at most five messages; it was developed and tested on a microcomputer with 64Kb memory. The system achieved expert-level performance in 24,000 time steps. The rule generation process was triggered after every 200 time steps, i.e., the genetic algorithm required roughly 120 generations.

An example rule generated by this system was:

```
IF [input pressure low,
    output pressure low,
    rate of change of pressure very negative],
THEN [send 'leak' message]
```

Example 5.7 Holmes [20] describes a learning classifier system, EpiCS, used to derive a measure of disease risk in humans. EpiCS is an object-oriented version of Bonelli's NEWBOOLE system [3].

Population sizes of about 1000 were found to be the best for this problem. To control overgeneralization, a "governor" was implemented, modifying excessively general classifiers (where the fraction of *don't care* components exceeded 85%) by introducing randomly assigned components. To avoid eliminating non-specific classifiers altogether, the penalty factor penalizing classifiers that advocate incorrect decisions was lowered to 50% (compared to 95% in NEWBOOLE).

Although individual classifiers predict a positive or negative outcome (regarding presence of disease), the output of the entire system is a real-valued *risk of disease*, examining the fraction of matching classifiers (weighted with probabilities) that predict the disease.

Classification accuracy was found to be highly sensitive and highly specific, and EpiCS classified new test cases also with high accuracy. The results of this system were found to be statistically better than the probabilities obtained by logistic regression.

5.8   Bibliographic Notes

Holland's early papers and book [15, 16, 17] are the earliest references on classifier systems, and are rich in ideas pursued in later work. However, the development of practical classifier systems required much further work, and a short survey article by Wilson and Goldberg [43] summarizes the state of the art and challenges in 1989, proposing solutions that have since been implemented by other researchers. A survey paper by Booker, Goldberg and Holland [6] introduces the topics of classifier systems and genetic algorithms presenting the evolution of a simple learning organism that receives visual input from its environment. Goldberg's book [13] also gives a good description of classifier systems. Wilson [42] and Kovacs [26] describe the framework of XCS, which differs significantly from that of Holland's classifier system. Information on other classifier system literature can be found on the internet at

http://www.cs.bham.ac.uk/ tyk/lcs/

Bibliography

[1] S. Ashley, "Engineous Explores the Design Space," *Mechanical Engineering,* Feb. 1992, pp. 49-52.

[2] P. Baffes and L. Wang, "Mobile Transporter Path Planning Using a Genetic Algorithm Approach," *SPIE Cambridge Symp. on Advances in Intelligent Robotic Systems,* 1988.

[3] P. Bonelli, A. Parodi, S. Sen, and S. Wilson, "NEWBOOLE: A fast GBML system," in B. Porter and R. Mooney (Eds.), *Proc. Seventh International Conference on Machine Learning,* San Mateo (CA): Morgan Kaufmann, June 1990, pp. 153-159.

[4] L.B. Booker, *Intelligent behavior as an adaptation to the task environment,* Ph.D. Dissertation, Computer and Communication Sciences, University of Michigan, Ann Arbor (MI), 1982.

[5] L.B. Booker, "Representing Attribute-Based Concepts in Classifier Systems," in *Proc. Workshop on Foundations of Genetic Programming,* G.J.E. Rawlins (Ed.), Morgan Kaufmann, 1991, pp. 115-127.

[6] L.B. Booker, D.E. Goldberg and J.H. Holland, "Classifier Systems and Genetic Algorithms," *Artificial Intelligence,* 1989, 40:235-282 (also in J.W. Shavlik and T.G. Dietterich (Eds.), *Readings in Machine Learning,* Morgan Kaufmann, 1990).

[7] K.J. Callahan, *Strength-to-weight and Stiffness-to-weight Optimization of Laminates using a genetic algorithm,* M.S. Thesis, Dept. of Aerospace Engineering, University of Alabama, Tuscaloosa (AL), 1991.

[8] R.A. Caruana and J.D. Schaffer, "Representation and hidden bias: Gray vs. binary coding for genetic algorithms," *Proc. Fifth International Conf. on Machine Learning,* Ann Arbor (MI), Morgan Kaufmann, pp.153-161.

[9] D. Cliff and S. Ross, "Adding Temporary Memory to ZCS," *Adaptive Behavior*, 1995, 3(2):101-150,.

[10] K. Deb, "Optimal Design of a class of welded structures via Genetic Algorithm," in *Proc. 31st Structures, Structural Dynamics and Materials Conf.*, April 1990, pp. 444-453.

[11] A.K. Dhingra, *A Unified Approach to Multiple Objective Design of Engineering Systems*, Ph.D. Dissertation, Purdue University, Lafayette (IN), 1990.

[12] D.E. Goldberg, *Computer-aided Gas Pipeline Operation using Genetic Algorithms and Rule Learning*, Ph.D. Dissertation, Univ. of Michigan, 1983.

[13] D.E. Goldberg, *Genetic Algorithms in search, optimization, and machine learning*, Addison-Wesley, Reading (MA), 1989.

[14] R. Hayes-Roth, "Patterns of induction and associated knowledge acquisition algorithms," in C.H. Chen (Ed.), *Pattern Recognition and Artificial Intelligence*, Academic Press, 1976.

[15] J.H. Holland, "Processing and Processors for Schemata," in E.L.Jacks (Ed.), *Associative Information Processing*, American Elsevier, New York, 1971, pp. 127-146.

[16] J.H. Holland, *Adaptation in Natural and Artificial Systems*, Univ. of Michigan Press, Ann Arbor, 1975.

[17] J.H. Holland, "Adaptation," in R. Rosen and F.M. Snell (Eds.), *Progress in Theoretical Biology IV*, Academic Press, New York, 1976, pp. 263-293.

[18] J.H. Holland, "Escaping Brittleness: The possibilities of general purpose learning algorithms applied to parallel rule-based systems," in R.S. Michalski, J.G. Carbonell, and T.M. Mitchell (Eds.), *Machine Learning: An Artificial Intelligence Approach* **2**, Morgan Kaufmann, Los Altos (CA), 1986, pp. 593-623.

[19] J.H. Holland, K.J. Holyoak, R.E. Nisbett, and P.R. Thagard, *Induction: Processes of Inference, Learning, and Discovery*, MIT Press, 1986.

[20] J.H. Holmes, "Discovering Risk of Disease with a Learning Classifier System," in *Proc. International Conf. on Genetic Algorithms*, 1997.

[21] H. Ishibuchi, T. Nakashima, and T. Murata, "A fuzzy classifier system that generates fuzzy if-then rules for pattern classification problems," in *Proc. 1995 IEEE International Conf. on Evolutionary Computation,* Dec. 1995, pp.759-764.

[22] E.D. Jensen, *Topological Structural Design using Genetic Algorithms,* Ph.D. Dissertation, Purdue University, Lafayette (IN), 1992.

[23] C.L. Karr and D.E. Goldberg, "Genetic Algorithm based Design of an Air-Injected Hydrocyclone," *Mineral and Metallurgical Processing (Control 90),* 1990, pp. 265-272.

[24] E.G. King, Jr., *Flow vectoring of supersonic exhaust nozzles using a genetic algorithm to define optimally shaped contours,* M.S. Thesis, University of Alabama, Tuscaloosa (AL), 1991.

[25] R.M. Kling and P. Banerjee, "Empirical and Theoretical Studies of the Simulated Evolution Method Applied to Standard Cell Placement," *IEEE Transactions on CAD*(10), Oct. 1991.

[26] T. Kovacs, "Evolving Optimal Populations with XCS Classifier Systems," Technical Report CSRP-96-17, Univ. of B'ham, U.K., 1996.

[27] J. Koza, *Genetic Programming,* MIT Press, Cambridge (MA), 1992.

[28] P.L. Lanzi, "Extending the Representations of Classifier Conditions – Part I: From Binary to Messy Coding," in *Proc. Genetic and Evolutionary Computation Conference (GECCO),* Orlando (FL), July 1999, pp. 337-344.

[29] Z. Michalewicz, *Genetic Algorithms + Data Structures = Evolution Programs,* Third Edition, 1995.

[30] M. Mitchell, *Genetic Algorithms,* MIT Press, 1996.

[31] W.F. Punch, R.C. Averill, E.D. Goodman, S.-C. Lin and Y. Ding, "Design Using Genetic Algorithms – Some Results for Laminated Composite Structures," *IEEE Expert,* February 1995, 10(1):42-49.

[32] R.L. Riolo, "The emergence of coupled sequences of classifiers," in J.D. Schaffer (Ed.), *Proc. Third International Conference on Genetic Algorithms,* Morgan Kaufmann, 1989, pp. 256-264.

[33] R.E. Smith, *A learning system based on genetic algorithms,* Ph.D. Dissertation, Computer Science Department, University of Pittsburgh, Pittsburgh (PA), 1980.

[34] R.E. Smith and D.E. Goldberg, "Reinforcement learning with classifier systems: adaptive default hierarchy formation," *Applied Artificial Intelligence,* 1992, 6:79-102.

[35] A. Tomlinson and L. Bull, "A Corporate Classifier System," in A.E. Eiben, T. Back, M. Schoenauer, and H.P. Schwefel (Eds.), *Parallel Problem Solving from Nature - PPSN V,* Springer, 1998, pp. 550-559.

[36] A. Tomlinson and L. Bull, "On Corporate Classifier Systems: Increasing the Benefits of Rule Linkage," in *Proc. Genetic and Evolutionary Computation Conference (GECCO),* Orlando (FL), July 1999, pp. 649-656.

[37] C. Watkins, *Learning from Delayed Rewards,* Ph.D. Dissertation, Cambridge University (U.K.), 1989.

[38] S.M. Weiss and C.A. Kulikowski, *Computer Systems That Learn,* Morgan Kaufmann, 1991.

[39] S.W. Wilson, "Classifier Systems and the Animat Problem," in *Machine Learning,* 1987, 2:199-228.

[40] S.W. Wilson, "ZCS: A Zeroeth Level Classifier System," *Evolutionary Computation,* 1994, 2(1):1-18.

[41] S.W. Wilson, "Classifier fitness based on accuracy," *Evolutionary Computation,* 1995, 3(2):149-175.

[42] S.W. Wilson, "Generalization in the XCS Classifier System,' in *Proc. Third Annual Conf. on Genetic Programming,* 1998.

[43] S.W.Wilson and D.E.Goldberg, "A Critical Review of Classifier Systems," in *Proc. Third International Conf. on Genetic Algorithms,* Morgan Kaufmann, 1989.

Chapter 6

Connectionist Systems

A man's brain is stored powder; it cannot be touched off by itself; the
fire must come from the outside. _____Mark Twain, 1898

Since 1986, there has been an explosion of research and results in the field of connectionist systems or artificial neural networks. These are often applied to the same tasks as traditional expert systems, such as classification and prediction, although their methodology differs drastically from that of other expert systems.

Neural networks are primarily distinguished from traditional rule-based expert systems by their repudiation of the need to explicitly store knowledge in symbolic form: instead, they apply learning algorithms to modify connection weights in network structures. These connection weights are often uninterpretable, although the adaptation of this technique to the expert systems context has resulted in attempts to formulate weight interpretation techniques. In addition to the possibility of using a neural network directly as an expert system by itself, another motivation has been the development of hybrid systems, in which expert systems using other methodologies rely on neural networks for some learning tasks.

Neural networks are nonparametric estimators, making no assumptions about input distributions, and use nonlinear node functions; it is much easier to implement these than to implement non-parametric and non-linear statistical procedures. However, unlike statistical procedures, measures of confidence cannot be formulated easily for results generated by neural networks.

If knowledge is readily available and expressible, a traditional expert system may suffice. By contrast, neural networks can be applied more easily if raw data is available, and the knowledge acquisition task is difficult. Systems based on connectionist models are 'data-driven'; there is much scope for parallelism and fault-tolerant behavior; inputs from different sources can be processed together. Networks can be trained even when there is no underlying causal model or theory that connects input and output variables. In this respect, some neural networks are analogous to case-based reasoning (cf. Chapter 7). As in inductive learning and case-based reasoning systems, each neural network is presented only with the inputs and outputs from experts' decisions, not the rationale or causal models underlying such decisions. The choice between neural networks and case-based systems is dictated by the form of the data and the amount of expert assistance available .

The next section presents an overview of neural networks, focusing on commonly used networks for the tasks of importance to expert systems. Sections 6.2 and 6.3 describe two connectionist expert system models (KBCNN and MA-CIE) with mechanisms to facilitate human comprehension, use and explanation of neural network performance.

6.1   Neural Networks

Artificial neural networks (also referred to as "neural nets," "artificial neural systems," "parallel distributed processing systems," and "connectionist systems") are computing systems developed using the analogy of biological neural networks. Each neural network has a labeled directed graph structure, in which nodes perform simple computations, and connections (edges/links/arcs) convey signals between nodes. Each connection is labeled by a number called the *connection strength* or *connection weight* indicating the extent to which a signal is amplified or diminished by a connection. Neural networks can be built with sufficiently general node functions to be capable of solving many problems. Learning (training) algorithms are used to determine the weight values appropriate for a specific task.

Section 6.1.1 describes computations performed by single nodes (neurons). Section 6.1.2 outlines the neural network architecture most frequently used in the expert system context. Section 6.1.3 describes principles of neural learning and learning algorithms. Section 6.1.4 discusses how neural networks may be used in expert systems.

6.1.1 Node Functions

Most[1] neural network nodes apply simple functions to the weighted sum of inputs to the node coming from other nodes or the system's input interface, with node output $= f(w_0 + w_1 x_1 + \cdots + w_n x_n)$ or $f(net)$, where $net = w_0 + \sum_{i=1}^{n} w_i x_i$.

Perceptrons are simple neural networks in which each node function is a step function, often defined as follows:

$$f(net) = \begin{cases} 0 \text{ (or } -1) & \text{if } net \leq 0 \\ 1 & \text{if } net > 0 \end{cases} \tag{6.1}$$

The output of a step function is sometimes interpreted as a class identifier. One may also interpret nodes in the interior of a network as identifying high level features of the input, whereas output nodes compute application-specific output.

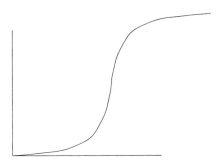

Figure 6.1: A sigmoid function

Many networks use *sigmoid* (S-shaped) functions, illustrated in Figure 6.1, such as

$$z + \frac{1}{1 + \exp(-x \cdot net + y)}$$

and

$$\tanh(x \cdot net - y) + z,$$

where *net* is the net input to a node. These functions are differentiable everywhere, rotationally symmetric about some point, and asymptotically approach their saturation values, e.g.,

$$\lim_{net \to \infty} f(net) = 1,$$

---

[1] Exceptions exist, e.g., some nodes in "sigma-pi" networks compute the product of node inputs.

and

$$\lim_{net \to -\infty} f(net) = 0 \text{ (or -1)}.$$

Their smoothness makes it easy to devise learning algorithms and understand the behavior of large networks.

Radial basis function networks and competitive networks (that perform clustering) often use Gaussian (bell-shaped) node functions, e.g.,

$$f(net) = \frac{1}{\sqrt{2\pi}\sigma} \exp\left(-\frac{1}{2}\left(\frac{net - \mu}{\sigma}\right)^2\right).$$

This node function can be extended to use a different μ_i and σ_i, for each input dimension. Unlike the step and sigmoid node functions, $f(net)$ asymptotically approaches 0 (or some constant) for large magnitudes of net, and $f(net)$ has a single maximum for $net = \mu$.

6.1.2   Network Architecture

Nodes in a network that receive external inputs are called *input nodes*, nodes whose outputs are transmitted to the external environment are *output nodes*, and all others are *hidden nodes* whose interaction with the external environment is indirect. Some nodes may receive an input as well as generate an output.

Association problems are sometimes solved using symmetric networks, in which the strength of a connection is the same along both directions. These networks are implicitly *recurrent*, and computations iterate through cycles of node activations.

By contrast, most networks used for classification and function approximation problems are *feedforward* ('layered' or 'acyclic') with nodes partitioned into subsets called layers, with no connections that lead from layer j to layer k if $j \geq k$. Terminological conventions vary; we call a network *strictly feedforward* if every connection from layer j leads to layer $j + 1$. In our notation, each external input arrives at and is distributed to other nodes by each node of the "input layer" or "layer 0" where no other computation occurs. The size and structure of such a network can be described by a sequence whose elements denote the number of nodes in each successive layer, e.g., the '3-2-3-2' network of Figure 6.2 accepts 3-dimensional inputs, has 2 nodes in the first hidden layer (layer 1), 3 nodes in the second hidden layer (layer 2), and the last layer generates 2-dimensional outputs.

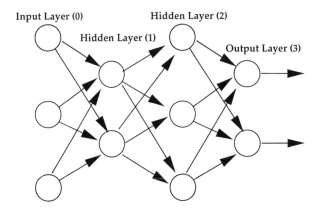

Figure 6.2: A strictly feedforward network of size 2-3-2-3, with two hidden layers of nodes

6.1.3 Neural Learning

A few fundamental learning principles underlie most neural network learning algorithms:

1. *Correlation (Hebbian) learning:* This approach reinforces the strength of connections among nodes having similar outputs when presented with the same input. Connection strengths eventually represent the correlations between node outputs. This approach is generally used in representing associations, e.g., applications such as character recognition.

2. *Competitive learning:* When an input pattern is presented to a network, different nodes compete to be *winners* that specialize to specific regions in the data space. The connections between input nodes and the winner node are then modified to increase the likelihood that the same winner continues to win future competitions for inputs similar to the one which caused the adaptation. Each node comes to represent a prototype or a cluster centroid in the data space.

3. *Feedback-based learning:* Each interaction of the system with the environment is evaluated, and results in a small change in the system directed towards improving performance in the future. For instance, if increasing a particular weight leads to diminished performance or larger error, then that weight is decreased as the network is trained to perform better.

The most frequently used neural network learning algorithm, *error back-propagation (BP)* [12], applies this principle in the context of feedforward networks. When an input vector is supplied to the network, nodes in its successive layers generate outputs, resulting in an output vector for the network as a whole. This 'actual' output vector is compared with the desired output vector for the input vector in question, and the mean squared error between actual and desired output vectors provides the feedback used to modify connection weights, beginning with the connections incident on the output nodes. Stochastic gradient descent is carried out in the space of connection weights; the change in each connection weight is proportional to the partial derivative of the mean squared error with respect to the connection weight to be modified.

The use of well known sigmoid node functions (such as tanh) makes these computations easy to perform, using the changes in later layers of weights to compute the changes in preceding layers of weights. For a network with one hidden layer, for instance, in response to presentation of an input vector x_p, the change in a connection weight from the jth hidden node (in layer 1) to the kth output node (in layer 2) is

$$\eta(d_{p,k} - o_{p,k})S'(net^{(2)}_{p,k})x^{(1)}_{p,j}$$

and the change in the connection weight from the ith input node (in layer 0) to the jth hidden node (in layer 1) is

$$\eta \sum_k \left((d_{p,k} - o_{p,k})S'(net^{(2)}_{p,k})w^{(2,1)}_{k,j} \right) S'(net^{(1)}_{p,j})x^{(0)}_{p,i},$$

where

- η is a positive learning rate (usually constant),

- $d_{p,k}$ is the kth desired output,

- $o_{p,k}$ is the network's actual kth output,

- S' is the first derivative of the sigmoid node function (e.g., $S'(net) = S(net) \times (1 - S(net))$ if $S(x)$ is defined to be $1/(1 + e^{-x})$),

- $net^{(2)}_{p,k}$ is the net input to the kth node in layer 2,

- $net^{(1)}_{p,j}$ is the net input to the jth node in layer 1,

- $x^{(1)}_{p,j}$ is the output of the jth node in layer 1, and

- $x^{(0)}_{p,i}$ is the output of the ith node in layer 0.

Many variations to this algorithm have been proposed, e.g., assuming $(d_{p,k} - o_{p,k}) = 0$ if its magnitude is smaller than a predetermined threshold (e.g., 0.05).

The magnitude of changes in connection weights in a single learning step must be small enough to ensure that a network does not stray too far from its partially evolved state, but large enough so that overall learning time is not excessive.

6.1.4 Connectionism and Expert Systems

Neural networks have been introduced into the field of knowledge-based expert systems in two ways:

1. A hybrid system may be developed in one or more of the following ways:

   (a) A neural network may preprocess data to be supplied to a traditional expert system.

   (b) A neural network may postprocess outputs of a traditional expert system.

   (c) A neural network may work alongside (in parallel with) a traditional expert system, in a modular cooperative framework.

   (d) A neural network may be embedded in the context of a large expert system.

   (e) Small components of the neural network may embed traditional expert systems or reasoning techniques.

2. A neural network may be built to process knowledge, essentially replacing a traditional expert system. The neural network must then be augmented with some components of traditional expert systems, such as a preprocessing procedure to translate knowledge into a form usable by a neural network, and an explanation facility that interprets network outputs and describes network structure and behavior. Network size and architecture may be determined using expert knowledge. Two examples of this approach, KBCNN and MACIE, are discussed in the rest of this chapter.

6.2 KBCNN

To develop rule-based connectionist networks, Fu [2] suggests a procedure in which rules are first written in Horn clause form, $l_1 \& l_2 \& \ldots \& l_n \supset r$, where r and each l_i denote a hypothesis. Each rule is translated into parts of a neural network; n different nodes in a lower layer correspond to $l_1, \ldots, l_n$, with connections into a hidden node called a *conjunction node*. Another higher layer node corresponds to r, receiving inputs from all the conjunction nodes corresponding to rules in which r occurs as the right-hand-side of the rule; this node is called a *disjunction node*. The resulting network contains alternating layers of conjunction and disjunction nodes.

Connection strengths are initially set to 1 (or -1 if the relevant rule's antecedent contains the negation of an input hypothesis l_i). If the nature of the relationships between problem variables is only hypothesized but not known with certainty, nodes representing the hypothesized premise may be connected to the relevant conjunction node using connection strengths of smaller magnitude, e.g., 0.1.

A learning algorithm such as backpropagation can then be applied to the neural network containing many such rule representations. The learning procedure improves upon the original rule-based representation from which the network structure was derived. When the connection weights are intended to be interpreted as uncertainty measures, the learning algorithm is constrained so that it cannot modify them beyond a prespecified interval, e.g., $[-1, 1]$ if uncertainty is to be expressed using certainty factors (cf. Chapter 3).

In KBCNN [3], if the network performance remains unsatisfactory after applying the learning algorithm, then new hidden nodes can be added to the network, and the learning procedure is restarted. Each new conjunction node is connected to all existing nodes in adjacent layers, as well as to a new disjunction node at a higher layer that only receives inputs from new conjunction nodes. Figure 6.3 (adapted from [2]) illustrates this for a network developed from three rules:

1. $P \,\&\, Q \;\supset\; O$

2. $I_1 \,\&\, I_2 \,\&\, I_3 \,\&\;$ possibly $I_4 \;\supset\; P$

3. $I_3 \,\&\, I_4 \,\&\, I_5 \;\supset\; Q.$

Conjunction nodes corresponding to these rules are $\&_1, \&_2, \&_3$. A weak link is shown from I_4 to $\&_2$, with low connection strength. New hidden nodes $(\&_{h1}, \&_{h2})$ are added to the network when the learning algorithm fails to achieve good performance using the original network. Thicker arrows identify connections in the original network before adding new hidden nodes. A new disjunction node, H, is also added to the network, to allow direct flow of information between the two conjunction hidden nodes, unmediated by P, Q.

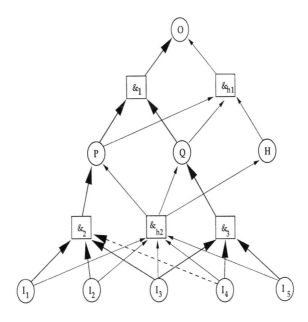

Figure 6.3: A rule-based KBCNN; the dashed line represents a tentative connection (low initial weight), and smaller arrows identify connections incident on new hidden nodes

If the input nodes of a connectionist expert system are intended to be categorical, but the inputs from the problem are numerical, then the range of such an input variable may be broken up into overlapping sub-intervals, as in the KBANN system [11]. Each sub-interval is associated with an input node in the network, and an input value may activate one or more nodes corresponding to sub-intervals within which it occurs.

In the KBCNN algorithm, an application of the backpropagation learning algorithm is followed by roughly clustering the hidden nodes using a single pass through the nodes, in which each node is allotted to one of the clusters already determined, if near enough, or to a new cluster. Old hidden nodes are replaced by nodes that represent the clusters thus obtained. Weights on connections incident on such a new node are obtained by averaging corresponding weights of connections incident on the old nodes being replaced by the new node.

6.3   MACIE

The MACIE connectionist expert system (developed by Gallant) also attempts to perform inferencing with partial information (when some data is unavailable). This system has facilities for interactive acquisition of data, in which the system may seek information from the user when such information is necessary for reliable inference. For instance, in a medical diagnostic domain, specialized blood tests may not normally be performed, but the network may contain nodes and connections related to the same. In many cases, MACIE may generate reasonable answers without requiring specialized blood test results, but may ask for the results of a specialized blood test if such results are considered most useful to establish or disprove a tentative disease hypothesis. After MACIE generates an answer in response to available data, it may be asked to justify its conclusions, and does so by constructing (post-hoc) a rationalization in the form of previously nonexistent 'rules' that explain its behavior, constructed by tracing over the most relevant node activations in the network.

As with most other connectionist expert systems, MACIE is restricted to classification problems, a Boolean dichotomy in the simplest case (e.g., presence or absence of a specific disease). By using multiple Boolean variables, continuous values may be approximated to some degree of precision. The main applications are in diagnosis, fault detection, and pattern recognition, but not design or configuration.

MACIE uses feedforward networks in which a step function is computed by each node. Values of input nodes $(u_1, \ldots, u_p)$ are discrete, drawn from the set

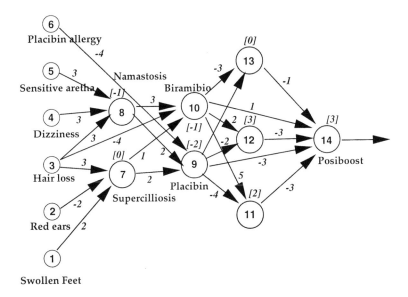

Figure 6.4: MACIE network for sarcophagal disease diagnosis and treatment, adapted from [5]; node numbers are indicated in the circles denoting nodes treatment nodes (numbered 9, 10, and 14) generate output to the environment; bias weights are given in square brackets, and connection weights are shown next to all edges

$\{-1, 0, 1\}$, in which '0' refers to an unknown value, whereas -1 and 1 correspond to the input hypothesis being false/true. Connection weights are restricted to be positive or negative integers, to facilitate explanation. Nodes are numbered such that $i > j$ if a connection is directed from node u_j to node u_i.

MACIE is a 'matrix-controlled inference engine' with each row in the weight matrix corresponding to an intermediate or output node; there is one column for each node. In the weight matrix W, the connection weight $w_{i,j}$ corresponds to the link from u_j to u_i. The bias value (the constant term in the node function) for the ith node is denoted $w_{i,0}$; MACIE assumes the convention that there is a special node u_0 whose activation value always equals 1.

Figure 6.4 illustrates a simplified network developed by MACIE for the diagnosis and treatment of acute sarcophagal disease.

Connections represent the dependency information from input variables (e.g., symptoms) and intermediate variables (e.g., diseases) to output variables (e.g., treatments), showing which variables' values are sufficient to compute each node's value.

Since not every Boolean function can be represented as a linear discriminant, additional hidden nodes are introduced into the system. Too many such nodes should not be added, otherwise the network may perform very well on the training data without generalizing well to test data (new input cases).

Once the structure and size of the network are determined, any network training algorithm can be used; Gallant proposes the *pocket algorithm* [4], suitable for classification tasks when the network nodes compute a step function and not a sigmoid. This algorithm presents data randomly to a node, updating the vector of connection weights by $\pm\eta x$, where $\eta > 0$ is a small learning rate constant, and x is an input vector misclassified by the node; the sign is positive if x belongs to the class for which desired output is positive. The pocket algorithm stores (in a 'pocket') the best set of connection weights so far encountered, judged in terms of the number of data elements classified correctly in the current run. A variant, the *pocket algorithm with ratchet*, replaces pocket contents only after first checking that the new set of weights has better performance on the entire data set.

The user interface queries regarding the presence of each possible symptom (input variable), to obtain relevant information from the user. Variables can be initialized to known values (± 1) or 'unknown' (0).

After obtaining initial information, MACIE's inference engine repeatedly executes the following sequence of steps:

1. Forward chain to make inferences.

2. Quit if output is satisfactory; generate explanation if needed.

3. Backward chain to find useful unknown variable values, and query user.

Forward inferences for all nodes are performed in one pass, as follows. In the forward inference for node u_i, MACIE computes the quantity

$$Known_i = \sum_{known\ u_j} w_{i,j} u_j$$

as well as

$$Max\_Unknown_i = \sum_{unknown\ u_k} |w_{i,k}|,$$

the maximum possible change when we find values for all currently unknown variables. Whenever $|Known_i| > Max\_Unknown_i$, any additional information will not change the sign for the discriminant, so the output can depend just on the sign of $Known_i$. This procedure addresses the problem of knowing when the available information is inadequate to make a decision.

MACIE attempts to estimate the confidence '$Conf(u_i)$,' i.e., the likelihood that an unknown variable will eventually be deduced to be true or false. This measure is useful for comparing unknown variables, but should not be confused with probability. It is computed using the following heuristics:

1. For a node that represents a known hypothesis, $Conf(u_i) = u_i$.

2. For an unknown input node, $Conf(u_i) = 0$.

3. For other unknown nodes, the computation is carried out in the order of increasing index:

$$Conf(u_i) = \frac{\sum_{j=0}^{i-1} w_{i,j} Conf(u_j)}{\sum_{u_j \text{ unknown}} |w_{i,j}|}.$$

Clearly, $-1 \leq Conf(u_i) \leq 1$.

MACIE has a *Question Generation* component, used when the system must find an input node with unknown activation and ask for its value. MACIE uses the following approach:

1. 'Pursue' the unknown variable u_i such that $Conf(u_i)$ is maximum, starting with an output node.

2. If pursuing the node u_i, find the unknown cell u_j with the greatest absolute influence on u_i, i.e., maximize $|w_{i,j}|$. If u_j is an input variable, query the user for its value, else pursue u_j. Acyclicity ensures that backtracking is not needed.

Other heuristics are to emphasize positive evidence (maximizing $Conf(u_j)$), or to maximize $|w_{i,j}|.(|Conf(u_j)| + 1/level(u_j))$ taking into account both confidence estimates and $level(u_j) = 1+$distance to closest input node. Gallant reports that the results are not very sensitive to the choice of heuristics.

The user may respond 'unobtainable' to a query, in which case the system treats the variable as having activation 0. This is to be distinguished from 'unknown', where the value may change in the future.

A variant of MACIE, suggested by Ghalwash [7], modifies the pursuit mechanism used to decide which nodes must be chosen as targets for future firing, leading to queries regarding unknown input values. In this variant, additional variables (with a parameter denoting time) are maintained per node, initialized as follows:

$$
\begin{aligned}
knet_i(0) &= -\theta_i \text{ (threshold)} \\
unk_i(0) &= \sum_j |w_{i,j}|
\end{aligned}
$$

where u_i denotes the output of the ith node in the network, $knet_i$ its net input from known values, and unk_i the largest possible weighted sum of unknown values at the input of the ith node.

These variables are updated (at time instant $\lambda + 1$) to

$$knet_i(\lambda + 1) = knet_i(\lambda) + \sum_{j:\text{new}(\lambda)} w_{i,j} u_j(\lambda)$$

$$unk_i(\lambda + 1) = unk_i(\lambda) - \sum_{j:\text{new}(\lambda)} \sum_j |w_{i,j}|$$

where $new(\lambda)$ identifies the nodes that have become newly activated at time λ.

Among the nodes that have most recently gained additional input but were unable to fire, the node with maximum $knet_i/unk_i$ is chosen to be 'pursued' (successively examining nodes closer to the input layer) as in MACIE. Ghalwash reports that this approach resulted in the system reaching its conclusions faster than MACIE, requiring fewer known inputs.

MACIE has an explanation generation facility to help explain the conclusions reached by the network. If the user queries why the system has asked the user a particular question, MACIE lists the backward-chaining logic (node sequence, in reverse chronological order) used to produce that particular question. Explanations are expressed using if-then rules, in response to a user's query as to how a conclusion was reached. A minimal subset of the currently known information that is sufficient to make the inference is extracted as follows:

1. List all known inputs that contributed $w_i u_i$ with the same sign as the output. Contradictory and unknown evidence is omitted.

2. Sort the list of weights in the order of decreasing absolute values.

3. Generate a conjunction of the most significant of these for the conditional of an if-then rule, taking elements from the list until

$$\left(\sum_{u_i \text{ used}} |w_i| \right) > \left(\sum_{u_j \text{ unused}} |w_i| \right).$$

For small networks, the set of rules can be extracted directly, and these can be used to form the knowledge base of a rule-based expert system. However, the possible number of rules grows exponentially with size of the network, hence it may be preferable to continue to represent the knowledge using the neural network, possibly caching answers to frequently encountered queries.

MACIE has been used to diagnose causes for infantile diarrhoea, where performance (70%) and explanatory rules were judged to be as good as those of experts. MACIE has also been applied to management decision-making (whether to continue with the development of a new product), a chemical process fault diagnosis model that includes temporal information, and other medical and economic problems.

Connectionist expert systems such as MACIE can be extended in various ways. Online learning can be combined with the operation of the expert system, using a method that stores the most recent inputs. To improve robustness so that the system can handle noisy data effectively, training data may be corrupted deliberately by injecting noise, before the learning process is initiated. For instance, the signs of some training input features may be reversed with a fixed low probability.

As with other connectionist learning algorithms, it is necessary to guard against overtraining a network: sufficiently large amounts of data must be used, the network size should not be too large, and training should be terminated if error on test cases (that do not belong to the training set) begins to rise.

6.4 Bibliographic Notes

The 1980s are considered the "renaissance" period for neural networks, beginning with the publication of the book by (D. Rumelhart and J. McClelland [10]. Several introductory-level books on neural networks are now available, such as [9]. For the more mathematically inclined reader, a useful comprehensive text is by Haykin[8]. There are several books on specific applications of neural networks, in areas as wide-ranging as chemistry and geography. Many neural network tools are also freely available on the internet.

Early work on connectionist inferencing was done by J.A. Anderson using an autoassociative model, where a system is trained to reproduce input patterns, and subsequently becomes robust to partial/noisy inputs [1]. Connectionist expert systems are discussed in considerable detail in the books by Fu [2] and Gallant [6].

Bibliography

[1] J.A. Anderson, J.W. Silverstein, S.A. Ritz, and R.S. Jones, "Distinctive features, categorical perception, and probability learning: Some applications of a neural model," *Psychological Review*, 1977, 84:413-451.

[2] L. Fu, *Neural Networks in Expert Systems*, McGraw Hill, 1994.

[3] L. Fu, "Knowledge-based connectionism for revising domain theories," *IEEE Transactions on Systems, Man and Cybernetics*, 1993, 23(1):173-182.

[4] S.I. Gallant, "Optimal Linear Discriminants," in *Proc. International Conf. on Pattern Recognition*, Paris (France), 1986, pp.849-952.

[5] S.I. Gallant, "Connectionist Expert Systems," *Communications of the ACM*, Feb. 1988, 31(2):152-169.

[6] S.I. Gallant, *Neural Network Learning and Expert Systems*, MIT Press, 1993.

[7] A.Z. Ghalwash, "A Recency Inference Engine for Connectionist Knowledge Bases," *Applied Intelligence*, 1998, 9(3):201-216.

[8] S. Haykin, *Neural Networks: A Comprehensive Foundation*, second edition, Prentice-Hall, 1999.

[9] K. Mehrotra, C.K. Mohan, and S. Ranka, *Elements of Artificial Neural Networks*, MIT Press, 1997.

[10] D. Rumelhart and J. McClelland, *Parallel Distributed Processing: Explorations in the microstructure of cognition* (2 Vols.), MIT Press, 1986.

[11] G.G. Towell, J.W. Shavlik, and M.O. Noordewier, "Refinement of approximate domain theories by knowledge-based neural networks," in *Proc. AAAI-90*, Boston (MA), 1990, pp.861-866.

[12] P. Werbos, *Beyond Regression: New tools for prediction and analysis in the behavioral sciences,* Ph.D. dissertation, Harvard University, 1974.

6.5 Exercises

1. For which of the Exercise problems mentioned in Chapter 2 (pages 129 to 131) would a connectionist expert system be useful?

2. What are the relative advantages and disadvantages of backpropagation *vs.* the pocket algorithm for systems such as MACIE?

3. Develop and evaluate a variant of MACIE in which each node is associated with a collection of functions, one per possible subset of missing input values. For example, if a node is to receive two inputs x, y, it would be associated with four functions, $f_0(), f_1(x), f_2(y), f_3(x, y)$, with the choice of the function depending on which inputs $\in \{x, y\}$ are available for computation.

4. In a connectionist expert system, should restrictions be placed on the extent to which connection weights given by an expert are modified by a neural network algorithm?

5. Compare the computational effort involved in developing systems using MACIE and KBCNN.

Chapter 7

Case Based Reasoning Systems

We should be careful to get out of an experience only the wisdom that's in it – and stop there; lest we be like the cat that sits down on a hot stove-lid. She will never sit down on a hot stove-lid again – and that is well; but also she will never sit down on a cold one any more. —————————————————— Mark Twain, 1897

In many real-world situations, it is impossible or impractical to fully specify all rules involved, yet it is easy to generate working solutions for commonly encountered situations. *Case-Based Reasoning (CBR)* is an expert systems methodology in which reasoning and learning are based on examples, significantly reducing the cost and effort previously spent in acquiring rules in the knowledge acquisition phase. CBR has emerged as a strong alternative to rule-based systems.

CBR resembles interpolation when multiplying numbers using a table of logarithms; the numbers we need may not occur in the table, but we do not have to learn how to compute logarithms from first principles. Instead, computation proceeds by looking for the closest matching numbers in the table, and modifying corresponding entries in the table to suit the specific numbers for which an answer is desired. Similarly, in a CBR system, new problems are solved by adapting relevant cases from the case library. CBR is generally applied to problems characterized by discrete or categorical attributes; in particular, classification problems are the easiest for CBR since class identity requires no adaptation.

Section 7.1 presents an overview of CBR systems and their development. Section 7.2 addresses the primary issue of how the most relevant cases may be extracted from a case library, and Section 7.3 discusses how cases are adapted to fit new problems. This is followed by a discussion in Section 7.4 of the case library and how it may be constructed. Section 7.5 addresses how the system is modified using feedback, and also the interfaces and tools useful in building and interacting with the CBR system. Section 7.6 discusses the use of learning techniques to automatically modify cases in a library. Some large-scale practical examples of CBR systems are given in Section 7.7. Finally, a closely related reasoning technique, *Analogical Reasoning*, is discussed in Section 7.8.

7.1 Overview

Unlike traditional rule-based expert systems, CBR systems are based on direct representations of example cases, without explicitly acquiring and representing the knowledge as separate from the cases. New cases are solved by retrieving and modifying solutions from previous cases. At a high level, this methodology has much in common with problem-solving techniques that perform clustering, or divide up the input data space into small regions within which the output variables are expected to have similar values. All these techniques perform well when reasoning is restricted to narrow ranges within the problem domain for which reliable examples exist, but not when considerable extrapolation is required.

Although a CBR system will be restricted to small variations of known situations, it is expected to quickly generate answers grounded in reality. Its reasoning is similar to those of experts on the field who must make quick decisions, where reasoning from fundamental principles is unlikely to occur. With CBR, there is always a short connection between the input case and the retrieved solution. For instance, a cargo-loading foreman will use cases from his previous knowledge to determine how a pulley will behave when used to lift a weight, unlike the reasoning used by a physicist sitting in a laboratory.

In addressing a new task, the first question to be asked is whether a rule-based system or a CBR system is more appropriate. As with any problem for which expert systems must be built, the problem must require expertise, which must be available, and there should be significant expected payback as a result of developing an expert system for the problem. In addition, a CBR approach would be more appropriate if there is a narrow focus, with a large set of closely related problems and solutions. Difficulties may arise if the domain changes

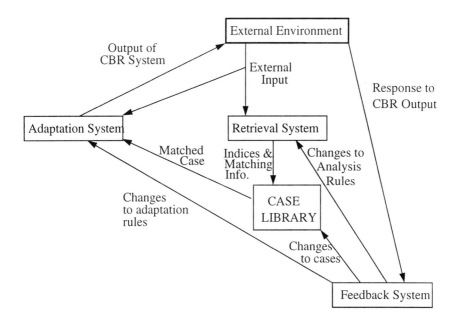

Figure 7.1: Architecture of a CBR System

with time. The problem context should be stable, and not subject to drastic and frequent changes. In some problems, although the system environment may change with time, a CBR approach may be applicable to subtasks that are stable.

Once a decision is made to develop a CBR system, the following components of a CBR system must be developed: a *Case Library*, a *Retrieval System*, an *Adaptation System*, and a *Feedback System*, whose interconnections are illustrated in Figure 7.1. The case library contains the cases organized using abstraction hierarchies and indexed using problem attributes and features. The retrieval system extracts the best matched cases from the case library, in response to new inputs from the environment. The adaptation system determines what is different between the input and the retrieved case, and then modifies the solution stored in the retrieved case (taking those differences into account). The feedback system uses external evaluations of CBR system outputs to modify the above three components, as needed. These components are discussed in greater detail in the sections that follow.

7.2   Retrieval

This section addresses the primary task in case based reasoning: *retrieval*, i.e., extracting from the case library those cases that most resemble new input problem descriptions.

The Retrieval System relies on an *analyzer* to find the most relevant information describing an input case. This extracts important features of the input, such as the values of important attributes, conjunctions of attributes, and relationships between attributes, and numerical constraints. Analysis rules are task-specific, and obtained from the domain expert.

After such analysis, the retriever applies *matching rules* to compare features of the input case with the cases stored in the case library. The result is one (or a few) best matching case(s) from the case library. Two subtasks are involved in retrieval: *indexed retrieval* and *similarity ranking*.

1. **Indexed Retrieval:**   Since exhaustive matching can be computationally expensive for large case libraries, the CBR system indexes cases using features chosen to speed up the retrieval process. Each index is a predicate on the features, analogous to a branch in a classification tree (cf. Section 8.4), identifying a region in the input data space and a subset of cases in the case library. The indexed retrieval process extracts cases that share a sufficient number of indices with the new input. Sophisticated indexing schemes are used to ensure fast retrieval.

2. **Similarity Ranking:**   Cases extracted by the retriever are ranked according to how well they match the input, using task-specific ranking rules. Cases most similar to the input are selected for adaptation. Similarity of cases is evaluated by examining the relative importance and similarity of individual attributes and features, where importance is determined by the domain expert as the case library is being built.

Example 7.1 Consider the problem of determining the amount that a bank may loan to an applicant. Attribute importance rules may assert that attributes such as the amount of the loan and the applicant's income are more important than the applicant's phone number and name. The best matching case from the case library may indicate that a loan of $9000 was approved for (and repaid by) an applicant with similar features. Should the new loan application for $10000 be approved, denied altogether, or should a smaller amount of loan be approved? Here, the primary decision is to determine whether $9000 and $10000 are similar enough to warrant loan approval, although $9000 \neq 10000$. A few alternatives are outlined below:

1. One approach is to divide up possible loan amounts into intervals, such as *under $1000, $1000 to $3000,* etc., so that two values may be considered to match with each other if they lie in the same interval.

2. Another alternative is to allow intervals to overlap, and determine similarity by counting the number of common intervals to which two entries belong.

3. Instead of using intervals, the expert may predetermine the excess amounts (beyond the loan amount from the retrieved case) upto which a new loan may be permitted, e.g., approving the loan for $10,000 in this case if $(10000 - 9000)/9000$ does not exceed a predetermined threshold.

A *Match formula* assigns a similarity rating to each pair of cases, which increases when the attribute values match better, and when the relative weights (importance) of matching attributes are higher. Linear combinations of the similarities of attribute value pairs are often used.

Example 7.2 In the bank loan example, the domain expert may assign a relative importance of 0.001 to annual income, and -1 to problems with credit history. For instance, if the applicant's annual income is $35,000 vs. $30,000 for the retrieved case, and the applicant had 6 late payments on his credit history vs. 4 for the retrieved case, the match formula may compute a similarity rating of

$$(0.001)(35000 - 30000) + (-1)(6 - 4) = 3.$$

The same input matches less well with another case in the case library with the attributes of $40,000 annual income and 7 late payments, for which the similarity rating computed is lower:

$$(0.001)(35000 - 40000) + (-1)(6 - 7) = -4.$$

The similarity rating and the results of retrieval would have been different if the relative weights had instead been 0.0001 and -1.

Abstraction hierarchies can be used to determine how well two attribute values match, based on the average distance to the nearest common ancestors. Using this approach, if b is a parent of a in the hierarchy, their similarity

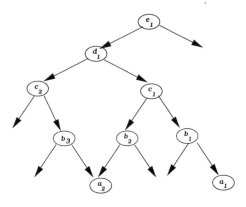

Figure 7.2: An abstraction hierarchy

$sim(a, b) = sim(b, a)$ is defined to be the *concreteness* of b, where *concreteness* of a node $\in [0, 1]$, valued 0 at the root and 1 at leaves; formally, we may define

$$concreteness(X) = \frac{d_R(X)}{d_L(X) + d_R(X)}$$

where X is a node in the abstraction hierarchy, $d_L(X)$ is the distance from X to its nearest descendant leaf, and $d_R(X)$ is the distance from X to the root. If b is not an abstraction of a, then $sim(a, b)$ may be computed as $\sum_{c \in A(b)} sim(a, c)/|A(b)|$, where $A(b)$ is the set of parents of b in the abstraction hierarchy, i.e., each $c \in A(b)$ is an immediate abstraction of b.

Example 7.3 Consider the portion of an abstraction hierarchy depicted in Figure 7.2, with a_1, a_2 as the lowest level nodes with concreteness 1; b_1, b_2, b_3 with concreteness $3/4$; c_1, c_2 with concreteness $1/2$; d_1, d_2 with concreteness $1/4$; and root node e_1 with concreteness 0. The similarity between nodes b_1 and a_2 in this hierarchy is computed as follows:

$$
\begin{aligned}
sim(b_1, a_2) &= (0.5)(sim(b_1, b_2) + sim(b_1, b_3)) \\
&= (0.5)(sim(b_1, c_1) + sim(b_1, c_2)) \\
&= (0.5)(concreteness(c_1) + sim(b_1, d_1)) \\
&= (0.5)(concreteness(c_1) + concreteness(d_1)) \\
&= (0.5)(0.5 + 0.25) \quad = \quad 0.375
\end{aligned}
$$

7.3 Adaptation

This section discusses *Adaptation*, the modification of the solutions of retrieved cases to make them more appropriate to new data for which a solution is required. In the simplest problems (e.g., classification tasks) no adaptation is needed, but many other problems require substantial adaptations.

When a retrieved case does not match a new input perfectly, its solution component must be adjusted to fit the new situation better. The problem-specific knowledge that helps accomplish this task is generally represented using *Adaptation Rules*. These rules determine how to modify the solution of the retrieved case, returning an answer to the new input situation. The adaptation process looks for salient differences between the retrieved case and the input, and applies rules that take these differences into account. Unlike interpolation methods, these rules adapt the solution from only a single retrieved case.

If a considerable amount of knowledge is stored in adaptation rules, a small number of cases would suffice, illustrating the tradeoff between procedural knowledge and memory requirements. Minor variants of cases need not be stored if they can be derived by adaptation rules. Conversely, if the case library is large enough, a very small amount of adaptation may be sufficient without affecting the quality of the final results generated by the CBR system.

Adaptation rules are generally more complex than analysis and retrieval rules. They require a well-defined structure to the solution part of a case, just as analysis and retrieval rules require a well-defined structure for the problem part of a case.

Adaptation depends on domain-specific knowledge, hence adaptation rules must be formulated primarily by domain experts. The domain expert can parameterize the solution by treating it as a form in which values need to be filled in using predefined formulas. These formulas would depend on the relative values of attributes in the input and the retrieved case.

Example 7.4 The maximum amount loaned by a bank to a loan applicant may be determined using the formula

$$\text{Amt. loaned in retrieved case} \times \frac{\text{Annual Income of new applicant}}{\text{Annual Income in retrieved case}}$$

If the new applicant's annual income is \$35,000, the annual income in the retrieved case is \$30,000, and the amount loaned in the retrieved case was \$9,000, then the bank would be willing to loan at most $\$9000 \times 35000/30000 = \$10,500$ to the new applicant. If the requested amount was \$10,000, then the loan application would be approved for the entire amount since it is less than the upper limit computed above ($10,500).

Example 7.5 Hammond's *CHEF* program [9] generates new Chinese stir-fry and souffle recipes by adapting recipes retrieved from a case library containing known recipes. In an attempt to construct a recipe for *chicken and green beans*, CHEF's CBR system retrieves a recipe for *beef and broccoli*, and attempts to adapt it. The first step is the substitution of *chicken* for *beef* and *green beans* for *broccoli*. The retrieved recipe has *chop broccoli into small pieces*, but the corresponding step *chop green beans into small pieces* is not necessary and is hence deleted. On the other hand, *chop chicken* requires an additional step of removing bone, which the original *chop beef* did not have, and must be added.

In a planning domain, adaptation rules must examine preconditions to actions that may have to be carried out, and find plans to achieve them. In a diagnostic task, they must find gaps in an explanation and fill in missing causal relationships. Although non-trivial, adaptation rules are expected to be simpler than the rules in a purely rule-based system. Changes made are local to parts of a single case, and should lead to only minor modifications of the retrieved case.

Adaptation rules may be of two kinds, *structural* or *derivational*, discussed below in greater detail.

7.3.1   Derivational Adaptation

In *Derivational Adaptation*, rules that generated the original solution are re-executed to generate the new solution. This requires storing the planning sequence that constructed the solution. When a case is retrieved, the reasoner checks to see if the differences (between the retrieved case and the new input) affect any of the decisions underlying the solution stored in the case. If so, those decisions are re-evaluated with the new values. Parts of the original solution process are re-executed. Fewer *ad hoc* rules are needed, and problem-solving knowledge from other domains can be used (as in *analogical reasoning*, cf. Section 7.8). One example of derivational adaptation is *reinstantiation* of the method used to generate a solution.

Example 7.6 Simpson's MEDIATOR program [18] proposes possible compromises to resolve disputes between parties with conflicting goals. When a proposed solution (based on a retrieved case) is unsatisfactory, MEDIATOR generates a new proposal, and also records the failure of the previous solution, so that the right action is taken in similar future cases. The dispute between Egypt and Israel over control of the Sinai was solved by MEDIATOR by using a solution for the Panama canal conflict between USA and Panama. In the Panama canal case, the relevant plan that generated the solution was *divide into different parts,* separating control of the canal along political and military lines. Reinstantiating this plan for the Egypt-Israel conflict, the proposed solution was to divide control of the Sinai.

A related adaptation technique is *abstraction and respecialization.* If a piece of the retrieved solution does not apply to the new problem, this technique looks for relevant abstractions of that piece of solution, and re-specializes the abstraction.

7.3.2 Structural Adaptation

In *Structural Adaptation*, the adaptation rules apply directly to the solution stored in a case. The most frequently used adaptation technique is the method of *parameterized solutions.* Each problem parameter is associated with one or more solution parameters. When a case is retrieved, the old case and new problem descriptions are compared along the specified parameters. These differences are then used to modify the solution parameters as determined by structural adaptation rules.

Example 7.7 Bain's JUDGE program [2] attempts to pronounce sentences for convicted criminals, based on a case library describing sentences for past crimes. JUDGE slowly builds the (initially empty) case library as it makes decisions for new crimes, using general heuristics. Input attributes include the crime, the event sequence leading to the crime, and the range of possible sentences for the crime (as per legal statutes). The sentence from a retrieved case is adapted by increasing or decreasing the severity of the sentence, based on how the new crime compares to the retrieved one. The more heinous the crime, the harsher the sentence.

In *critic-based adaptation*, a critic looks for some combination of features that can cause a problem in a plan. Critic-based adaptation rules scan the output and make local modifications, applying changes to each part of the retrieved case solution. Critics can only make small local patches in solutions, possibly using high-level repair strategies.

Example 7.8 Suppose a plan is needed to paint a ladder and a ceiling. First these problems are solved separately, leading to a sequence of actions such as:

Paint ladder; Climb ladder; Paint ceiling.

A critic checks for any step with a side-effect that makes a later step difficult, e.g., painting the ladder makes it wet, and a ladder must be dry before it can be climbed. The critic suggests a high-level repair strategy such as

Rearrange the sequence of steps in the current plan.

This may lead to generating another sequence such as:

Climb ladder; Paint ceiling; Paint ladder.

Other constraints and preconditions eliminate sequences such as

Paint ceiling; Climb ladder; Paint ladder.

If an adaptation attempt is unsuccessful, an *adaptation failure* is said to occur, driving a learning process that modifies the adaptation rules.

7.4   Case Library

The Case Library contains a collection of *Cases*, where each case describes a problem and a solution to the problem.

Cases should be represented using a scheme that is capable of representing all relevant facts, objects, and relationships. Frames are the most natural choice for representing knowledge in CBR. Within each case frame, there are two main parts: problem and solution, each with *slots* (also referred to as 'fields' or 'attributes') describing various aspects of the problem and solution.

Example 7.9 CBR systems that solve diagnosis problems contain cases in which the problem part is a set of symptoms and the solution part is a hypothesis regarding the unobservable state of a system. For instance, a case library for plumbing system diagnosis may contain a *valve leak* case frame with problem part:

alarm light is ON and gauge B reads low,

and solution part:

valve C is leaking.

The frame structure contains several slots, such as 'alarm light,' 'gauge A', and 'gauge B', of which some may be unknown or irrelevant to the problem being considered.

7.4.1 Constructing the Case Library

The domain expert supplies the solved examples to the system. The expert also helps organize the collection of examples, telling the system which examples are similar and which are not, which are exceptions, and which are prototypical. Experts must look for inconsistent or missing data, interactions between different attributes, and their relative importance. Ideally, examples should be detailed records available in machine-readable form, such as online databases. Least preferable are idealized examples artificially generated by the expert, since these are likely to omit many real-world details.

The database of examples is transformed into a usable case library expressed using the chosen knowledge representation language. The domain expert gathers a representative set of cases, large enough to provide a good testbed for structuring the case library, including classic prototypes of the domain as well as important exceptions to the prototypes. All additions and modifications to the case library must be with reference to actual examples rather than hypothesized relationships or rules.

The expert organizes an initial set of cases, and then tries new examples to see what the CBR system retrieves and how it adapts them. When the expert presents an input example I, the system may retrieve a case C whereas the expert expects a different case T to be retrieved. This may occur due to one of the following reasons:

- The case library may not contain an appropriate case; the expert must then introduce I or some variant of it as a case.

- The organization of cases and matching criteria may need correction; the expert must then modify the rules until I results in retrieving T instead of C.

Results of retrieval may be modified in several ways:

1. Make certain attribute values match better than others by creating new numeric intervals or abstraction classes. For example, we can make $5000 match $5200 by converting the numeric attribute into a set of ranges of values, e.g, [0, 1000], [1001, 2000], etc. For a categorical attribute such as profession, we can make *carpenter* match *plumber* by creating an abstraction class *home repair* that includes both.

2. Change the relative weightage (importance) associated with various attributes.

3. Introduce a new derived (calculated) attribute, whose importance is a function of the importance of the attributes on which it depends.

New changes to the case library may effectively reverse earlier changes (that made previous matches work). Therefore, consistency checks must be performed when the case library is changed, with any new errors being reported to the expert. These may point to the need for new abstractions, especially if the system can identify errors before the latest change is actually installed in the field. Resolving conflicts between two changes may require finding a compromise (e.g., an intermediate importance level) or a new calculated attribute.

After building a reasonably large case library, the system is field-tested with end-users. Every case solved by the user becomes available for future problem-solving sessions. Problem cases are to be logged and submitted to the domain expert for inspection; end-users do not make major changes in the case library.

7.4.2   Hierarchical Organization of Cases

Each case in the case library is represented as a node in an *abstraction hierarchy*, with its generalizations as parents, and specializations and instances as children. Some nodes may represent collections of cases rather than single cases. Leaf nodes are specific cases. Higher levels of the hierarchy represent more general knowledge, whereas lower levels represent exceptions and specialized knowledge. The properties of each node are inherited by the nodes below it in the hierarchy. When the solution corresponding to a node X conflicts with its parent node Y, the lower level node is presumed to be more appropriate for all cases that match both parent and child. Hence, whenever an input I matches the parent Y, it is also necessary to check whether I matches X. Node Y is flagged, with a *failure link* to X.

The case library may also contain a *part-whole hierarchy*, with lower level nodes representing parts or sub-events of concepts represented by their parents.

A node may have *index links* to its specializations. Index links connect nodes into a discrimination network, linked by sequences of predicates and predicate values. Attributes used to index cases are essential to case descriptions.

Some CBR systems maintain explicit connections between cases and problem-solving goals, capturing domain-independent problem-solving knowledge, and representing goal-subgoal relationships.

7.5 Interfaces and Feedback

Three kinds of interfaces are required in a CBR system, possibly constructed using a 'shell' that provides a starting point in developing each interface:

The Programmer Interface enables construction of utilities. This should include tools for programming domain-specific *forms* and graphics for input and output to domain experts and end users. Each form is a presentation of a frame structure intended to be filled in by experts or end-users. This interface should also facilitate writing code that ties visual displays to the internal knowledge representation language. A library of functions must be available, and the interface must allow the programmer to add domain-specific functions to the function library.

The Domain Expert Interface enables building the case library. The domain expert uses this interface, along with various forms and functions created by the programmer, to supply examples and organize cases, build abstraction hierarchies, adjust matching weights, build calculated attributes, and describe rules for analyzing, retrieving, adapting, and repairing cases. The goal is to capture the expert's classification scheme, as well as the techniques used by experts in adapting old cases to new situations. The interface must also offer tools for:

1. case browsing (to look for relevant cases that the retriever is unable to find in response to an input),

2. editing abstraction hierarchies, and

3. defining formulas (relationships between features and attributes).

These facilitate representing analysis information (what to look for in input cases), matching information (how to match cases), and adaptation information (how to make old solutions fit new problems).

The End-user Interface permits use of the case library and the forms created by the programmer. In response to a form filled in by the user, the interface returns another form containing an adapted version of the solution from the retrieved (most relevant) case in the library.

These interfaces facilitate feedback from experts and end-users. The feedback system is expected to contain a mechanism to allow external evaluation of the answers returned by the adaptation system, possibly with a human in the loop. When the system's answers are deemed unsatisfactory, an explanation system should help determine why. CBR systems explain answers by giving the prior case from which the answer was adapted, and reasons for adapting the prior case in the manner that the system did. Such explanations are easy to understand and evaluate. Retrieved cases do not have to be hidden, and can be revealed in a user interface, for ease of understanding and modification of the CBR system.

The *repair system*, invoked if the solutions generated by the system are unsatisfactory, adds new cases to the case library or modifies existing rules. This enables the CBR system to perform better if a case similar to the current input is presented again.

7.6   Case Based Learning

In basic CBR, the domain experts are responsible for entering cases and rules needed to store, retrieve, and adapt cases; in some systems, a *Case-based learner* is invoked for this task, to modify a case library without human intervention. A case-based learner may modify the case library in three ways:

1. New cases can be added.

2. Old abstractions (of cases) can be removed, and new abstractions can be generated, e.g., when several cases are discovered to share some common set of features. For example, after seeing several examples of accidents in parking lots, an abstraction for parking lot accidents may be created. Some abstractions formed in this manner may not be considered important by human experts, e.g., the case-based learner may create an abstraction for accidents that result in exactly two fatalities, but this abstraction may be useless for the task at hand. *Similarity-based generalization* defines new general categories, using learning strategies based on similarity metrics or explanations.

3. Indices (features used to structure the case library) can be generated or modified. Indices are generated by looking for features of collections of cases that distinguish them from other cases and abstractions. A good index would be distinctive and would identify a subset of cases that is not too small. Indices can be determined using an information-theoretic approach (as in the ID3 algorithm discussed in Chapter 8) or other feature-extraction algorithms (cf. Chapter 9). Certain attributes may be marked as being predictive in certain contexts, and strongly correlated with other features.

Repair rules start with a solution and a failure report and modify the solution to remove the failure. An explanation, if available, may help determine what repair is needed. When no explanation facility is available, the failure report may be used to augment the case and then retrieve the best match, with the new information included. Some systems invoke *explanation-based learning*, wherein domain-dependent heuristics are used to deduce causal structures and identify causal reasoning chains.

Failures can direct attention to possible weak spots in causal explanations. Beliefs change when failures are detected, using a feedback loop that involves failure diagnosis, learning, and strategies for memory repair. The last step involves reorganizing the case library so that the effect of the repair will be retrieved in future. This may be accomplished by storing a *failure link* from the case that failed to apply to the case that finally worked. If the failure reoccurs, the system can look for exceptions associated with the failure case, and attempt to explore the path taken in the previous failure case.

7.7 Examples

This section presents a few large-scale applications of CBR, to illustrate the usefulness of the methodology.

Example 7.10 Cheetham and Graf [6] have developed a case-based reasoning system that determines the combination of colorants needed to produce a specific color of plastic. This system is in use at several Generic Electric Company sites, with significant cost savings.

A color sample is provided by the customer, and its spectrum is obtained using a spectrophotometer. A case library is searched, using key information including the color spectrum and the resin and grade of plastic material to be used. In addition to matching the color, criteria to be satisfied by the retrieved case include the presence of a sufficient amount of pigment to hide the color of the plastic, optical density (amount of light permitted to pass through), color stability despite temperature changes needed in molding, and cost of production. Adaptation of retrieved cases is performed by iteratively modifying the retrieved solution and evaluating the result, until a satisfactory solution is obtained.

Example 7.11 Jarmulak and associates [10] have developed a case-based reasoning system for interpreting image data obtained from an ultrasonic rail-inspection system. Rails are inspected using a special coach carrying transducers that take measurements of each rail at 2mm. intervals. Ultrasonic images thus obtained must be analyzed to determine abnormalities identifying defects such as cracks. Clustering is performed on the raw data, generating a hierarchical representation of the image. An existing rule-base of knowledge is first invoked, and only the cases not satisfactorily classified in this manner are passed on to the case-based reasoning system.

The main reason to prefer a case-based reasoning approach for this problem is the difficulty of knowledge acquisition. Future enhancements to the system would also be easier using case-based learning. A case-based reasoning system was preferred to a neural network solution, since the scope of applicability of the case-based reasoning system can be delineated more easily. Statistical approaches require feature extraction and representation in a manner that is not feasible for this problem.

About 12000 cases are organized hierarchically, based on the channels present, the number of subclusters, and the length of a cluster. Matching retrieves the best case from among the leaves of the relevant subtree of the hierarchy. The evaluation phase compares the retrieved case to the input case. Unlike a generic case-based reasoning system, however, this system does not perform adaptation; changes to the classification scheme must be performed manually.

Example 7.12 Several case-based reasoning systems have been built for knowledge retrieval in the legal domain, where the problem domain itself is logically organized by cases [3]. For instance, *HYPO* is a case-based reasoning system that creates legal arguments for cases drawn from the domain of trade secret law [1]. A more recent and larger example is a CBR system that performs retrieval, searching for legal cases indexed by attributes called *descriptors* [19]. About 90,000 complete descriptions of legal cases are maintained in the case library. The CBR approach is combined with a natural language processing system that extracts descriptors from various parts of a legal case.

Example 7.13 Schmidt and Gierl [16] report the development of several case-based reasoning system for the medical domain, emphasizing the importance of continued physician involvement in development and use of such systems.

1. *GS.52* is a diagnostic support system for non-random combinations of different disorders, used in the children's hospital at the University of Munich since 1990. Cases are clustered into diagnosis 'prototypes' (cases) acquired by expert consultation, based on the relative frequency of occurrences of different features. For instance, a prototype may be associated with 30% frequency for heart murmur, 23% for depressed nasal bridge, and 75% for

prenatal onset, where these fractions indicate the frequency with which the associated conditions occur in patients whose description matches this prototype. The retrieval process ranks prototypes based on similarity with an input feature description. Adaptation relies on expert review, checking the results of retrieval against general constraints as well as specific diagnoses.

2. One component of the *ICONS* project, that reached subclinical status, generates rapid antibiotic therapy advice for intensive care patients who have developed infections as additional complications. The precise diagnosis is unknown, and a combination of antibiotics is first determined that cover all current symptoms while not being contraindicated for the patient at hand. A physician makes the final decision, examining potential side effects of the antibiotics, and the ICONS system computes the recommended dosage. Adaptation involves modifying therapies previously advised for a similar case, taking the current patient's contraindications into account. When the actual infection-causing agent is determined via laboratory tests, the therapy already initiated is re-evaluated and modified, as are the relevant cases in the library.

3. Another component of the ICONS project conducts time course prognoses (predictions) of kidney function, determining therapeutic interventions as needed. The renal reports generated by another program (with 13 measured attributes and 33 calculated features) are abstracted using a model of kidney function, based on increasing severity of kidney condition (from 'normal' to 'failure'), used to evaluate daily kidney status. Trends of different durations (short-term, medium-term and long-term) are generated based on sequences of daily status reports. Case-Based Reasoning is used to compare these trends for a patient with the trends in stored cases, and the prognosis is based upon the best matching retrieved case. Adaptation can only be performed by a physician.

7.8 Analogical Reasoning

This section describes *Analogical Reasoning*, an approach that closely resembles CBR. Analogical Reasoning assumes that if two entities agree in some respects, they are also likely to agree in other respects. Analogical Reasoning also compares new input situations with previously stored cases, as in CBR, but some important differences exist:

1. Case-Based Reasoning assumes that cases are drawn from the same domain and are closely related to the input scenarios for which solutions are required. By contrast, Analogical Reasoning allows comparisons across domains.

2. Case-Based Reasoning attempts to obtain actual detailed solutions, making minor adaptations from retrieved cases. Analogical Reasoning extracts only high level solution schema or plans from retrieved cases, and requires significant changes to such solutions before they can be used for the problem in a new domain.

Analogical Reasoning consists of the following four phases:

Access: An analogous situation (the 'source' or 'base'), for which a solution or sufficiently complete description exists, must be discovered. This may involve searching through a collection of indexed situation descriptions, as in retrieval in case-based reasoning.

Mapping: The objects in the new (*target*) situation must be mapped to those in the source situation, based on syntactic form or semantic relationships among objects in each situation. In *structure mapping* [8, 7], relationships among source objects determine the mapping, with more interconnected relations given greater importance.

Evaluation: There must be some way of determining whether the results (inferences about the target problem) are reasonable, e.g., by involving a human user, or by carrying out qualitative simulations.

Learning: The knowledge obtained by Analogical Reasoning may be expressed using an abstract representation that facilitates future reasoning steps. In some cases, when Analogical Reasoning fails, learning prevents the same kinds of analogical inferences from being drawn again.

Example 7.14 If a problem relating to atomic structure is to be solved, the access process may identify the structure of the solar system as a possible source. The nucleus of the atom is mapped to the sun, and electrons to planets. Structure mapping emphasizes interconnected relations: the sun *attracts* the planets, *causing* them to *revolve* around the sun; these are considered more important than isolated relations such as that the sun is older than the planets. The resulting inferences may be evaluated by reviewing existing evidence about the behavior of atoms, or by new experiments designed to support or falsify the inferences. If atoms could be modeled using the same physical laws as the solar system, then one may predict that the electrons would quickly radiate energy and spiral into the nucleus. The analogy hence needs to be repaired, e.g., asserting that electrons may exist in predetermined orbits without radiating energy. From the Analogical Reasoning process, one may learn the abstract concept that a central force can cause revolutions.

The use of multiple analogies may reduce some errors that arise from Analogical Reasoning, as suggested by Burstein [4]. Carbonell [5] advocates storing information about the process of application of Analogical Reasoning, including failed search paths, rejected alternatives, and dependencies among decisions; similar ideas have been used in case-based reasoning. Early reasoning steps (when solving the target problem) are compared to the steps in solving previous problems. Similarity in these steps guides the selection of the source; the subsequent reasoning steps of such a source are then adapted to the target problem. In some Analogical Reasoning systems [11], the nature and goals of the problems are considered important in determining the source; target goals are satisfied by adapting a domain-specific explanation of the problem-solving steps used by the source to achieve its goals.

7.9 Bibliographic Notes

Bain's dissertation [2] provides a good starting point for an application oriented study of case based reasoning systems. Two recent books on Case-Based Reasoning are those by Riesbeck and Schank [15] and Kolodner [12]. Another useful collection of survey articles is in the book by Leake [13]. A number of application papers are contained in recent conference proceedings such as [14]. A collection of important papers on analogical reasoning is contained in [17].

Bibliography

[1] K. Ashley and E.L. Rissland, "Compare and Contrast: A Test of Expertise," *Proc. AAAI National Conf. on Artificial Intelligence*, 1987.

[2] W.M. Bain, *Case-based Reasoning: A Computer Model of Subjective Assessment*, Ph.D. Dissertation, Computer Science Department, Yale University, New Haven (CT), April 1986.

[3] T.J.M. Bench-Capon, *Argument in Artificial Intelligence and Law*, JURIX 1995.

[4] M.H. Burstein, "Combining Analogies in Mental Models," in D.H. Helman (Ed.), *Analogical Reasoning*, Kluwer, 1988.

[5] J.G. Carbonell, "Derivational Analogy: A theory of reconstructive problem solving and expertise acquisition," in R. Michalski, J. Carbonell, and T. Mitchell (Eds.), *Machine Learning: An Artificial Intelligence Approach*, Morgan Kaufmann, San Mateo (CA), 1986.

[6] W. Cheetham and J. Graf, "Case-Based Reasoning in Color Matching," D.B. Leake and E. Plaza (Eds.), Case-Based Reasoning Research and Development, *Proc. ICCBR-97*, Springer, July 1997, pp.1-12.

[7] B. Falkenhainer, K.D. Forbus, and D. Gentner, "The structure-mapping engine," *Proc. AAAI*, Philadelphia (PA), 1986, pp.272-277.

[8] D. Gentner, "The mechanisms of analogical learning," in S. Vosniadou and A. Ortony (Eds.), *Similarity and Analogical Reasoning*, Cambridge University Press, London (U.K.), 1983.

[9] K. Hammond, "CHEF: A Model of Case-Based Planning," *Proc. Sixth AAAI Conf.*, Philadelphia (PA), 1986.

[10] J. Jarmulak, E.G.H. Kerckhoffs, and P.P. van't Veen, D.B. Leake and E. Plaza (Eds.), Case-Based Reasoning Research and Development, *Proc. ICCBR-97*, Springer, July 1997, pp.43-52.

[11] S. Kedar-Cabelli, "Toward a computational model of purpose-directed analogy," in A. Prieditis (Ed.), *Analogics*, Morgan Kaufmann, San Mateo (CA), 1985.

[12] J. Kolodner, *Case-Based Reasoning*, Morgan-Kaufmann, 1993.

[13] D.B. Leake (Editor), *Case-Based Reasoning: Experiences, Lessons, & Future Directions*, MIT Press, 1997.

[14] D.B. Leake and E. Plaza (Eds.), Case-Based Reasoning Research and Development, *Proc. ICCBR-97*, Springer, July 1997.

[15] R.C. Schank and C. Riesbeck, *Inside Case-Based Reasoning*, Lawrence Erlbaum Associates, Hillsdale, NJ, 1989.

[16] R. Schmidt and L. Gierl, "Experiences with Prototype Designs and Retrieval Methods in Medical Case-Based Reasoning System," B. Smyth and P. Cunningham (Eds.), *Advances in Case-Based Reasoning*, Proc. 4th European Workshop, Dublin (Ireland), Sept. 1998., pp. 370-381.

[17] J.W. Shavlik and T.G. Dietterich (Eds.), *Readings in Machine Learning*, Morgan Kaufmann, 1990.

[18] R.L. Simpson, *A Computer Model of Case-Based Reasoning in Problem Solving: An investigation in the domain of dispute mediation*, Ph.D. Dissertation, Tech.Rep. GIT-ICS-85/18, School of Information and Computer Science, Georgia Institute of Technology, Atlanta (GA), 1985.

[19] R. Weber-Lee, R.M. Barcia, M.C. da Costa, I.W.R. Filho, H.C. Hoeschl, T.C.D'Agostini Bueno, A. Martins, and R.C. Pacheco, "A Large Case-Based Reasoner for Legal Cases," D.B. Leake and E. Plaza (Eds.), Case-Based Reasoning Research and Development, *Proc. ICCBR-97*, Springer, July 1997, pp.190-199.

7.10 Exercises

1. Connectionist learning algorithms as well as CBR work with example data rather than acquired rules. Compare these approaches with respect to applicability and computational effort.

2. Give examples of problems for which case-based reasoning is inappropriate, and where a rule-based representation would be preferable.

3. For each of the following problems, discuss whether case-based reasoning is more appropriate than traditional rule-based system development, and suggest the frame structure to be used in representing cases. An extensive programming project would involve subsequent development of an actual case-based reasoning system for one of these problems.

   (a) Determining the amount of credit to be extended to a loan applicant

   (b) Determining the optimal allocation of a financial portfolio (stocks of varying price volatility, bonds issued by governments and companies, currencies of different countries, etc.)

   (c) Patent dispute litigation

   (d) Developing a marketing strategy for a new product

   (e) Selecting candidates to be hired from a large pool of applicants

   (f) Allocating employees to various tasks in a software development project

4. Show whether sim (cf. page 182) is a well-defined function, with $sim(X, Y)$ being computed to be the same irrespective of the sequence of nodes examined in the computation. Recompute $sim(b_1, a_2)$ for Example 7.3, using a modified Figure 7.2 in which b_1 is a leaf node, i.e., pruning edges and nodes below b_1.

Chapter 8

Knowledge Acquisition

It is better to ask some of the questions than to know all the answers.

—————————————————————James Thurber,1940

Knowledge Acquisition involves eliciting, analyzing and interpreting the knowledge that a human expert uses when solving problems. This aspect of expert system building is often the most serious bottleneck, being the least automated and involving significant amount of communication (in imprecise natural language) between experts and expert system builders. Approaches to knowledge acquisition are based on lessons and ideas drawn from the fields of requirements analysis, human psychology, learning theory, and cognitive science.

Knowledge acquisition is a daunting task: can all of an expert's knowledge, gained over many years of experience and study, be abstracted and transferred to someone who begins without knowing anything about the problem domain? Can the knowledge engineer be trained to be an expert in a short period of time? The immensity of this task leaves only one way out: the knowledge engineer must serve as a medium or intermediary to assist the formalization of knowledge, and must help delineate a subset of the expert's knowledge sufficient for the problem-solving task for which an expert system is to be built.

This chapter addresses this principal bottleneck in expert system development. The next section contains a general overview of knowledge acquisition procedures, including discussion of the difficulties often encountered in the process. Subsequent sections present specific knowledge acquisition approaches. Section 8.2 discusses knowledge elicitation procedures that involve human interaction, including the nominal-group technique, the Delphi method, Blackboarding, structured interviews, and case studies. Section 8.3 discusses the application of personal construct technology and repertory grids from cognitive psychology, along with the logic of confirmation, and its use for automatically generating expert system rules. Section 8.4 discusses inductive machine learning, focusing on learning classification trees using the 'ID3' algorithm.

8.1 Key Concerns

Newcomers often treat the topic of knowledge acquisition as a non-issue. What more is involved in knowledge acquisition than sitting down with the expert and asking for all the information relevant to a problem? Unfortunately, the paradigm of 'mining for diamonds from an expert's brain' is grossly inadequate. The expert system builder may not know what questions to ask, may not understand the expert's answers, and may be unable to set up a framework within which an expert system must be built for the task. Some experts are themselves problems rather than problem-solvers[7]: the wimp expert, the cynical expert, the 'high priest of the domain' expert, the paternalistic expert, the uncommunicative expert, the uncaring expert, and the pseudo-AI-literate expert.

In the jargon of software engineering, knowledge acquisition is essentially *requirements analysis*, combined with interface specification and some aspects of high level design. Requirements analysis primarily concerns understanding the problem domain, not proposing solutions nor designing software following a specific methodology [10]; this is the central issue of knowledge acquisition as well. Interpretation of elicited data results in construction of the system's knowledge base, which is itself a model or theory of the expert's domain knowledge.

8.1.1 Hurdles

The knowledge engineer faces many hurdles such as language problems, complexity, fallibility, resistance, and interpretation, detailed below.

8.1.1.1 Language problems

Knowledge Acquisition becomes more difficult as the language used by the expert becomes specialized and unfamiliar to the expert system builder. For instance, a person who knows the rules of many card games would find it relatively easy to learn the rules of a new card game, since several card games share terminology and basic approach. On the other hand, attempting to teach a card game to someone who has never played cards would be much more challenging.

At the other end of the process, the success of knowledge acquisition also depends on the choice of formal language used to represent the knowledge in the system. The choice of an appropriate language is guided by three criteria: expressiveness (in the ability to model the specific problem), computational efficiency (in reasoning), and ease of use.

8.1.1.2 Difficulty

Not all knowledge acquisition tasks are equally difficult. Greater complexity of the problem domain implies greater difficulty in the knowledge acquisition process. The difficulty of the knowledge acquisition task can sometimes be estimated in terms of the number (and sizes) of rules and special cases or exceptions to such rules. This is illustrated, for instance, by comparing the relative difficulty of teaching chess *vs.* teaching checkers to someone who has not played similar games before. Problem difficulty also depends on the choice of representation; sometimes, a feature extraction step is useful in transforming a difficult problem space to a much simpler one.

8.1.1.3 Fallibility

Experts cannot easily give detailed descriptions of their knowledge and how they use it. In many real-life domains, the experts themselves are not fully aware of the procedures they intuitively use to solve problems, much as an expert at a physical sport may not be able to express formally the precise physical movements needed to accomplish his task. Furthermore, the rules formally learned at school and enshrined in textbooks may not be used by humans in actual problem-solving tasks: in areas of active research, the development of knowledge tends to transcend very soon its most recent formalization. Thirdly, when an expert is asked to explain his actions, the procedure that is vocalized may only be an idealized retrospective reconstruction which is historically inaccurate: a long-winded explanation may be given by the expert instead of an honest answer such as: "I can't say why, I just had a strong hunch based on other similar cases encountered in the past." The very process of knowledge elicitation can alter the expert's view of what he does.

When an expert system is intended to work alongside an expert in an advisory or decision support capacity, its usefulness is maximized if it can compensate for weaknesses in human reasoning that can be easily overcome in an automated system. For instance, humans are often fixated on a specific aspect of the problem, studying it in depth, instead of reviewing a large body of evidence. When they have a significant amount of evidence in favor of a favorite hypothesis, human experts often ignore or dismiss negative evidence, possibly leading to a wrong decision. When the number of variables or parameters is large, human experts may find it difficult to identify the data most relevant to solving the problem at hand. Human reasoning tends to work well in domains where no more than a few rules or principles need to be combined or chained together to produce a conclusion; complex interactions among many rules are not handled easily. Human experts also do not find it easy to carry out reasoning that involves counterfactuals, e.g., hypothesizing "if X had been true, then Y would have been observed, but Y has not been observed, hence X is unlikely." It is advisable to automate such reasoning processes.

8.1.1.4   Resistance

Knowledge engineers may be confronted with overt or subtle resistance from the experts being interviewed. It is natural for an expert to worry about being displaced by the development of an expert system – notwithstanding assurances to the contrary. Sometimes, the source of the resistance is a belief that the expert system building task is doomed to fail, since the expertise acquired by the experts over many years cannot possibly be automated. In some other cases, experts view their time as valuable and hate to fritter it away by answering the rudimentary questions of an uninformed knowledge engineer. Resistance may also be traced to the difficulty of formalizing empirically gained knowledge whose nature is ill-understood by the practitioners themselves. Progress in the knowledge acquisition process depends crucially on understanding the reason for resistance or lack of progress.

8.1.1.5   Interpretation

Knowledge Acquisition does not merely consist of eliciting verbal data. The expert system builder must also *interpret* such data to *infer* what might be the expert's knowledge. This interpretation must be used to construct a model or language that describes the expert's knowledge and performance. Naturally, the main difficulty in knowledge acquisition is not in the process of asking questions and recording answers, but rather in the interpretation and inference tasks, as well as in deciding what questions to ask.

8.1.2 Procedure

Once it is decided that a given domain or task is suitable for expert system development, the knowledge engineer must address several important questions before jumping into the knowledge acquisition task:

- What type of knowledge acquisition is needed for the task at hand?

- What is the language that human experts use for the specific domain under consideration? In some cases, no such language may be available, and a suitable language may have to be evolved during the knowledge acquisition process.

- Is there a machine representation that adequately supports the language?

Buchanan and Shortliffe [4] analyze knowledge acquisition as consisting of five different phases: identification of problems and resources, discovery of relevant concepts, design of knowledge representation scheme, expression of knowledge using the chosen representation scheme, and evaluation of the system built in this manner. Of these phases, most discussions of knowledge acquisition emphasize aspects related to knowledge *elicitation*, i.e., the transfer of knowledge from the expert to the knowledge engineer.

A formal top-down approach to expert system building requires that the knowledge engineer must identify and isolate the problem-solving *task*, without being lost in the maze of knowledge associated with the problem domain. The knowledge engineer must then attempt to analyze and describe types of knowledge necessary to solve the problem. It is important not to be constrained by any particular implementation considerations; understanding the problem thoroughly is a prerequisite for representing the relevant knowledge and implementing the expert system. A complete knowledge-level description must be generated; this will enable developing each of the following aspects of the expert system:

1. A clear description of what it means to solve the problem;

2. An intermediate representation of the knowledge that can be used to guide the elicitation and interpretation, and decisions about an appropriate machine representation;

3. A rigorous specification of what the finished expert system should be able to do;

4. A framework for addressing problems of internal consistency, correspondence with outside world (validity), completeness (whether all cases are covered), and maintenance of expert knowledge bases; and

5. A basis for explaining why a system is successful or unsuccessful in a particular application, to guide usage in other applications.

Roles vs. Tasks

A well-designed expert system should clearly distinguish between *roles* or *modalities* (e.g., whether the system is to function as a completely automated expert, or as a consultant, or a tutor) and *problem-solving tasks* to be addressed by the system (cf. Section 1.2). Accordingly, one of the first steps in designing an expert system is to decide on the appropriate modality, and then to identify the set of problem-solving tasks.

Example 8.1 The role played by a medical expert system may be to assist instruction of medical students, to be distinguished from the task of diagnosis, for which instruction is needed. A system that addresses the same diagnostic task may instead be used in a different role, e.g., to assist a physician in diagnosing new patients. Similarly, a medical expert system intended for instructional usage may address a different task, such as determining the medication that must be administered to a patient with given symptoms or disease.

It is necessary to formulate a knowledge-level description of the selected problem-solving task; this will specify minimal requirements for expert systems, guide the types of knowledge to be acquired, and enable successful generalization to related problem areas. Knowledge Acquisition may play a role even in task identification; for instance, determination of the precise nature of the problem-solving tasks may involve recording and understanding consultation dialogues between experts and clients. In most domains, consultation includes the following three tasks:

1. Formulating the problem in domain terms, in collaboration with the user

2. Answering questions about the domain, such as:

   - Why did an event occur?
   - How can a specific goal be achieved?
   - Will a certain action achieve a specified goal?

3. Communicating advice in a focused, intelligible and convincing form

User's knowledge

An expert system developer needs to be aware of the capabilities, knowledge, and perspectives of users. To enable good design decisions, knowledge acquisition should hence include the following steps:

1. Identifying different classes of users likely to use the system, and their needs

2. Analyzing user requirements:

   - What are the common classes of problems and questions?
   - What advice does the user require? In what form?
   - What type of justification does the user require?

3. Analyzing what types of knowledge the user brings to bear on the problem-solving process:

   - Goals of users
   - Constraints on acceptable solutions (*e.g.*, time, availability, cost)
   - How users model the problem
   - What users expect of the expert system's capabilities

Brachman [1] distinguishes between several levels of representation of static knowledge in expert systems:

1. Identification of domain-dependent concepts

2. Establishing relations between concepts

3. Uncovering structural properties of expertise

4. Mapping structures to a formalism

5. Implementation using a programming language

Of these, the knowledge engineer is primarily concerned with the first three levels, including the identification of objects, classes, subclasses, knowledge sources, models, structures, and strategies. Examples of structures are hierarchies (subclass-superclass, part-whole, specific-general, etc.), sequences, clusters, and relational networks. Strategies provide plans for invoking knowledge sources, such as forward chaining or backward chaining. Models provide a basis for justification, and enable establishing relations between reasoning strategies and knowledge structures; these include causal models, process models (representing relations between events and operations), formal models, empirical models, and spatial models.

The *Knowledge Acquisition and Document Structuring (KADS)* methodology and system, proposed by Breuker and Wielinga [3], suggests cycling through several steps of analysis and elicitation processes:

1. *Orientation*: Acquisition of vocabulary, main features, and domain characteristics

2. *Problem identification*: Uncovering structures of domain concepts (e.g., frame hierarchies), functional analysis, and task analysis

3. *Problem analysis*: Analysis of the user and environment of the expert system (to be developed), and analysis of the expertise in action (how problems are solved in practice)

The last phase also provides constraints and data for design and implementation.

Some expert system shells have inbuilt knowledge acquisition facilities. For instance, the MYCIN project included a program called TEIRESIAS [5] to help develop and manage knowledge bases, mostly using syntactic analysis of rules. Musen [11] developed a knowledge acquisition system called OPAL, associated with the ONCOCIN expert system of Shortliffe *et al.* [16]. OPAL conducts direct interviews with experts, attempting to elicit knowledge without the knowledge engineer as intermediary. For this purpose, OPAL has a specific model of the cancer-diagnosis problem domain addressed by ONCOCIN. In other words, OPAL is not a general-purpose knowledge acquisition tool, but illustrates that a knowledge acquisition tool may be developed specifically tailored to an existing expert system's problem domain.

8.2   Interacting with Experts

In this section, we discuss knowledge acquisition procedures that involve direct interaction in face-to-face meetings between the knowledge engineer and the expert, including unstructured meetings, nominal-group technique, the Delphi method, blackboarding, structured interviews, case studies (observational and retrospective), and combinations of these techniques.

8.2.1   Unstructured Meetings

In unstructured interviews, an expert is invited to describe the knowledge do-main, the problems, and solution methods used by the expert to solve such problems. The main role of the interviewer is similar to that of a journalist or a discussion moderator, attempting to prevent rambling in irrelevant directions, asking questions to clarify the meanings of new terms and concepts mentioned by the expert, requesting elaborations on points mentioned so far, asking for the reasons for statements and claims made, and inviting opinions on specific issues.

New ideas and viewpoints often spark other new ideas, and better results may be obtained by having several people getting together to address a topic than by separately interviewing each member of the same group of people. *Brain-storming* sessions are helpful when many experts are to be involved in the knowledge acquisition process, and meetings can be held with multiple experts at the same time. The primary purpose of brain-storming is constructive, not analytical; participants are invited to make suggestions and contribute new ideas that are recorded for later analysis. Such sessions are not the appropriate forum for criticism or evaluation of each idea, which is an activity distinct from brain-storming. However, brain-storming sessions are often dominated by two or three individuals; hence it is more productive to have small groups (in which most participants are vocal) than large groups in which most members silently nod to a few highly vocal individuals.

8.2.2   Nominal-Group Technique

The *Nominal-Group Technique (NGT)* is similar to brainstorming, but is based on the idea that written communication is helpful prior to oral discussion. NGT is useful in problem domains involving uncertainty, where multiple experts are involved. NGT involves the following steps:

1. First, each expert lists (in writing) the positive and negative aspects of alternative solutions.

2. All these lists (from different experts) are merged by the knowledge en-gineer and the resulting mega-list is circulated among all experts, who prioritize various items on the list for discussion.

3. A discussion then ensues, focusing on the priorities and reasoning attached with each item on the list.

4. Alternative solutions are then compiled.

5. This is followed by a group discussion to determine the best alternative.

Since the process is time-consuming, voting may occur at various steps, with an upper bound on the amount of discussion permitted on any topic.

8.2.3 Delphi Method

The *Delphi method* involves polling experts repeatedly. Its main features are anonymous response, controlled feedback in a small set of rounds, and the ability to influence each expert's opinion based on what others say.

In the first round, each expert provides anonymous opinions about a problem or problem domain. The results are repeatedly collected, summarized and circulated to all experts, and new opinions and answers are sought from each expert. Eventually, a final summary is prepared, narrowing the solution space to a small size.

8.2.4 Blackboarding

Experts with multiple fields of expertise are allowed to communicate via a central "blackboard" whose contents initially describe the problem, parts of which are iteratively modified by experts to evolve a complete solution. A typical blackboard system consists of knowledge sources, the blackboard, and a control mechanism. This model is discussed in Chapter 10 in greater detail, as an alternative expert system paradigm rather than for use in the knowledge acquisition phase alone.

8.2.5 Structured Interviews

Unstructured interviews are most useful in the early phases of knowledge acquisition, helping to identify the important concepts and jargon specific to the domain. This can be followed by a *structured* interview, a "concept-driven" elicitation technique that maintains a focus on one issue at a time. This provides detailed knowledge and uncovers related topics and new concepts that can be explored later. The whole process is analogous to conducting depth-first search in the concept space.

The first step is to define a list of topics to be covered. One of the topics is chosen and questions on this topic are posed. Probing questions are used to delve into each new topic raised by the expert in response to preceding questions.

Surprises are less likely in structured interviews than in unstructured interviews, if the interviewer understands the important issues well enough to pose sensible questions to direct the interview. The main problem with interviewing is that introspection may be ineffective in obtaining a complete or reliable account of a person's problem-solving knowledge.

8.2.6 Case Studies

A *case* is an actual problem that has been solved in the past, and contains the solution and the problem-solving method used. Case-based reasoning is discussed in Chapter 7 as an expert system paradigm by itself; in this section, we discuss how knowledge may be extracted by asking an expert to review specific cases and make appropriate recommendations.

Typical (frequently occurring) cases as well as unusual cases need to be considered. Typical cases yield information applicable to a large number of other problem instances, wheras unusual cases involve detailed analysis, possibly invoking first principles. Deeper introspection may occur with unusual cases; different and more elaborate models and theories may then be invoked, whereas typical cases are solved using simpler rules and models. Selecting appropriate unusual cases is non-trivial: the best approach is to find another expert to generate such cases. Presentation of an unfamiliar case can result in uncovering new concepts and new information relevant even for typical cases.

The process of information collection is known as a *protocol*, which may be a set of written notes, tape recording or video, and may include the expert "thinking aloud."

Case studies can be "retrospective" or "observational," as described below.

8.2.6.1 Retrospective Case Study

This addresses the situation when an expert is asked to review a case and explain (in retrospect) how the problem was solved.

The expert is goal-driven, and first reviews major findings of the case, attempting to show how the basic problem information supports those findings. Most experts approach the problem with a well-established procedure for gathering information, identifying and classifying the relevant problems, subgoals, and solutions. The knowledge engineer has to record the major problem-solving tasks, information collected during each task, how information is used, and various decisions made by the expert while problem-solving. During or after this process, standard interviewing questions may be used to gain insight into issues raised during problem solving.

This approach involves memory recall which may be inaccurate since the expert may speculate on how the problem was solved, instead of remembering what was actually done. Since the approach involves a review, many details may be omitted. Experts may also offer information biased by assuming that the new case is similar to other cases they have seen before.

8.2.6.2   Observational Case Study

The expert is asked to solve the problem, thinking aloud while being observed by the knowledge engineer, answering questions such as:

- What are the goals?

- What issues are important?

- How are these issues addressed?

- What data is used?

In some cases, however, verbalization influences the problem-solving thought process. Further, some problems may not be amenable to verbalization.

8.2.7   Combining Different Techniques

The ideas discussed above are not exclusive of one another, and may be profitably combined as follows:

- Start with an unstructured interview to obtain a basic understanding.

- Conduct a structured interview.

- Conduct familiar case studies.

- Conduct unfamiliar case studies.

- Carefully interpret and analyze the collected information using appropriate graphical representations and reviewing these with the experts.

8.3   Personal Construct Technology

The problem in communication between expert and knowledge engineer often results from cognitive defenses. This section discusses *personal construct technology*, an approach developed to overcome such cognitive defenses, assisting knowledge acquisition by identifying important concepts specific to the problem domain

Personal Constructs are frameworks that an individual creates and attempts to fit over realities [8]. Constructs are internalized by an expert and used to make predictions, but may not have been stated explicitly. The knowledge engineer must make an expert's construct system explicit, to provide a suitable language of discourse and facilitate understanding the problem-solving approach used by the expert. This process results in a *Repertory Grid*, which represents personal constructs as mappings from individuals (data items) to numeric values.

The *Triad method* may be used to identify personal constructs. Data items are presented to the expert in groups of three, asking in what way two are alike and different from the third. This leads to the identification of "interesting" concepts, excluding any attribute that is unique to a single data item, as well as attributes that are common to all data items.

Example 8.2 A manager may be asked in what respects his subordinates A and B resemble each other but differ from another subordinate C. He answers that A and B are both highly intelligent, introspective, motivated, and creative when compared to C, but much more sloppy. This leads to identifying five of the personal constructs shown in Table 8.1. He may also assert that both A and B live in the same neighborhood, differing from C in this respect, but such an attribute may be far too specialized to merit further consideration as a personal construct (unless one discovers a hidden bias in favor of employees living in certain neighborhoods).

The expert is then asked to rate each individual or data element with respect to possible extreme values for each personal construct identified in this manner. It is commonly presumed that experts are incapable of reasoning with decimal fractions, hence ratings in a scale such as 1-5 are first obtained and then linearly transformed to the $[0, 1]$ interval. To avoid forcing incorrect evaluations, one must allow gaps in the grid, when an expert is unable to evaluate a data element along a construct.

The degree to which two experts agree may be determined by comparing pairs of grids formulated separately by them for the same data.

8.3.1 Grid Analysis

The purpose of grid analysis is not to evaluate a specific data item, but to extract the relationships between various personal constructs. For this purpose, each

Table 8.1: Staff appraisal repertory grid, adapted from [9], evaluating individuals A-J along 11 constructs, after linear transformation of grid elements to the interval [0,1]

Construct	Meaning of value 1	A	B	C	D	E	F	G	H	I	J
Intelligence	intelligent	1	1	$\frac{1}{4}$	0	$\frac{1}{2}$	$\frac{1}{2}$	0	$\frac{3}{4}$	$\frac{1}{2}$	0
Personality	introspective	1	1	0	$\frac{1}{4}$	$\frac{3}{4}$	$\frac{1}{2}$	1	$\frac{1}{2}$	$\frac{1}{4}$	$\frac{1}{4}$
Experience	beginner	1	$\frac{3}{4}$	$\frac{1}{2}$	0	$\frac{1}{4}$	$\frac{1}{4}$	$\frac{1}{4}$	1	$\frac{1}{4}$	$\frac{1}{2}$
Motivation	motivated	1	1	$\frac{1}{4}$	0	$\frac{3}{4}$	$\frac{3}{4}$	0	$\frac{1}{2}$	$\frac{1}{2}$	$\frac{3}{4}$
Reliability	dependable	$\frac{1}{2}$	$\frac{3}{4}$	$\frac{3}{4}$	0	1	1	0	1	$\frac{3}{4}$	$\frac{1}{2}$
Interactions	mellow	$\frac{1}{2}$	$\frac{1}{4}$	0	$\frac{3}{4}$	$\frac{3}{4}$	$\frac{1}{2}$	1	0	$\frac{1}{4}$	0
Creativity	creative	1	1	0	0	$\frac{3}{4}$	$\frac{1}{2}$	$\frac{1}{4}$	$\frac{1}{2}$	$\frac{1}{4}$	0
Helpfulness	helpful	$\frac{1}{4}$	$\frac{1}{2}$	$\frac{1}{4}$	$\frac{3}{4}$	$\frac{1}{2}$	0	1	$\frac{1}{4}$	0	0
Attitude	professional	1	$\frac{3}{4}$	$\frac{1}{2}$	$\frac{1}{2}$	$\frac{3}{4}$	1	0	$\frac{3}{4}$	$\frac{1}{4}$	$\frac{1}{4}$
Neatness	sloppy	$\frac{3}{4}$	$\frac{3}{4}$	0	$\frac{1}{4}$	$\frac{1}{4}$	0	1	0	$\frac{1}{2}$	1
Overall	superior	$\frac{3}{4}$	1	$\frac{1}{2}$	$\frac{1}{4}$	1	$\frac{3}{4}$	0	$\frac{3}{4}$	$\frac{1}{2}$	$\frac{1}{4}$

personal construct can be considered to be a point in a multidimensional space whose dimension is the number of elements involved. Distances between two personal constructs can be calculated in this space, assuming that the elicited constructs are roughly similar in complexity, and span the problem domain as fully as possible.

Example 8.3 Table 8.1 shows a repertory grid for personnel evaluation (adapted from [15]), obtained by questioning an expert to identify relevant personal constructs. Each of ten individuals (A-J) was rated along each construct, using a 1-5 range. The values obtained from the expert (1,...,5) are first mapped linearly into *membership levels* (1.0, 0.75, 0.5, 0.25, 0.0) (cf. fuzzy sets, discussed in Section 3.11). The membership levels are shown in Table 8.1, where each column of numeric entries represents the evaluation of a member of the staff using eleven criteria (personal constructs). The personal constructs lie in a 10-dimensional space, where each dimension corresponds to one of the evaluated personnel. The "Intelligence" construct is represented in this space by the point $(1, 1, \frac{1}{4}, 0, \frac{1}{2}, \frac{1}{2}, 0, \frac{3}{4}, \frac{1}{2}, 0)$, i.e., the first row of the table, and the "Personality" construct by the point $(1, 1, 0, \frac{1}{4}, \frac{3}{4}, \frac{1}{2}, 1, \frac{1}{2}, \frac{1}{4}, \frac{1}{4})$, i.e., the second row of the table. The Euclidean distance between these points is ≈ 1.17, which is fairly small compared to the maximum possible distance between two points $= \sqrt{10} \approx 3.16$ (since the dimensionality of the space is 10). In other words, analysis of the repertory grid based on Euclidean distance reveals that the Intelligence and Personality constructs are closely correlated, with the most intelligent individuals being most introspective.

In the space of personal constructs, we can determine the most informative linear combinations of constructs by performing *Principal Components Analysis (PCA)*. Let T be an n-dimensional data set, linearly normalized to have mean vector $(0, 0, \ldots, 0)$, and with variance-covariance matrix $S(T)$. The (linear) PCA procedure computes the eigen-vector $\mathbf{b}$ of $S(T)$ that corresponds to the largest magnitude eigen-value of $S(T)$. Then, among all possible n-dimensional unit vectors, $\mathbf{b}$ maximizes the variance of $\mathbf{b.x}$, where $\mathbf{x} \in T$. In other words, among all possible axes to which we could project elements $\mathbf{x} \in T$, the projection to $\mathbf{b}$ maximizes the separation of projected elements. This is expected to preserve as much information as possible, since this projection (compared to others) allows us to maximally distinguish among elements in T.

Alternatively, we may perform *cluster analysis,* placing in each cluster all those constructs that are at small distances from each other. Further analysis may be carried out in a smaller dimensional space, representing each cluster by a single construct from the cluster.

Distance-based approaches capture only symmetric relations, but not inferential relations (such as implications and rules) needed in expert systems. The rest of this section addresses the extraction of rules from repertory grids, using an approach based on fuzzy sets [15]. In this approach, each extreme value of a construct is considered a predicate that defines a fuzzy set (cf. Section 3.11). A candidate rule is evaluated by examining whether the fuzzy implication (between constructs in the *lhs* and *rhs* of the rule) holds to a reasonable degree for the available data elements.

Example 8.4 The repertory grid in Table 8.1 can be analyzed as follows, to extract rules from the values for various personal constructs.

- A threshold membership level is chosen to represent a natural language characterization of values for a personal construct. For example, the individuals A,B,E,F, and H have membership levels ≥ 0.50 for the first construct (intelligence), and this threshold value may be considered to characterize the set of individuals with "at least average intelligence."

- This forms the basis for answering queries such as "which individuals satisfy a specified membership level for a construct."

- The simplest rules involve associations between two personal constructs, e.g, *Overall* superiority and *Intelligence*. Each such rule has an antecedent (and a consequent) of the form $Construct \geq \alpha$ or $Construct \leq \alpha$, where *alpha* is a threshold value $\in [0, 1]$, e.g.,

$$Overall(x) \geq \alpha_1 \quad \Rightarrow \quad Intelligence(x) \geq \alpha_2.$$

- The subset of rules of possible interest in the application is identified. In the personnel appraisal task, it may be most important to find out which other personal constructs provide necessary or sufficient conditions for overall superiority, hence rules in which this construct appears in the antecedent or consequent would be of most interest.

- Rules of possible interest are tested using all available data, over individuals A-J in the current example. For instance, the rule "at least average intelligence is required to consider an individual to be of above average superiority" is written as

$$Overall(x) \geq 0.75 \quad \Rightarrow \quad Intelligence(x) \geq 0.5.$$

The antecedent of this rule is true for five individuals (A, B, E, F, and H), for whom the consequent is also true. This is hence a rule that expresses significant knowledge acquired from the repertory grid.

- The converse of this rule,

$$Intelligence(x) \geq 0.5 \quad \Rightarrow \quad Overall(x) \geq 0.75,$$

is violated by an individual (I), since $Intelligence(\text{I}) \geq 0.5$ but $Overall(\text{I}) < 0.75$.

Relationships and hypotheses connecting various personal constructs can be built in this manner, and generalized to the greatest extent possible. For instance, a rule such as

$$Reliability(x) \geq 1.0 \quad \Rightarrow \quad Overall(x) \geq 0.5$$

can be generalized to

$$Reliability(x) \geq 1.0 \quad \Rightarrow \quad Overall(x) \geq 0.75,$$

whose interpretation is "extremely reliable individuals are of above average superiority," but the even more general rule

$$Reliability(x) \geq 1.0 \quad \Rightarrow \quad Overall(x) \geq 1.0$$

is violated by the data.

When such implications have been constructed, we can apply them for prediction tasks, hypothesizing how a new data element might be placed along one construct, given its placement on other constructs. The criteria for determining which rules are useful are discussed in Chapter 9 in greater detail, in the context of knowledge discovery for Data Mining applications.

8.3.2 Logic of Confirmation

When assembling combinations of personal constructs to manufacture production rules for an expert system, a central issue is that of *relevance*: a classical logic statement of the form "*A* implies *B*" does not address whether *A* is actually relevant to *B*. When an example is presented, we are often interested in the question of whether that example confirms or contradicts a hypothesis or rule. A logic of confirmation consists of the explicit formulation of rules for deciding to what extent a hypothesis is supported by some particular evidence.

Example 8.5 Hempel's raven paradox was constructed to show that classical logic cannot be viewed as a reasonable logic of confirmation. The hypothesis that '*All non-black items are non-ravens*' is supported by finding a white handkerchief among available data items. But in classical logic, this hypothesis $(\forall x.\neg Black(x) \rightarrow \neg Raven(x))$ is logically equivalent to '*All ravens are black*' $(\forall x.Raven(x) \rightarrow Black(x))$. Using this equivalence, finding a white handkerchief appears to confirm the hypothesis that all ravens are black!

In a more appropriate logic of confirmation, logically equivalent hypotheses may not be confirmed by the same evidence. The rest of this section sketches such a logic based on Bundy's *incidence calculus*, defined below.

Let $W = \{x_1, x_2, \cdots, x_n\}$ be the world of discourse, i.e., the collection of data elements. Let $\Phi, \Psi, \Omega, \cdots$ be subsets of $\{x_1, \cdots, x_n\}$, or unary predicates. Each such set Ψ can be written as an n-dimensional binary string $\mathcal{I}(\Psi)$, such that the ith element of $\mathcal{I}(\Psi)$ is 1 or 0 depending on whether $x_i \in \Psi$. $\mathcal{I}(\Psi)$ is called the *incidence* of Ψ. For instance, if $n = 11$ and Ψ contains only x_1, x_3, and x_4, then $\mathcal{I}(\Psi) = 10110000000$. Bundy's incidence calculus associates set-theoretic functions with logical connectives from propositional logic, as follows.

$$\mathcal{I}(true) = W; \qquad\qquad \mathcal{I}(false) = \{\}$$
$$\mathcal{I}(\neg\Psi) = W - \mathcal{I}(\Psi) \qquad \mathcal{I}(\Psi\&\Pi) = \mathcal{I}(\Psi) \cap \mathcal{I}(\Pi)$$
$$\mathcal{I}(\Psi \vee \Pi) = \mathcal{I}(\Psi) \cup \mathcal{I}(\Pi)$$

The function occ counts the number of non-zero elements occurring in its argument incidence string. For example, $occ(10011000) = 3$. An epistemic probability measure is derived: $P(\Psi) = \text{occ}(\mathcal{I}(\Psi))/\text{occ}(\mathcal{I}(W))$, where the denominator is the length of the incidence string, i.e., the number of objects in the world.

The problem is to associate a degree of confirmation with the non-material conditional 'if x is in Ψ then x is in Π'. This is treated as $P(\Pi|\Psi)$, which is considered equivalent to $P(\Pi \cap \Psi)/P(\Psi) = \text{occ}(\mathcal{I}(\Psi) \cap \mathcal{I}(\Pi))/\text{occ}(\mathcal{I}(\Psi))$, by analogy to Bayes rule (cf. Chapter 3).

Example 8.6 If $\mathcal{I}(\Psi) = 00100001010$ and $\mathcal{I}(\Pi) = 11100001000$, then

$$P(\Pi|\Psi) = \text{occ}(00100001010 \cap 11100001000)/\text{occ}(00100001010)$$

$$= \text{occ}(00100001000)/3 = 2/3.$$

Hence the degree of confirmation associated with the statement "all Ψ's are Π's" is 0.67. Note that this is different from $P(\neg\Psi|\neg\Pi) = 6/7 = 0.86$, a degree of confirmation associated with the statement "all not-Π's are not-Ψ's".

Unlike standard probability, only relevant evidence is used in computing the degree of confirmation. For instance, if two propositions are not related by any relevant evidence, the degree of confirmation $P(B|A) = $ (number of individuals that satisfy propositions A and B)/(number that satisfy A) = 0.

8.3.3   Rule Generation Procedure

This section applies the logic of confirmation discussed above to extract rules from a repertory grid.

For each possible rating for each attribute (of a repertory grid), incidence strings are obtained by examining which individuals have that rating. If no data is missing, then for each attribute (row in the repertory grid), the union of incidence strings over all ratings is a string of 1s, since each individual has one of the ratings for each attribute. Simple rules can be generated as pairs of attribute-rating pairs, and their degrees of confirmation can be estimated using this procedure.

Example 8.7 If Ψ corresponds to 'hates broccoli' to an extreme degree (say 5 on a scale of 1-5), and Π corresponds to 'is rich' to an extreme degree, with $\mathcal{I}(\Psi) = 00100001010$ and $\mathcal{I}(\Pi) = 11100001000$ as in Example 8.6, then the hypothesis "all those who hate broccoli extremely are extremely rich" is confirmed to the degree 0.67, whereas "all those who are not extremely rich do not hate broccoli extremely" is confirmed to the degree 0.86.

Some incidence strings can be combined; for instance, we may generate a new incidence string with the intended meaning 'hates broccoli considerably' by taking the union of the 4-rating and 5-rating incidence strings for 'hates broccoli'. Such combination strings may also be used to generate rules, for which the degree of confirmation is obtained in a same manner.

NICOD is a semi-automated medical knowledge acquisition system developed by Adams-Webber using these methods (repertory grid and logic of confirmation), and has been successfully applied to radiological diagnosis, generating useful hypotheses which were not articulated by experts, but with which they agreed [6].

8.4 Induction of Knowledge

Machine learning algorithms based on the inductive learning paradigm can be used to translate case-specific information into a more general form that can be used to address other cases. This section discusses the *ID3 algorithm*, which uses an information-theoretic measure to construct classification trees from example data, thereby avoiding some of the effort involved in knowledge acquisition.

Whereas "deduction" refers to the application of (general) knowledge to specific cases, "induction" involves constructing general rules from specific cases. The task of a knowledge engineer may be viewed as that of constructing an appropriate model of an expert's problem-solving machinery, based on viewing the results when an expert solves various specific problems (cases). Hence, the results of prior research in inductive (human and machine) learning can be brought to bear on the knowledge acquisition problem. Even if inductive learning does not answer all questions, it may highlight the interesting ones.

In this section, we focus on a specific inductive learning algorithm that may be used to construct a decision-making model, or to develop a set of rules pertinent to categorizing various data items.

The *ID3* ('Iterative Dichotomizer 3') Algorithm of Quinlan (1973) induces a classification tree from a training set of examples consisting of classes and attributes. A classification tree[1] is a tree in which each interior node is a *decision node*, examining an attribute value to decide on routing a data element to one of the subtrees below this node. When a data element is routed to a leaf node, it is considered to belong to the class associated with the leaf node during the

---

[1] The phrase *decision tree* is frequently used in this context than *classification tree*, but the latter terminology is preferred in this book to maintain a distinction from the notion of 'decision tree' as defined in Chapter 3.

ID3_Learning (S): /* where S is the set of training data */
IF most elements in S belong to the same class,
THEN associate the current node with this class
ELSE {

      Find suitable attribute for splitting S into S^+ and S^-, and create a
      new node N in the classification tree;
      Create the right-subtree below N, calling ID3_Learning(S^+);
      Create the left-subtree below N, calling ID3_Learning(S^-).

}

Figure 8.1: The ID3 learning algorithm

ID3_Use (x, T): /* where x is to be classified using classification tree T */
IF T consists of a node with no children,
THEN allocate x to the class associated with this node;
ELSE if the condition associated with the root of T evaluates to *true* for x,
then ID3_Use(x, right subtree of T)
else ID3_Use(x, left subtree of T).

Figure 8.2: Using ID3 to determine the class of a new data element

learning process. An example of such a classification tree is depicted in Figure
8.3 (page 225)..

    Classes are determined by the expert, and the attributes are those he thinks
are relevant to the decision. Attributes may be categorical (*e.g.*, color) or numerical. The tree may be used to explain the underlying pattern and effects of
the attributes, as well as to predict outcomes for new examples. An induction
algorithm requires criteria for splitting the set into successive subsets, criteria
for stopping, and a method of allocating the class at a terminal node.

    As described in Figure 8.1, the ID3 algorithm continues splitting until a
node is 'pure', i.e., a subset contains elements of a single class. Any element
that corresponds to a terminal node is associated with the class corresponding to
members of the subset corresponding to that (pure) node. The next subsection
describes the splitting criterion used by ID3.

8.4.1 Splitting

At each splitting step, the algorithm selects an unused attribute that subdivides the current set of data in the 'best' way.

To determine the 'best' split, a statistic based on Shannon's information function is maximized, where *Information* is quantified as the number of bits needed to represent an object or abstraction. *Information gain* refers to the decrease in the number of bits needed for representation, when our knowledge relevant to a scenario improves. Since various alternative states may not be equally likely, information gain is expressed in terms of a measure called "entropy" that takes into account the probabilities of different states. *Entropy* is a measure of disorder or lack of knowledge, formally defined as $-\sum_x p(x) \log_2 p(x)$ when the variable x ranges over a discrete number of states, and as $-\int_x p(x) \log_2 p(x) dx$ when x ranges over continuous space with a probability distribution $p(x)$.

Example 8.8 If our initial knowledge indicates that a cat is equally likely to be in any of sixteen rooms, the probability that a cat is in a specified room is $1/16$, and we need $\log_2 16 = 4$ bits to specify exactly which room the cat is located in. If our knowledge improves later so that the cat is now constrained to be in eight of those rooms, only $\log_2 8 = 3$ bits are now needed to identify the specific room containing the cat. Hence, the information gain is $4 - 3 = 1$ bit.

If our initial knowledge indicated that the cat could be in any of sixteen rooms, but is more likely to be in the eight rooms upstairs than in the eight rooms downstairs, with probability $1/12$ for each room upstairs and probability $1/24$ for each room downstairs, and if our final knowledge ruled out downstairs rooms completely (so that the new probabilities are $1/8$ for each upstairs room and 0 for each downstairs room), then the information gain is better described by the change in entropy. The old entropy is

$$-8 \left(\frac{1}{12} \log_2(\frac{1}{12}) \right) - 8 \left(\frac{1}{24} \log_2(\frac{1}{24}) \right) \approx 3.92.$$

We may express the probability for the downstairs rooms as $0 = \lim_{x \to \infty} 1/x$ so that $0 \log_2 0 = \lim_{x \to \infty} \frac{1}{x} \log_2(\frac{1}{x}) = 0$. Hence the new entropy is

$$-8 \left(\frac{1}{8} \log_2(\frac{1}{8}) \right) - 8(0 \log_2 0) = 3 + 0 = 3.$$

The information gain is hence $\approx 3.92 - 3 = 0.92$ bits, which is smaller than the corresponding information gain of 1 bit obtained earlier. In other words, the first initial state (in which all rooms were equally likely) contained less information than the second initial state (in which upstairs rooms were likelier), and the final states were the same in both cases, hence the information gain was more in the first case than the second.

If p_j is the proportion of samples in class j, the information value of that set is given by $I_0 = -\Sigma p_j \log_2(p_j)$, maximized when all classes are equally likely. If the given set is subdivided into n subsets using some attribute, and the information value of the kth subset is i_k, then the new (proportionally averaged) information value is $I_1 = \Sigma p_k i_k$. ID3 selects the attribute which maximizes $(I_0 - I_1)$, i.e., minimizes I_1 for a given I_0, measuring how well the attribute has discriminated between the different samples.

Example 8.9 Consider three-attribute (3-dimensional) data, with data items (1,1,1), (1,0,1), (1,0,0) belonging to class C_1 and (0,1,1), (0,0,1) belonging to class C_0. In this simple case, the value for each attribute is binary and hence can be directly interpreted as an answer to a yes-no question. The probability is 3/5 that an element in the data set belongs to C_1, and 2/5 that it belongs to C_0. Hence the initial information value (before applying the ID3 algorithm) is

$$I_0 = -(3/5)(\log_2(3/5)) - (2/5)(\log_2(2/5)) = 0.96$$

If we choose the first attribute as the "root" of the classification tree, dividing samples into the 'pure' sets $S_1 = \{(1,1,1), (1,0,1), (1,0,0)\}$ and $S_0 = \{(0,1,1), (0,0,1)\}$, the information associated with S_1 is

$$I(S_1) = -(3/3)(\log_2(3/3)) - (0/3)(\log_2(0/3)) = 0.$$

Similarly,

$$I(S_0) = -(0/2)(\log_2(0/2)) - (2/2)(\log_2(2/2)) = 0.$$

Indeed, the information associated with any pure set is 0. Weighting these measures by the relative proportions of samples that are in S_1 and S_0 respectively, the total information is now

$$I_1 = (3/5)I(S_1) + (2/5)I(S_0) = 0 + 0 = 0,$$

so that the information gain is

$$G_1 = I_0 - I_1 = 0.96 - 0 = 0.96.$$

If we instead choose the second attribute as the root of the classification tree, dividing samples into the sets $S_1' = \{(1,1,1), (0,1,1)\}$ and $S_0' = \{(1,0,1), (1,0,0), (0,0,1)\}$, we obtain

$$I(S_1') = -(1/2)(\log_2(1/2)) - (1/2)(\log_2(1/2)) = 1.$$

Indeed, information value of 1 is associated with any set in which exactly half the samples belong to each of two classes. Similarly, we may calculate

$$I(S_0') = -(2/3)(\log_2(2/3)) - (1/3)(\log_2(1/3)) = 0.91$$

so that the information gain is

$$G_2 = I_0 - \frac{2}{5}I(S_1') - \frac{3}{5}I(S_0') = 0.96 - 0.4 - (0.6)(0.91) = 0.01.$$

Finally, we consider the choice of the third attribute as the root of the classification tree, dividing samples into the sets $S_1'' = \{(1,1,1), (1,0,1), (0,1,1), (0,0,1)\}$ and $S_0'' = \{(1,0,0)\}$, of which only the latter is pure (with $I(S_0'') = 0$), obtaining the information gain

$$G_3 = I_0 - \frac{4}{5}I(S_1'') - \frac{1}{5}I(S_0'') = 0.96 - (0.8)(1) - 0 = 0.16.$$

Although $G_3 > G_2$, indicating that the third attribute is preferable to the second attribute (as a choice for the root of the classification tree), we find that $G_3 < G_1$, supporting the obvious choice of the first attribute. Since we find that sets S_1, S_0 (associated with the children of such a root node) are pure, no further work is necessary, and the classification tree is complete.

Note that since the initial information I_0 is the same for all cases, it is sufficient to examine the new net entropy (when a decision node is selected) instead of computing the difference with I_0.

Example 8.10 We now consider a more complex problem, illustrating the development of a larger classification tree in the medical domain. A nurse must determine, on the basis of initial observations, whether a patient needs immediate attention from a physician. For conciseness, each data sample will be represented as a binary string containing six bits, omitting commas and spaces. Some data elements belonging to class C_1 (requiring immediate physician attention) are $\{100010, 010010, 001001, 100100, 011010, 000011\}$ and data elements belonging to class C_2 (not requiring immediate physician attention) are $\{000010, 100001, 010001, 110000, 110001\}$.

To begin with, we must decide which of the six attributes to select as the root of the classification tree. If the first attribute x_1 is chosen, the two subsets of samples obtained contain five and six samples respectively; of these the first subset contains two elements of C_1, and the second subset contains four elements of C_2. The resulting information gain is $G_1 =$

$$I_0 - \frac{5}{11}\left(-(\frac{2}{5})\log_2(\frac{2}{5}) - (\frac{3}{5})\log_2(\frac{3}{5})\right) - \frac{6}{11}\left(-(\frac{4}{6})\log_2(\frac{4}{6}) - (\frac{2}{6})\log_2(\frac{2}{6})\right)$$

$$\approx I_0 - 0.93,$$

where I_0 is the initial information. Similarly, the respective information gains obtained by examining the possibilities of using each of the other variables $(x_2, \ldots, x_6)$ are:

$$G_2 = I_0 - \frac{5}{11}(0.96) - \frac{6}{11}(0.91) = I_0 - 0.93,$$

$$G_3 = I_0 - \frac{2}{11}(0) - \frac{9}{11}(0.99) = I_0 - 0.81,$$

$$G_4 = I_0 - \frac{1}{11}(0) - \frac{10}{11}(1) = I_0 - 0.98,$$

$$G_5 = I_0 - \frac{5}{11}(0.72) - \frac{6}{11}(0.91) = I_0 - 0.82,$$

and

$$G_6 = I_0 - \frac{5}{11}(0.96) - \frac{6}{11}(0.91) = I_0 - 0.93.$$

Comparing these values, we find that G_3 is highest, hence the variable x_3 is chosen as the root node for the classification tree. The ID3 algorithm is then invoked separately on the resulting subsets, viz., $S_1 = \{001001, 0111010\}$ and its complement S_0 containing all the other samples. Since S_1 is pure, containing only samples of the first class, no further elaboration of this subtree is necessary. For the remaining set of nine samples, with information value I_3, we again evaluate the information gain obtained if we use x_1, x_2, x_4, x_5, or x_6 as the decision variable:

$$G_1 = I_3 - \frac{5}{9}(0.96) - \frac{4}{9}(1) = I_3 - 0.98,$$

$$G_2 = I_3 - \frac{4}{9}(0.81) - \frac{5}{9}(0.96) = I_3 - 0.89,$$

$$G_4 = I_3 - \frac{1}{9}(0) - \frac{8}{9}(0.95) = I_3 - 0.85,$$

$$G_5 = I_3 - \frac{4}{9}(0.81) - \frac{5}{9}(0.72) = I_3 - 0.76,$$

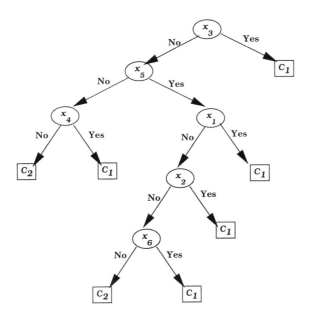

Figure 8.3: Classification tree derived using the ID3 algorithm for Example 8.10

and

$$G_6 = I_3 - \frac{4}{9}(0.81) - \frac{5}{9}(0.96) = I_3 - 0.89.$$

Clearly, the fifth variable is the best, dividing S_0 into the subsets

$$S_{0,1} = \{100010, \ 010010, \ 000011, \ 000010\}$$

in which only the last element belongs to class C_2, and

$$S_{0,0} = \{100100, \ 100001, \ 010001, \ 110000, \ 110001\}$$

in which only the first element belongs to class C_1. Each of these subsets requires elaboration of the tree to one more level, once again by comparing the information gain obtained by selecting variables x_1, x_2, x_4, and x_6. We would then find that $S_{0,0}$ is separated into pure subsets by x_4, but $S_{0,1}$ requires three more levels of elaboration of the tree in order to obtain pure subsets using this method, e.g., using x_1 followed by x_2 followed by x_6.

The classification tree of Figure 8.3 results, with x_3 as root, one leaf child, the other subtree has x_5 as root, etc.

Viewed as a set of production rules, this classification tree may be interpreted as follows:

$$x_3 \ \Rightarrow \ C_1$$

$$\neg x_3 \& x_5 \& x_1 \ \Rightarrow \ C_1$$

$$\neg x_3 \& x_5 \& \neg x_1 \& x_2 \ \Rightarrow \ C_1$$

$$\neg x_3 \& x_5 \& \neg x_1 \& \neg x_2 \& x_6 \ \Rightarrow \ C_1$$

$$\neg x_3 \& x_5 \& \neg x_1 \& \neg x_2 \& \neg x_6 \ \Rightarrow \ C_2$$

$$\neg x_3 \& \neg x_5 \& x_4 \ \Rightarrow \ C_1$$

$$\neg x_3 \& \neg x_5 \& \neg x_4 \ \Rightarrow \ C_2$$

Obvious meanings may be attached to these rules, considering that the data elements were constructed with the following interpretations for the variables:

x_1 :   high temperature

x_2 :   high blood pressure

x_3 :   bleeding

x_4 :   unconscious

x_5 :   politically important

x_6 :   loudly demanding immediate attention

When attributes take real values, a potential cutoff point has to be chosen, perhaps as a midpoint (median) between the various values, minimizing the value of I_1.

Example 8.11 In the previous example, instead of a binary variable x_1 whose intended meaning is "patient has high temperature," we may instead have a continuous-valued variable θ (=temperature) available for each patient, with values such as (103, 98, 99, 102, 99, 100) for the six patients of C_1, and values (98, 101, 99, 102, 103) for the five patients of C_2, respectively. There are now many different possible alternatives for the decision variable, such $\theta \geq 98$, $\theta \geq 99.5$, etc., with each possibility corresponding to the interval between two temperature values in the given data. We may begin from the median value (=100 for the current data), evaluating the information gain corresponding to the decision variable $\theta \geq 100$, and comparing this with the information gain corresponding to other choices for the decision variable that are different, e.g., $\theta \geq 99$ and $\theta \geq 101$. If we find that the latter is better, we would then compare it with the information gain for other similar decision variables that involve the temperature, until an optimal value is found.

8.4.2   Multi-class problems

The ID3 algorithm can also be applied to problems with three or more classes. In the previous example, the nurse may instead have to choose from three possible decisions:

(a) perhaps a physician is to be seen immediately (class C_1),

(b) perhaps the patient is asked to wait until the physician is free (class C_2), or

(c) the patient is discharged as being healthy enough with the prescription of a broad-spectrum antibiotic, assuming that physician's attention is unnecessary for this patient (class C_3).

The information gain calculations and procedures to determine the best possible variable are similar to those performed earlier, except that three classes are taken into account. If S is the complete data set, and the answer to the decision variable is "yes" for $S_1 \subseteq S$, the information measure computed is

$$-(\sum_{i=1}^{3} p_i \log_2 p_i) \left(\frac{|S_1|}{|S|} \right) \quad - \quad (\sum_{i=1}^{3} q_i \log_2 q_i) \left(1 - \frac{|S_1|}{|S|} \right)$$

where p_1, p_2, p_3 are the relative proportions of elements in S_1 belonging to classes C_1, C_2, C_3, and q_1, q_2, q_3 are the relative proportions of elements in $S \setminus S_1$ belonging to classes C_1, C_2, C_3.

Instead of entropy, another widely used splitting criterion is the *Gini Index*, defined as

$$Gini(S) = 1 - \sum_i p_i^2$$

where S is current data set, and p_i is the proportion of data elements in S that belong to class i.

8.4.3   Termination condition

In some cases, too large a classification tree results if we continue the splitting process until subsets associated with all leaf nodes are pure. If we started with a thousand data items, for instance, it may not be worthwhile continuing the splitting process when the subset size associated with a node has shrunk to under ten data items. In other words, the relative size of the data set associated with a node may be used as an additional criterion to determine whether to terminate the splitting process. We may also require that the information gain obtained by adding a node should exceed some absolute or relative threshold value — however, any such proposal leaves to the developer the task of determining the appropriate threshold; too small a threshold makes it irrelevant, while too large a threshold may rule out the choice of relevant attributes as well. The *Gain Ratio* criterion can be used to evaluate the relative information content associated with an attribute, where

$$\text{Gain Ratio for attribute } A = \frac{\text{Information Gain using } A}{\sum_i \left(\left(\frac{p_i + n_i}{p + n} \right) \log \left(\frac{p_i + n_i}{p + n} \right) \right)},$$

where p_i and n_i indicate the number of samples in each class for the ith child of the decision node corresponding to A, $p = \sum_i p_i$, and $n = \sum_i n_i$.

These methods may be viewed as instances of the "regularization" approach of Tikhonov [17]: the cost associated with the increased complexity of the model (classification tree) is being balanced against the improvement in performance obtained by elaborating the classification tree by one further level. This approach has the added advantage that it is more tolerant to noisy input data: the tree's size will not grow inordinately when a few errors exist in classifying some data items, or if some rare cases exist that do not warrant a separate rule for each such exceptional case. Indeed, training data may even be artificially corrupted beforehand, to improve the likelihood that an expert system will perform reasonably well when tested on corrupted data. Each impure leaf node in a classification tree is categorized with the class corresponding to the majority of the data elements in the set associated with that node.

Another possible approach is to use the statistical approach of confidence intervals, to determine the confidence with which one can reject the hypothesis that an attribute is irrelevant to the classification problem at hand. Alternatively, the fractions of training data elements belonging to each class (of data associated with an impure node) may be interpreted as probabilities to be attached to the production rules extracted from the classification tree.

8.4.4   Multivalued attributes

Some classification trees allow each decision node to have more than two children, e.g., if a node in the classification tree corresponds to checking the "color" attribute, each of its children may correspond to one possible color (red, blue, green, etc.). However, the information gain analysis has an inherent bias in favoring attributes with more values per attribute; a node that has more children is likely to accomplish better classification than a node with fewer children. To eliminate such bias, we may "binarize" trees, transforming each multi-valued attribute into a sequence of two-valued attributes. Such binarization can lead to the growth of tall trees that inhibit comprehension; also, computation costs increase since multiple tests are performed on the same attribute.

Another reasonable approach is to establish a relationship between the relative complexity of different tests (when attributes are multivalued): an attribute with n possible values can be considered equivalent in complexity to $\log_2 n$ different tests with binary attributes. Instead of binarizing the tree, we may use this factor in the relative information gain comparisons.

8.4.5 Computational Cost

The computational expense associated with the ID3 algorithm does not increase exponentially with problem size. At every interior (non-leaf) decision node in the tree, every data item must be examined to determine its class and its value for each attribute, with the associated computational expense proportional to the product of the number of classes and the number of attributes.

8.4.6 Guidelines for Inductive Learning

For inductive learning to be successful, we need efficient learning algorithms as well as informative examples. The need for the former is obvious: a perfect learning system is of absolutely no use if the learning process is extremely slow. The need for informative examples may be seen from considering the extreme cases wherein crucial data is missing, so that what is learned is not adequate for handling cases similar to those of the missing crucial data. A new data item is considered informative if it can lead the system to learn something beyond what has already been learned.

Selection of examples is not trivial. Borderline cases may be needed, not just the most frequent cases. The example set may need to be refined to get satisfactory results. Further, the inductive process may itself be used to identify contradictions and gaps in the initially provided samples. Subjective assessment of data should be done in conjunction with the expert.

The selection of attributes requires skill. Sometimes it helps to group some attributes together into one. The chosen attributes should be the most relevant and natural from the expert's viewpoint, and should be as independent as possible. Care is also needed in introducing new attributes to distinguish contradictory data; a solution should not be imposed by the knowledge engineer, it is the task of the expert to determine relevance of various attributes and features synthesized by combining existing attributes.

Misleading results can be obtained if we use attributes that are labels. For example, due to a chance feature found in the data supplied, a medical diagnostic system may come up with the interesting conclusion that we can determine that a patient is diabetic by checking if his social security number ends with a zero. Such a conclusion is clearly invalid and would not apply to other data in general. As in this case, the vagaries of data may lead to the illusion that information gain results from selecting an attribute for a decision node, even when the values of an attribute are irrelevant to expert decision-making. It is hence necessary for an expert to review the classification tree extracted by the ID3 algorithm, to ensure that spurious relationships are not emphasized in the expert system being built based on the classification tree.

The goal of induction is to gain knowledge and learn rules that can be applied to data other than those cases used to develop the system. Methods for evaluating results should be built into the system. The system, when developed, should be tested on both easy and hard cases, both typical and rare cases, and cases on which some of the attribute measurements may be partially in error. The size of the training set should be large enough to engender confidence in the generalizability of the conclusions and the applicability of the classification tree. A statistician's rule-of-thumb is to use 5-10 times as many examples as the number of free parameters in the system, in order to have sufficient confidence that the system developed will continue to do well on new data not previously encountered by the system. A safer estimate is $2^{no.\ of\ attributes}$, corresponding to the number of leaves in a complete binary classification tree; however, this requires expensive computations using a very large data set, which may not be feasible for a given problem. For problems of very high dimensionality, a better approach may be to perform feature extraction using methods such as linear principal components analysis, and then construct the classification tree using the extracted features rather than the raw data field values.

Considerable ambiguity and lack of clarity may be expected even in the process of constructing the data set. Where possible, the expert must be encouraged to be specific, and to identify key phrases that enable judgement of text. In identifying that a data item belongs to a specific class, the expert may be able to specify a confidence measure indicating his belief in the hypothesis that the item belongs to that class. Rules constructed by an inductive system may be probabilistic, not categorical; for instance if 70% of the training set (corresponding to a leaf node in the classification tree) belongs to Class I, the constructed rule may indicate 70% as the probability associating that node with Class I. In some cases, making a wrong decision of one kind may be much more expensive or hazardous than another, calling for the use of a table of misclassification costs. The combination of the cost measure and the probability of class membership may then be used to make the final decision, minimizing expected cost.

Some amount of pre-induction analysis may help simplify the task of the induction algorithm. For instance, a structured or hierarchical approach may be used, clearly identifying subproblems for which classification trees can be constructed by induction. Classification trees constructed may be further analyzed and modified, after their construction by the induction procedure. For instance, trees may be pruned to eliminate leaf nodes that correspond to very few data elements.

We conclude this section by noting that inductive knowledge acquisition
- does not distinguish between necessary and confirmatory data;
- assumes the training set is complete and correct; and
- provides no guarantee that the results are applicable outside the training set.

Well-known and oft-used variations of the ID3 algorithms include *CART* [2], often mentioned in statistical literature, and *C4.5* [13], which accounts for numeric attributes.

8.5 Bibliographic Notes

Chapters in the book edited by Kidd [9] provide a broad introduction to various techniques for knowledge elicitation and acquisition. Repertory grids have been implemented in a suite of computer programs called 'PLANET' [14]. Inductive machine learning algorithms such as ID3 are discussed in Weiss and Kulikowski [18]; the book by Breiman, *et al.* [2] contains a detailed presentation of the closely related 'CART' algorithm and its variations. Kovitz's book [10] is a useful introduction to requirements analysis, that may provide a useful background before launching on knowledge acquisition tasks.

Bibliography

[1] R.J. Brachman, "On the epistemological status of semantic networks," in N.V. Findler (Ed.), *Associative Networks*, Academic Press, New York, 1979.

[2] L. Breiman, J. Friedman, R. Olshen and C. Stone, *Classification and Regression Trees*, Chapman and Hall/CRC Press, Boca Raton (FL), 1998.

[3] J.A. Breuker and B.J. Wielinga, "KADS: Structured knowledge acquisition for expert systems," in *Proc. Fifth International Workshop on Expert Systems and their Applications*, Avignon (France), 1985.

[4] B.G. Buchanan and E.H. Shortliffe, *Rule-based expert systems*, Addison-Wesley, Reading (MA), 1984.

[5] R. Davis, "Meta-rules: Reasoning about control," *Artificial Intelligence*, 1980, 15:179-222.

[6] K.M.Ford, F.E.Petry, J.R.Adams-Webber, and P.J.Chang, "An Approach to Knowledge Acquisition Based on the Structure of Personal Construct Systems," *Transactions on KDE*, 1991, 3(1):78-88.

[7] A.J. Gonzalez and D.D. Dankel, *The Engineering of Knowledge-Based Systems: Theory and Practice*, Prentice-Hall, Englewood Cliffs (NJ), 1993.

[8] G.A. Kelly, *The Psychology of Personal Constructs*, Norton, New York, 1955.

[9] A. Kidd (Ed.), *Knowledge Acquisition for Expert Systems: A Practical Handbook*, Plenum Press, 1987.

[10] B.L. Kovitz, *Practical Software Requirements: A Manual of Content and Style*, Manning Press, 1999.

[11] M.A. Musen, "Automated support for building and extending expert models," *Machine Learning,* 1989, 4(3-4):347-376.

[12] J.R. Quinlan, "Induction of Decision Trees," *Machine Learning,* 1986, 1:81-106.

[13] J.R. Quinlan, *C4.5: Programming for Machine Learning,* Morgan Kaufmann, San Mateo (CA), 1993.

[14] M.L.G. Shaw, "PLANET: Some experience in creating an integrated system for repertory grid applications on a microcomputer," *International Journal of Man-Machine Studies,* 1982, 17(3):345-360.

[15] M.L.G. Shaw and B.R. Gaines, "An Interactive Knowledge-Elicitation Technique Using Personal Construct Technology," in A. Kidd (Ed.), *Knowledge Acquisition for Expert Systems: A Practical Handbook,* Plenum Press, 1987, pp.109-136.

[16] E.H. Shortliffe, A.C. Scott, M.B. Bischoff, W. van Melle and C.D. Jacobs, "ONCOCIN: an expert system for oncology protocol management," in *Proc. 7th International Joint Conf. on Artificial Intelligence (IJCAI),* 1981, pp.876-881.

[17] A. N. Tikhonov, "On solving incorrectly posed problems and method of regularization," *Doklady Akademii Nauk USSR,* 151:501-504, 1963.

[18] S.M. Weiss and C. Kulikowski, *Computer Systems that Learn: Classification and Prediction Methods from Statistics, Neural Nets, Machine Learning and Expert Systems,* Morgan Kaufmann, San Francisco (CA), 1991.

8.6 Exercises

1. Find someone, the "expert" in this context, who plays a game with which you are completely unfamiliar, and which uses tools or props that are also unfamiliar to you. Attempt to determine the rules of the game by quizzing the expert, with the expert truthfully answering your questions but not volunteering any information.

2. From the repertory grid in Table 8.1, develop rules that allow predicting overall superiority from the first five personal constructs listed in the table.

3. Compute the degree of confirmation associated with the following statements pertaining to the repertory grid in Table 8.1:

   (a) Above average motivation is needed if a staff member's overall superiority is to be considered at least average.

   (b) If an individual's overall superiority is above average, his helpfulnes is below average.

   (c) The overall superiority is above average for highly intelligent individuals with high motivation levels.

4. Develop a repertory grid for the purpose of understanding the decision-making procedure used by students in selecting courses. Each column in this grid corresponds to one course, and each row a personal construct formulated by asking a student (expert, in this case) to apply the Triad method to compare courses. The last row in the grid should refer to desirability of registering for a course.

   Extract rules from this grid.

5. One possible criticism of the repertory grid approach is that it cannot develop elaborate relations between different entities. For instance, one cannot develop rules for course selection that also depend on student attributes, since rows in the grid refer only to course attributes. Suggest a way around this problem.

6. Estimate the computational effort involved in extracting rules from a repertory grid of given size.

7. Apply the ID3 algorithm to the following 5-dimensional data, using binary strings to represent each data element, as in Example 8.10.
   Class C_1: {11100, 11111, 01111, 10111, 11011} }
   Class C_2: {00101, 10000, 10001, 00000, 01000}

8. Apply a multiclass variant of the ID3 algorithm to the following data, using binary strings to represent each data element, as in Example 8.10.
Class C_1: {11100, 11111, 01111, 10111, 11011}
Class C_2: {00101, 10001, 10010}
Class C_3: {00001, 10000, 00100}

9. In the preceding two problems, illustrate how the classification tree construction process would be simplified if an additional feature (an attribute derived from existing attributes) can be precomputed and allowed to be used by the ID3 algorithm for learning.
Feature 1: The number of 1s in a bit string
Feature 2: The sum of the first three bits in a bit string

10. Illustrate the result for Example 8.10 if the termination criterion of ID3 is modified so that a node is not further split up if at least 75% of the data elements belong to the same class. Class membership is then determined by the majority rule. How many misclassification errors occur if this criterion is used, and what is the number of nodes of the resulting tree relative to the tree of Figure 8.3?

11. Can the results of classification tree development (using ID3) differ if the Gini index is used instead of an information-theoretic measure? Verify your answer, using the data of Example 8.10.

12. Complete the analysis of Example 8.11, constructing a classification tree for the data of Example 8.10, using the numeric attribute of temperature instead of x_1. What is the additional amount of computational effort required, as compared to the original example?

Chapter 9

Data Mining

Dirt-covered, a diamond lay hidden in the marketplace;
fools passed, but only the wise would know its face.   Kabirdas, c.1450

Data Mining, sometimes referred to as *Knowledge Discovery in Databases (KDD)*, applies artificial intelligence, pattern recognition, and database techniques for the commercial analysis and exploitation of large amounts of data. No discussion of modern knowledge-based systems would be complete without mention of this important topic. Data Mining may be oriented towards discovering (a) summary descriptions and visualization of collections of data, (b) finding correlations among data attributes, (c) discriminating among classes using attribute values, (d) predicting values for output attributes, (e) identifying groups of similar data, or (f) using historical information to predict the future values of variables. The following are some examples of data mining applications:

- Fraud detection in the use of credit cards and accounts

- Determination of the most appropriate target markets for a product

- Association of market segments with specific marketing strategies

- Analysis of medical histories to evaluate the risk of inheriting a disease

- Determining consumption and usage patterns of customers

- Projections of demand and supply of consumer products

- Creditworthiness evaluation of loan applicants

- Stock market predictions

The difficulties that arise with various data processing tasks are further exacerbated in data mining, due to the much larger quantities of data involved. Many algorithms considered efficient in other tasks are unsatisfactory in data mining, requiring excessive amounts of computational time. Space constraints become very important: many algorithms are designed to work with the entire data set in main memory, which becomes impossible in data mining due to the huge volume of data that needs processing. Rather than search for optimal (best) solutions, data mining algorithms instead seek suboptimal solutions. This makes it necessary to evaluate the results obtained by data mining algorithms, to determine whether they are relevant, reliable, and usable for the current application. Interactive algorithms that ensure user involvement are likely to be successful, eliminating fruitless paths that may be followed by systems without a human in the loop.

The analysis of large amounts of data involves several major steps addressed in successive sections of this chapter:

- preprocessing to prepare data for subsequent analysis;

- transforming data representation to enable efficient data mining;

- knowledge discovery to identify interesting aspects of data (including approaches discussed in Chapter 8); and

- prediction of properties of new cases (test data), in static as well as time-varying domains.

9.1   Preprocessing

Raw data is often riddled with errors, inconsistencies, incomplete coverage of data space, and missing values. Data mining algorithms would be much more effective if at least some of these difficulties are addressed at an early stage. Preprocessing involves preparing the data and transforming the data into a usable form, including elimination of noise, where appropriate. Different kinds of data from multiple disparate sources have to be merged. Human involvement is necessary in some preprocessing steps, e.g., in deciding upon common formats for a unified database.

9.1.1   Overall Statistics

To assist in other preprocessing steps, as well as in later data processing steps, it is useful to perform preliminary statistical analysis of the numerical components of the data, collecting essential information such as means and standard deviations of input and output variables, pairwise correlation analysis, and top-level clustering (into a small number of clusters)[1]. Such analysis may be useful in reducing the volume of data, e.g., if it is determined that two variables are very highly correlated, one may be eliminated altogether without losing information essential to the problem.

Computations of means and standard deviations may not be meaningful for categorical (non-numerical) attributes such as color. Instead, one may then count the number of occurrences of different categorical values at this stage (e.g., how many data elements have color attribute 'red').

Human intervention may also be useful at this stage to determine whether the entire data must be processed together, or whether the data can be partitioned into substantially dissimilar subsets analyzed separately, based on the initial clustering analysis or on expert evaluations based on specific attributes. For instance, in medical diagnosis of certain diseases, it may be useful to separate patient cases by gender.

9.1.2 Noise

Data may be inherently noisy, or noise may have been introduced as a result of human or machine errors. If the nature of the noise is known, the preprocessing steps can clean the data to some extent. Noise elimination is facilitated by a careful prior definition of what constitutes noise in the specific application being examined. For instance, it is reasonable in some applications to assume that the data is corrupted by *additive white Gaussian noise*, consisting of random perturbations drawn from a Gaussian distribution, added to uncorrupted data.

Noise elimination algorithms often rely on the assumption that similar data elements should have similar behavior, so if a single output variable is assumed to be corrupted, it can be smoothed by averaging with values from other data elements that are very similar in other respects.

Example 9.1 For a data processing problem, let $I(X)$ refer to the input variable values of data element X, and let $O(X)$ refer to the output variable values of X. Let $N(X) = \{Y : ||I(X) - I(Y)|| < \epsilon\}$, consisting of all the data elements near X, for some small $\epsilon > 0$. Then $O(X)$ can be modified by an averaging process, to $\sum_{Z \in N(X)} O(Z)/|N(X)|$.

---

[1] In clustering, the goal is to partition the data into a small number of data clusters, maximizing intra-cluster similarity and minimizing inter-cluster similarity.

This approach can be varied in many ways, e.g., considering a fixed number of nearest neighbors of X rather than using a distance criterion. However, this approach does not address the problem of noise in input variables, nor the occurrence of noise in multiple variables or components.

The approach of Example 9.1 accounts for the case when the nearest neighbors of a data element X are associated with output variable values that are substantially different from those of X. This data processing step may be desirable in most tasks, but undesirable in some. In the data mining context, some cases of apparent noise may mask useful *nuggets* of data that need careful analysis, and may be of importance to the application.

There is a danger that noise-elimination algorithms may eliminate or throw away such important data. To avoid this possibility, we may restrict smoothing or averaging to cases where all the nearest neighbors of a data element have similar output values, e.g., modifying $O(X)$ to $\sum_{Z \in N(X)} O(Z)/|N(X)|$ only if $\max_{Y \in N(X), Z \in N(X)} \|O(Z) - O(Y)\| < \theta$, where $\theta > 0$ is a problem-dependent threshold.

Outliers (data elements distant from the rest of the data) are sometimes considered to be noise or the result of human or machine errors, and hence these may also be deleted in the noise elimination step, subject to the caveat mentioned in the previous paragraph: in some cases, outliers may represent useful nuggets of information to be extracted, not thrown away.

Example 9.2 As in Example 9.1, let $I(X), O(X)$, and $N(X)$ refer to the input variables, output variables and neighbors of data element X in the data set S. We may consider X to be an outlier if $\min_{Y \in N(X)} \|O(X) - O(Y)\| > \theta$, where $\theta \gg 0$ is a predetermined problem-dependent threshold, possibly a small multiple of the standard deviation of $\{\|O(Y) - O(Z)\|$ where $Y \in S$, $Z \in S\}$.

9.1.3   Missing Values

Some vexing data, especially from the medical domain, is characterized by the absence of values for some attributes; this may be caused, for instance, by a patient's refusal or inability to fill in some entries on standardized forms used to collect data, or by clerical errors generating meaningless values in the data entry process. Since a large proportion of cases may each miss some attribute value, we cannot just omit these cases; we risk losing important information.

Unknown attribute values must hence be estimated using some reasonable heuristic. This may be done by interpolating or averaging over the values for that attribute for data considered most relevant to the data element X under question, e.g., averaging over the desired attribute values for $\{Y : \|A(X) - A(Y)\| < \epsilon\}$, where $\epsilon > 0$ and $A(Y)$ is a vector of the other attribute values (not missing for these elements).

If preliminary analysis reveals known dependencies or correlations among various attributes, it may be possible to estimate the most probable value for one attribute, based on the values for other attributes.

9.2 Transforming Representations

Even after the preprocessing steps mentioned above, data may not be ready for direct analysis. In many problems, computational effort is significantly reduced if a suitable representation is found for the data. Attempts to transform the representation to a suitable form can be roughly categorized as normalization, dimensionality reduction, and data reduction, discussed below in greater detail.

9.2.1 Normalization

Data elements may have attribute values that vary widely and in different ranges. For example, one attribute value may range over the interval $[-100, 100]$, whereas another is restricted to the interval $[0, 1]$. The range depends on the unit of measurement, e.g., millimeters *vs.* meters. The problem is aggravated by the fact that some analysis techniques ignore dimensionality issues, focusing on numerical values alone.

To some extent, such problems are alleviated by prior normalization of data. Normalization may be performed by applying separate linear transformations to each attribute, into the range $[0, 1]$ or $[-1, 1]$. Such linear transformations can instead be applied after eliminating outliers, e.g., considering only values that lie within $[\mu - 3\sigma, \mu + 3\sigma]$, where μ and σ are the observed mean and standard deviation of values for the attribute under consideration. If the distribution of attribute values is asymmetric (e.g., with a 'heavy tail'), then a different interval may be more appropriate.

As an alternative to data normalization, the distance and similarity measures used in data analysis may be normalized, achieving similar effects.

9.2.2 Dimensionality Reduction

Data mining problems are often characterized by high data dimensionality that must be reduced drastically for computational efficiency as well as generalizability of results. In the simplest cases, it may be possible to eliminate many of the original problem dimensions using heuristic problem-specific knowledge. The remaining attributes may be the important *features* of the problem.

In other cases, the problem representation needs to be transformed to a different but smaller set of dimensions (axes), preserving most of the information in the data. This step involves *Feature Extraction*, i.e., determining useful features of data. For example, ratios or linear combinations of attribute values may carry the essential information in the problem, rather than raw attribute values themselves. The feature extraction process must determine the most useful such attribute combinations.

One well-known approach from the field of statistics is *Principal Component Analysis (PCA)* (cf. Section 8.3). PCA successively extracts linear combinations (of problem attributes) that capture the maximum diversity among data items; nonlinear versions of PCA exist, but are much more difficult to implement. PCA can be accomplished by computing the eigenvectors corresponding to the largest magnitude eigenvalues of the covariance matrix of normalized data. Several iterative methods have also been suggested that achieve close approximations to reaching the eigenvectors.

Relevant features may sometimes be discovered by applying machine learning algorithms, including neural networks. For instance, the LMS algorithm [38] or the pocket algorithm [11] may be used to obtain useful linear combinations of attribute values, for classification problems. More elaborate algorithms that extract useful features (before matching) exploit Fourier Transforms, singular value decompositions, or the Karhunen-Loeve transformation on covariance matrices (for details, see [15]). However, many of these algorithms are computationally expensive when the volume of data is large.

In addition to the usefulness of dimensionality reduction in data representation, data miners are also interested in the features themselves, since these describe important aspects of the problem that may not be previously known.

9.2.3   Data Reduction

Random sampling is a well-known data reduction technique that can be used with sufficiently large amounts of data, with theoretical basis in results such as the *law of large numbers*. Such results suggest that sampling can be a very accurate way of determining various aspects of data distributions, including means, variances, and proportions of elements that belong to specific classes. These results are robust and do not assume a specific data distribution. Reliability of results obtained from a random sample depend on sample size.

Some data miners have argued that random sampling is not satisfactory since small pockets of data may be of prime interest, and such pockets may not receive representation in the random sampling process, losing information important to the problem. For instance, in a credit card usage fraud detection application, only a very small fraction (0.1%) of the credit card transactions may be fraudulent [4], but these deserve careful analysis. This necessitates biased sampling procedures, exploring "interesting" regions of the data space more carefully than others. For instance, the entire data may be scanned, and neighborhoods of data elements of an important class (as specified by the user) may be sampled to a greater extent than the rest of the data space. An iterative focusing algorithm may be invoked, successively identifying and examining more closely the regions of interest identifying in earlier iterations.

Significant data reduction can be obtained by the application of clustering algorithms [19]. At the end of the clustering process, only the cluster centroids or *prototypes* are represented, with the rest of the data not used in subsequent analysis. A frequently used clustering algorithm is the *k-means algorithm*, in which cluster centroids are repeatedly updated, with data elements allocated to the nearest cluster centroid in each iteration. Some neural networks also achieve similar tasks, using simple competitive learning (cf. Chapter 6). A closely related approach is *Voronoi quantization* in which *codebook vectors* (prototypes) are obtained to represent different regions of data space. Clustering and quantization can be performed using statistical or connectionist algorithms. Among the latter, adaptive *radial basis function* networks and *self-organizing* networks both attempt to discover prototypes; details are beyond the scope of this book, and the reader is referred to the literature on neural networks, e.g., [26].

One problem with the clustering approach is that representation is often limited to the prototype, whereas it may be useful to retain information about the *shape* of the cluster. For instance, a cluster may extend a considerable distance away from the prototype in one direction, but much less in the opposite direction, depending on the density distribution within the cluster. This problem can be alleviated by computing and storing the representation of an approximation to the convex hull surrounding the bulk of the cluster, in addition to the prototype, as in [22]. Alternatively, we may invoke algorithms that attempt to approximate the probability distribution, although this does not result in as much space savings as the prototype based representations.

These approaches are closely related to the approach of case based reasoning, discussed earlier in Chapter 7, and each case in the case library can be considered a prototype. The use of a case hierarchy with exceptions (failure

links) identifies distinct sub-regions within the region associated with a prototype, which is difficult to represent using most clustering techniques.

9.3   Knowledge Discovery

Knowledge discovery entails the automated recognition of potentially useful
(previously unknown) patterns in the data, and generally involves the application of inductive machine learning and statistical algorithms. The kinds of
knowledge extracted may include rules, constraints and regularities. Some aspects of this task involve discovering important features of the problem, mentioned in the preceding section.

The ease of application of inductive machine learning algorithms depends
on the class of models through which the learning algorithm must search, hence
it is crucial for the the class of patterns of interest to be specified in a reasonable
manner. The class of models is restricted by the questions posed by the end-user
of mined data. For example, a marketing analyst may be interested in specific
questions such as:

Which pairs of items tend to be purchased together?
Who are the consumers more likely to purchase item X?

One of the major issues facing the data miner is the determination of
which 'nuggets' of data are interesting enough to merit careful analysis, or facilitate direct commercial exploitation for tasks such as marketing. Although
'interesting-ness' cannot be formally defined, machine learning researchers have
identified some useful notions, such as that a property must be parsimoniously
specifiable (i.e., should not require excessively elaborate descriptions), and must
hold for a nontrivial collection of data (i.e., neither too small nor too large). For
example, clustering analysis may reveal (as 'interesting') a small cluster of one
class embedded within a large region or cluster.

Incremental updating algorithms that make small changes to the existing knowledge obtained by data mining, are useful in many applications, e.g.,
in maintaining association rules extracted from large databases whose nature
changes slowly with time [7].

Subsections 9.3.1, 9.3.2, and 9.3.3 address knowledge discovery in the three
contexts most relevant to data mining: (a) classification trees[2], (b) clusters, and
(c) association rules.

---

[2]As mentioned in the footnote on page 219, we use the phrase *classification tree* instead of
the phrase *decision tree*, to distinguish from other usage of the latter phrase.

9.3.1 Classification Trees

The ID3 algorithm discussed in Section 8.4 falls under the first category. This algorithm and its variants attempt to discover which attributes to associate with each node in the classification tree, using a criterion such as information gain or Gini index. However, these algorithms require significant computational effort to process large data sets.

SLIQ [27] is another classification tree learning algorithm that uses several heuristic strategies (sorting attributes, pruning the tree, and breadth-first tree growing) to improve learning efficiency when amounts of data are so large that they cannot all be kept in main memory.

Another alternative is a divide-and-conquer approach, in which classification trees are constructed by combining classifiers obtained from subsets of data [5].

In addition to the problem of large data sets, another drawback of ID3 and similar classification tree learning algorithms is that the nodes in the tree examine only one problem attribute at a time, resulting in larger trees and poorer classification than if features (each a function of multiple problem attributes) are used at decision nodes. As mentioned earlier, simple neural network learning algorithms (e.g., the LMS [38] or pocket [11] algorithms) can be used for this purpose, possibly applied on a random sample of the data, for efficiency reasons. Alternatively, the classification trees obtained using ID3 (and its variants) may be simplified, determining linear combinations of attributes that can replace collections of nodes in the tree [17].

9.3.2 Clustering

Clustering algorithms such as k-means clustering can be applied for knowledge discovery. As mentioned earlier, the goal in clustering is to partition the data into a small number of data clusters, maximizing intra-cluster similarity and minimizing inter-cluster similarity. Dense regions in a large data space may be identified, and these may be of most interest for commercial exploitation.

The main problem with traditional clustering algorithms is that they often require distance computations with all the data available, which make them computationally unsuitable for data mining problems with very large amounts of data. Furthermore, if data changes with time, they require re-examination of the entire data set, rather than incrementally modify pre-existing cluster representations. This difficulty has been addressed in newer clustering algorithms fine-tuned for data mining, such as CLARANS [12] and BIRCH [39], outlined below.

- The CLARANS algorithm examines a small sample of the data at each instant, choosing different samples during its execution. For each sample, a *medoid*[3] prototype data element is determined for each cluster, and iteratively improved, examining other choices for the prototype among elements in the sample. In the process, outliers can be identified, and a reasonable choice can also be determined for the number of clusters. Computational effort in calculating inter-cluster distances can be reduced, using a tree-based representation for the clusters, focusing only on (a) representative data elements, (b) relevant clusters, and (c) a single cluster at a time [8]. In a practical application, segmentation of protein surfaces to facilitate docking queries, these techniques were found to decrease computational time by a factor of 50 without significant performance degradation.

- The BIRCH algorithm incrementally builds a balanced tree representation whose nodes contain essential *cluster feature* information, viz., the number of data elements in the cluster, their vector sum, and squared sum $(\sum_i X_i^2)$. The branching factor of the tree (number of children of a node) and the size of the subclusters associated with leaf nodes can be varied to find the best tree representation, without having to examine all data. Experimental evidence indicates that the algorithm produces satisfactory results while scaling up linearly with respect to the data set size.

---

[3]A *medoid* is a point that is centrally located with respect to all the data dimensions. For example, the medoid of the data set $\{(-18, 0.1), (8, 8.7), (10, 0.2)\}$, is $(8, 0.2)$ according to an accepted definition, obtained by concatenating median values for all data dimensions, whereas the centroid is $(0, 3)$. The medoid is a more robust measure than the centroid, swayed less by extreme values.

9.3.3 Association Rules

Association rules are rules that relate values of attributes or features of the problem domain to possible values of a desired output attribute, as discussed in Section 8.3. For instance, the *lhs* of an association rule may describe lower or upper limits on numeric attributes, and the *rhs* may indicate the class to which a data item belongs if the constraints on the *lhs* are satisfied. Such rules express associations among attributes in the data, rather than deep causal relationships or expert opinions.

The following criteria are generally used to evaluate itemsets[4] and rules:

Support: The support of a set S is the fraction of data elements that belong to S; the support of a rule ($lhs \rightarrow rhs$) is the fraction of data elements that satisfy both *lhs* and *rhs*.

Confidence: The confidence of a rule is the fraction of data elements satisfying *rhs* that also satisfy *lhs*, analogous to a conditional probability measure (cf. Section 8.3).

Size: The collection of rules should not be too large.

Interest: Subjectively, patterns are considered interesting if their results are surprising (unexpected) or if their results form the basis for actions to be carried out. A quantitative measure of whether a rule is interesting is the degree to which its support exceeds the average support expected if the attributes on the *lhs* and *rhs* of the rule were uncorrelated. The relative interest of a rule with respect to a more general rule can be expressed in terms of the ratio of their support (or confidence). A more refined measure [35] determines whether a collection of attribute values (or intervals) remains interesting even after deleting its more interesting specializations.

One approach to learning association rules has already been discussed in Section 8.3, in the context of extracting rules from repertory grid analysis. The machine learning literature suggests several other ways of learning rules, such as the 'conjunct dropping' technique. A number of steps are involved in the algorithms, outlined below.

---

[4] A transaction database consists of a set of transactions, where each transaction is described as a set of items. Each item may be present in multiple transactions, and is analogous to an input dimension. If there are n possible items, the presence of the ith item in a transaction is analogous to having a data element in discrete n-dimensional space (hypercube) valued 1 (instead of 0) at the ith dimension. An *itemset* is a collection of these items (input dimensions), considered significant if this collection occurs in a reasonably large number of transactions.

- It is first necessary to define the space of rules that are within the scope of the machine learning algorithm. Considering the problem as one of state space search, each 'state' for the algorithm is a collection of rules.

- We must define an initial state, i.e., a (possibly empty) collection of rules constituting the starting point for the algorithm. In some cases, the initial state is an exhaustive collection of specialized descriptions of all data elements, to be whittled down in the search process.

- The goal state may be defined as a collection of rules that account for all or most of the data available, possibly with a small number of errors permitted. The goal state may be required to contain only *strong rules*, with high support and confidence, exceeding minimum user-defined thresholds. However, the use of fixed thresholds can lead to misleading results; the confidence of a rule may exceed a threshold but be smaller than the fraction of data elements satisfying *rhs* alone. For example, the threshold may be 0.6, and the confidence of a rule 0.7, but 80% of the entire population may satisfy the *rhs* of the rule, i.e., the elements that satisfy the *lhs* of the rule actually have lower probability of satisfying the *rhs*. Such anomalies can arise if prior probabilities are ignored.

- The search strategy must be defined, e.g., some machine learning algorithms invoke depth first search with chronological backtracking. Many data mining algorithms use a two-phase strategy:

  - the first phase determines *frequent itemsets* (collections with support exceeding a predetermined threshold), and

  - the second phase generates rules from the frequent itemsets.

  The *DHP* and *Apriori*[5] algorithms are often used to obtain frequent itemsets. These algorithms begin with singleton itemsets, iteratively building up larger itemsets from the unions of smaller itemsets whose support has been found to exceed the required threshold (in earlier iterations).

- The 'moves' determine which collection of rules are visited from which state. These are specified in terms of mechanisms for:

  - Generating new rules, e.g., using the complete description of an existing data element (or a prototype) as a rule.

---

[5] Not to be confused with *a priori* probabilities.

- Specializing existing rules, e.g., a new conjunct may be added to the antecedent of a rule to prevent the rule from being applicable to a counterexample.

- Generalizing existing rules, e.g., a conjunct may be dropped from the antecedent of a rule, or a numeric interval constraint may be widened, or a disjunction introduced.

- Combining existing rules, e.g., two rules with similar consequents may be combined into a single rule whose antecedent is a disjunction of the antecedents of the rules being combined.

- Deleting rules, e.g., the algorithm may delete a rule which is subsumed by other rules, or a rule that holds for only a small number of examples, especially if these examples are considered uninteresting.

Since working with the entire set of data is immensely computationally expensive, a useful approach is to begin by applying the learning algorithm to a small random sample from the original data, and test performance of the resulting rules on the rest of the data or on a test set, i.e., another sample freshly drawn from the entire data set. If performance on the entire data set (or the test set) is unsatisfactory, we may apply the learning algorithm to a larger random sample, beginning with the rules learnt in the previous iteration. This process may be iterated, applying the learning algorithm to larger and larger data sets, until performance is satisfactory or computational limitations are exceeded.

The general goal is to come up with a small collection of simple rules that adequately describe all data; unfortunately, this may be impossible. Even when possible, determining the smallest such collection may involve exhaustive search through the space of possible rules, computationally intractable even for small data sets. Hence deterministic search strategies are defined, and the termination criteria are defined loosely enough so that suboptimal solutions are acceptable, rather than search for the optimal rule set. Chances of success are improved if the data can be reduced in size in any manner, or partitioned into clusters to which the learning algorithm can be separately applied.

Specialized algorithms have been suggested for learning association rules in the context of large databases, e.g., [1, 13, 36]. These have been extended to *Quantitative association rules* that contain numerical interval constraints, e.g.,

$$Age \in [20, 35] \& Income \in [\$40000, \$80000] \Rightarrow InterestedIn(CarXYZ).$$

Interval size is an important consideration: if the intervals are too large, rules may have low confidence; if the intervals are too small, rules may have low support. Specialized learning algorithms such as the *Equal Depth Partition (EDP)* algorithm [35], described below, have been developed to learn quantitative association rules.

The EDP algorithm attempts to determine frequent itemsets in the database while minimizing the number of intervals required to satisfy a user-specified *partial completeness* level (K).

Definition 1 If C is the set of all frequent itemsets in the database D, and $K \geq 1$, a subset $P \subseteq C$ is said to be K-*complete* iff

> P contains all subsets of all elements of P, and
> P contains some generalization X' of each itemset $X \in C$,
> such that
>
> $$P \text{ contains a generalization } Y' \subseteq X' \text{ of every } Y \subseteq X$$
> $$\text{satisfying } support(Y') \leq K \times support(X).$$

The size of the collection P decreases as K increases. C itself is the only 1-complete set.

Example 9.3 (adapted from [35]) For a problem with two numerical attributes A and C, let C contain seven frequent itemsets, enumerated below with their support values:

1. $support(\{A : 20..30\}) = 5\%$,

2. $support(\{A : 20..40\}) = 6\%$,

3. $support(\{A : 20..50\}) = 8\%$,

4. $support(\{C : 1..2\}) = 5\%$,

5. $support(\{C : 1..3\}) = 6\%$,

6. $support(\{A : 20..30, \ C : 1..2\}) = 4\%$,

7. $support(\{A : 20..40, \ C : 1..3\}) = 5\%$.

The collection of itemsets numbered 2, 3, 5 and 7 is a 1.5-complete set, but not the collection of itemsets numbered 3, 5 and 7, since
(i) support for itemset 3 (but not 2) exceeds 1.5× support for itemset 1,
(ii) itemset 5 does not generalize itemset 1, and
(iii) itemset 7 does not generalize itemset 1.

If R is a set of rules generated from C with minimum confidence level μ, and R_K is a set of rules generated from a set K-complete w.r.t. C with minimum confidence level μ/K, then for every rule $A \to B$ in R, there exists a rule $A' \to B'$ in R_K such that A' generalizes A, B' generalizes B, $support(A' \to B') \leq K \times support(A \to B)$, and

$$\text{confidence}(A \to B)/K \leq \text{confidence}(A' \to B') \leq K \times \text{confidence}(A \to B).$$

K-complete sets can generated by partitioning each of n quantitative attributes into disjoint *base intervals*, each of which is either a singleton set or has support $s < (K-1)m/2n$, where m is the prespecified minimum support threshold. Then the set of all frequent itemsets over the base intervals is K-complete w.r.t. the set of all frequent itemsets. If the highest support in the partition is s, the requirement $s < (K-1)m/2n$ implies that a partial completeness level $K = 1 + 2ns/m$ can be attained. The number of intervals can also be chosen using this approach: if the support s is split equally among intervals, the number of intervals must be $1/s \geq 2n/m(K-1)$ where K is the desired completeness level. As s decreases, the number of intervals increases, decreasing the partial completeness level and the information lost.

Fuzzy terms may also be included in such rules, e.g.,

$$Young \ \& \ Middle\_Income \ \Rightarrow \ Moderately(InterestedIn(CarXYZ)).$$

Zhang's *EDPFT algorithm* can learn such rules, using the EDP algorithm to determine intervals for numerical attributes, mapping values and fuzzy terms for each attribute into consecutive integers, determining the frequently occurring itemsets (using an extension of the Apriori algorithm), generating association rules from the frequent itemsets, and finally deleting rules with low confidence or low interest (precision, accuracy and certainty) [40]. Membership functions for the fuzzy sets are presumed to be trapezoidal, specified by a non-decreasing sequence of four parameters (a, b, c, d) such that the trapezoidal graph (plotting membership against attribute values) passes through the points $(a, 0)$, $(b, 1)$, $(c, 1)$, $(d, 0)$.

The itemset-oriented algorithms are of relevance in an important application, *mining path traversal patterns*. A typical internet user visits a large number of web-pages, and commercial organizations are interested in learning the patterns in user visits to different web-pages. Sequencing information is important in this application, unlike the itemsets and transactions in the database context. The traversal log (sequence of web-pages) is processed to determine which sequences of web-page visits occur most often, after eliminating spurious subsequences that arise when a user goes back to a previously visited web-page to access another page.

Example 9.4 [6] Using one letter to denote each web-page visited, the traversal log $ABCDCBEGHGWAOUOV$ contains a sequence of 'forward' and 'backward' movements. For instance, the segment $ABCDCBE$ ... suggests that the user started from A, visited B, C, D, then backtracked to C, B, and then moved forward again to E; C and D are deemed irrelevant for the visit to E, so that the relevant sequence (to reach E) is ABE. Hence the maximal reference sequences of interest (in the sequence $ABCDCBEGHGWAOUOV$) are $ABCD$, $ABEGH$, $ABEGW$, AOU, and AOV. Among these, we must find frequently occurring subsequences, e.g., AB occurs in three of the five maximal reference sequences.

The patterns of interest for data mining are the longest among such sequences. Unfortunately, results of such analyses are vitiated by the fact that the sequence of web-pages visited by users depends significantly on the links provided by previous web-pages, and is biased by search engines and service providers.

With all the algorithms discussed in this section, there is a danger of discovering and enshrining spurious correlations between attributes that may be completely unrelated in the real world. The end products of automated rule discovery algorithms must hence be subjected to expert scrutiny, before being put to production use.

9.4   Prediction

The purpose of data analysis is often to help characterize or predict properties of new test data, rather than just observe the patterns or discover interesting correlations. Into this category fall problems of classification and function approximation, including time-dependent prediction tasks. Neural networks and associated learning algorithms are popular choices for such tasks, though not the only ones possible. Statistical approaches have in the past emphasized linear models, whereas nonlinear models are easier to handle using neural networks.

Static Domains are those in which the nature of the data does not change with time, allowing repeated examination of different elements. The main task is to discover (and apply) the mapping from input variables to output variables, searching in a space of models (possible mappings). Ease of learning decreases with increase in expressive power (of the class of models being considered). In this respect, linear models are easiest to learn, followed by quadratic and other polynomial models; learning is hardest if the space of models is completely general and capable of capturing all functions, e.g., the class of all neural networks with sigmoid (e.g., tanh) functions at each node.

Static domains may be contrasted with *Time-varying Domains* in which the relationships between input and output variables depend on time, often captured by recent history of the values of both input and output variables. In *Tapped Delay Neural Networks (TDNNs)*, for instance, some of the inputs to the network (to be trained) are obtained by introducing delay elements with variables, so that values of a variable at several past instants may influence the final output. Moving averages of variables (over time) constitute other possible important inputs to the learning algorithm. Some algorithms are capable of modifying the function (being learnt) with time, as needed with nonstationary applications, by decreasing the relative weightage of less recent data, perhaps exponentially [29].

Several prediction applications involve matching new inputs (data elements not used in the learning phase) to stored cases or prototypes. This requires the use of similarity measures to determine the degree to which the new data element matches the prototype. Measures such as Euclidean distance are used when numeric attributes are involved, possibly normalized by within-attribute standard deviation. If the attributes are categorical or symbolic (even if a numeric coding is used to represent them), it is more appropriate to use an equality test between attribute values.

Sequences x, y of different lengths (with $|x| > |y|$) may be compared by computing correlation coefficients, or by comparing y to the most similar subsequence of x of size $|y|$, or to the most similar sequence of size $|y|$ that can be obtained by deleting some elements of x. Similarity measures are often computed on features extracted from the data (cf. Section 9.2.2) rather than the raw data. Heuristics and data compression techniques have been proposed to improve efficiency of sequence matching [9], but computational efficiency remains a major concern when data sequences are very long. The *HierarchyScan* algorithm [24] improves performance by iteratively selecting small subsets of features with the greatest discriminating ability, without using a tree structure for indexing. Yet another approach consists of finding small matching subsequences and iteratively combining these until the largest matching subsequences are discovered [2].

9.5   Bibliographic Notes

Data Mining is a new field, with terminology and concepts that are still evolving. Much of the published work is available in research papers and chapters in conference proceedings, e.g., [10]. Predictive data mining is well addressed by Weiss and Indurkhya [37], whereas a database perspective for knowledge discovery is presented in [31]. Two useful survey articles are [32, 6], written from different perspectives. Data mining relies significantly on approaches associated with other research areas, hence much additional useful material can be found in books on statistics, machine learning, neural networks, pattern recognition, classification, clustering, data visualization, and databases. Useful internet resources include

lib.stat.cmu.edu and *www.astro.psu.edu/statcodes/sc_multclass.html*,

with pointers to implementations of several statistical algorithms and packages, especially for classification and clustering, as well as many data sets.

Chen, Han and Yu [6] list many existing systems that perform data mining: Quest [3] (discovering association rules), KEFIR [25, 30] (analyzing health care data), DBMiner [13, 14] (mining rules at multiple abstraction levels), KnowledgeMiner [34] (integrating data mining with deductive database techniques), INLEN [28] (integrating multiple learning paradigms), Explora [23] (a multipattern and multistrategy discovery assistant), DataMine [16] (exploring query-directed mining) and IDEA [33] (interactive data exploration and analysis).

Bibliography

[1] R. Agrawal, T. Imilienski, and A. Swami, "Mining association rules between sets of items in large databases," in *Proc. ACM SIGMOD International Conf. on Management of Data,* 1993, pp.207-216.

[2] R. Agrawal, K.-I. Lin, H.S. Sawhney, and K. Shim, "Fast Similarity Search in the Presence of Noise, Scaling, and Translation in Time Series Databases," *Proc. 21st International Conf. on Very Large Data Bases,* Sept. 1995, pp.490-501.

[3] R. Agrawal, M. Mehta, J. Shafer, R. Srikant, A. Arning, and T. Bollinger, "The Quest data mining system," in *Proc. 1996 International Conf. on Data Mining and Knowledge Discovery (KDD'96),* Portland (OR), Aug. 1996.

[4] R. Brause, T. Langsdorf, and M. Hepp, "Neural data mining for credit card fraud detection," in *Proc.Eleventh International Conf. on Tools with Artificial Intelligence,* Nov. 1999, pp.103-106.

[5] P.K. Chan and S.J. Stolfo, "Learning arbiter and combiner trees from partitioned data for scaling machine learning," in *Proc. First International Conf. on Knowledge Discovery and Data Mining (KDD'95),* Aug. 1995, pp.39-44.

[6] M.-S. Chen, J. Han and P.S. Yu, "Data Mining: An Overview from Database Perspective," *IEEE Transactions on Knowledge and Data Engineering,* 1996, 8(6):866-883.

[7] D.W. Cheung, J. Han, V. Ng, and C.Y. Wong, "Maintenance of discovered association rules in large databases: An incremental updating technique," in *Proc. 1996 International Conf. on Data Engineering,* New Orleans (LA), Feb. 1996.

[8] M. Ester, H.P. Kriegel, and X. Xu, "Knowledge discovery in large spatial databases: Focusing techniques for efficient class identification," in *Proc. 4th International Symp. on Large Spatial Databases (SSD'95)*, Portland (ME), Aug. 1995, pp.67-82.

[9] C. Faloutsos and K.-I. Lin, "FastMap: A Fast Algorithm for Indexing, Data-Mining and Visualization of Traditional and Multimedia Datasets," in *Proc. ACM SIGMOD International Conf. on Management of Data*, May 1995, pp.163-174.

[10] U. Fayyad, G. Piatetsky-Shapiro, P. Smyth and U. Uthurasamy (Eds.), *Advances in Knowledge Discovery and Data Mining*, AAAI Press, Menlo Park (CA), 1996.

[11] S.I. Gallant, "Optimal linear discriminants," in *Proc. Eighth International Conf. on Pattern Recognition*, 1986, pp.849-852.

[12] J. Han, Y. Cai, and N. Cercone, "Data-driven discovery of quantitative rules in relational databases," *IEEE Trans. on Knowledge and Data Engineering*, 1993, 5:29-40.

[13] J. Han and Y. Fu, "Discovery of multi-level association rules from large databases," in *Proc. 21st International Conf. on Very Large Data Bases*, 1995, pp.420-431.

[14] J. Han and Y. Fu, "Exploration of the power of attribute-oriented induction in data mining," in U. Fayyad, G. Piatetsky-Shapiro, P. Smyth, and R. Uthurusamy (Eds.) *Advances in Knowledge Discovery and Data Mining*, AAAI/MIT Press, 1996, pp.399-421.

[15] S. Haykin, *Neural Networks: A Comprehensive Foundation*, second edition, Prentice-Hall, 1999.

[16] T. Imielinski and A. Virmani, "Datamine – application programming interface and query language for KDD applications," in *Proc. 1996 International Conf. on Data Mining and Knowledge Discovery (KDD'96)*, Portland (OR), Aug. 1996.

[17] V. Iyengar, "HOT: Heuristics for Oblique Trees," in *Proc.Eleventh International Conf. on Tools with Artificial Intelligence*, Nov. 1999, pp.91-98.

[18] M. James, *Classification Algorithms*, Wiley, NY, 1985.

[19] A.K. Jain and R.C. Dubes, *Algorithms for clustering data,* Prentice Hall, 1988.

[20] R.A. Johnson, *Miller and Freund's Probability and Statistics for Engineers,* fifth edition, Prentice-Hall, 1994.

[21] L. Kaufman and P.J.Rousseeeuw, *Finding Groups in Data: An Introduction to Cluster Analysis,* Wiley, 1990.

[22] W. Kim, K. Mehrotra and C.K. Mohan, "Fuzzy Adaptive Multimodule Approximation Network," in *Proc. NAFIPS International Conf.,* June 1999.

[23] W. Klosgen, "Explora: A multipattern and multistrategy discovery assistant," in U. Fayyad, G. Piatetsky-Shapiro, P. Smyth, and R. Uthurusamy (Eds.) *Advances in Knowledge Discovery and Data Mining,* AAAI/MIT Press, 1996, pp.249-271.

[24] C.S. Li, P.S,. Yu, and V. Castelli, "HierarchyScan: A Hierarchical Similarity Search Algorithm for Databases of Long Sequences," in *Proc. 12th International Conf. on Data Engineering,* Feb. 1996.

[25] C.J. Matheus, G. Piatetsky-Shapiro, and D. McNeil, "Selecting and reporting what is interesting: The KEFIR application to healthcare data," in U. Fayyad, G. Piatetsky-Shapiro, P. Smyth, and R. Uthurusamy (Eds.) *Advances in Knowledge Discovery and Data Mining,* AAAI/MIT Press, 1996, pp.495-516.

[26] K. Mehrotra, C.K. Mohan, and S. Ranka, *Elements of Neural Networks,* MIT Press, Cambridge, 1997.

[27] M. Mehta, R. Agrawal, and J. Rissanen, "SLIQ: A fast scalable classifier for data mining," in *Proc. 1996 International Conf. on Extending Database Technology (EDBT'96),* Avignon (France), March 1996.

[28] R.S. Michalski, L. Kerschberg, K.A. Kaufman, and J.S. Ribiero, "Mining for knowledge in databases: The INLEN architecture, initial implementation and first results," *Journal of Intelligent Information Systems,* 1992, 1:85-114.

[29] M.C. Mozer, "Neural Net Architectures for Temporal Sequence Processing," in A.S. Weigend and N.A.Gershenfeld (Eds.), *Time Series Prediction: Forecasting the Future and Understanding the Past,* Addison-Wesley, 1994.

[30] G. Piatetsky-Shapiro, "Discovery, analysis and presentation of strong rules," in G. Piatetsky-Shapiro and W.J. Frawley (Eds.), *Knowledge Discovery in Databases*, AAAI/MIT Press, 1991, pp.229-238.

[31] G. Piatetsky-Shapiro and W.J. Frawley, *Knowledge Discovery in Databases*, AAAI/MIT Press, 1991.

[32] G. Piatetsky-Shapiro, U. Fayyad, and P. Smyth, "From data mining to knowledge discovery: An overview," in U. Fayyad, G. Piatetsky-Shapiro, P. Smyth, and R. Uthurusamy (Eds.) *Advances in Knowledge Discovery and Data Mining*, AAAI/MIT Press, 1996, pp.1-35.

[33] P.G. Selfridge, D. Srivastava, and L.O. Wilson, "IDEA: Interactive data exploration and analysis," in *Proc. 1996 ACM-SIGMOD International Conf. Management of Data*, Montreal (Canada), June 1996.

[34] W. Shen, K. Ong, B. Mitbander, and C. Zaniolo, "Metaqueries for data mining," in U. Fayyad, G. Piatetsky-Shapiro, P. Smyth, and R. Uthurusamy (Eds.) *Advances in Knowledge Discovery and Data Mining*, AAAI/MIT Press, 1996, pp.375-398.

[35] R. Srikant and R. Agrawal, "Mining quantitative association rules in large relational tables," in *Proc. ACM SIGMOD International Conf. on Management of Data*, 1996, pp.1-12.

[36] H. Toivonen, "Sampling large databases for association rules," in *Proc. 22nd International Conf. on Very Large Data Bases*, 1996, pp.134-145.

[37] S.M. Weiss and N. Indurkhya, *Predictive Data Mining: A Practical Guide*, Morgan Kaufmann, 1998.

[38] B. Widrow and M. Hoff, "Adaptive switching circuits," in *Western Electronic Show and Convention, Convention Record*, Institute of Radio Engineers (now IEEE), 1960, 4:96-104.

[39] T. Zhang, R. Ramakrishnan, and M. Livny, "BIRCH: An efficient data clustering method for very large databases," in *Proc. ACM SIGMOD International Conf. on Management of Data*, June 1996.

[40] W. Zhang, "Mining fuzzy quantitative association rules," in *Proc.Eleventh International Conf. on Tools with Artificial Intelligence*, Nov. 1999, pp.99-102.

Chapter 10

Distributed Experts

E pluribus unum.
(From many, one.) 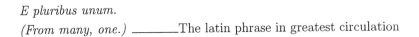The latin phrase in greatest circulation

Many complex real life problems require multiple kinds of expertise, applied using different problem-solving strategies. Recent advances in computer technology have made such multipronged approaches possible, thanks to the successful implementation of distributed computing systems and computer networks. "Distributed Artificial Intelligence" refers to the utilization of such systems by researchers in Artificial Intelligence, using multiple artificial expert systems that cooperate or collaborate in some manner. Such systems satisfy the practical need for large systems with multiple kinds of expertise that must sometimes be utilized effectively at multiple physical locations, where the use of a traditional monolithic expert system model would be far too cumbersome. For some limited tasks, it may be adequate to use a modular rule-based expert system, but the best solution is to use a collection of distributed experts (i.e., expert subsystems) that operate with some degree of autonomy, instead of being completely controlled by a single inference engine. DAI systems clearly separate control knowledge from the knowledge bases, and do not constrain the inference procedure by a fixed knowledge representation scheme. The development of a DAI system is additionally motivated if the components of the problem are themselves distributed; systems and data may belong to different organizations, each with its own concerns of privacy and security.

In this chapter, Section 10.1 highlights the main issues in DAI. Section 10.2 focuses on "blackboard systems," in which different components interact through a single shared data depository called the blackboard. Section 10.3

discusses "MultiAgent Systems," in which each of the multiple expert systems has considerably greater autonomy. Some researchers use the phrase "multiagent systems" to refer to the entire field of Distributed Artificial Intelligence, although this book distinguishes between the two. Section 10.4 discusses agent interactions and inter-agent communication protocols. Some examples of multiagent systems are presented in Section 10.5.

10.1　Distributed Artificial Intelligence

The field of Distributed Artificial Intelligence (DAI) is concerned with the development of systems consisting of loosely connected components that communicate, each of which has some specific expertise or knowledge base combined with problem-specific inference mechanisms. Much of the basis for proposing DAI approaches, sometimes well before their technological feasibility, comes from theories of how the human brain functions, and from cognitive psychology. DAI also owes many ideas to the field of sociology, borrowing theories of how societies and organizations function, given that the goals of each individual are different from the goals of an organization containing many such individuals.

The fundamental differences between DAI and AI (including traditional expert systems) are the following:

- DAI involves the use of several or many systems with expertise that are connected and communicate with one another.

- In DAI, intelligence is considered to be an attribute of the collection of communicating components, exhibited through their interactions.

- The primary concerns in DAI involve determining the nature of the interactions between different components, assuming that each component is equipped with the knowledge and reasoning mechanisms associated with a traditional expert system.

- In DAI, reasoning and control may be distributed, and successful activity is a joint effort of various components.

- The solution is often incrementally developed in DAI; in many traditional expert systems, by contrast, there is no notion of an intermediate solution.

The first issue faced by DAI system designers is to determine the nature of the main components that contain expertise; these components are variously known as "demons," "knowledge sources," or "agents." We use the latter terminology, although some practitioners make minor distinctions between these terms.

Problems to which the DAI methodology is applied are characterized by large amounts of information that is geographically distributed, with many components and dimensions, and broad scope. Furthermore, the environment may be dynamic and the data distribution topology may change with time. DAI provides four techniques to cope with such complexity: modularity, distribution (of agents), abstraction, and intelligence. In the simplest instances, agents may function as "wrappers" that encapsulate traditional computer programs. In more interesting cases, they may serve as active repositories of knowledge, available over a network to other agents.

Some of the most important questions faced by DAI designers are enumerated below:

1. How are agents created, modified or destroyed? Is the collection of agents static, or may it change with time? If dynamic, then how are different agents informed about changes in the agent pool?

2. How autonomous should each agent be? Does each agent determine its own goals and mode of operation? How are goals and capabilities communicated between agents?

3. What kind of knowledge should each agent possess? How is that knowledge to be represented?

4. Should there be uniformity between various agents? If not, how can successful communication be established between heterogeneous entities? Should there be a shared language between heterogeneous agents? What can each agent assume about other agents?

5. How can cooperation be ensured between agents that have different goals? Can the overall high level task be successfully accomplished by independent operation of multiple agents?

6. What is the control mechanism that governs the interrelationships between agents? Is control decentralized or distributed in some manner?

7. If implemented on a single processor, how should the activities of different agents be scheduled? If the number of processors does not equal the number of agents, how is execution to be scheduled?

Determining the appropriate answers to these questions is the starting point for building a DAI system. Different DAI systems may be characterized by the degree of autonomy possessed by each agent, the degree to which these agents are distributed over different machines, the communication model and protocols used, the presence or absence of a separate cognitive model (of intentions and beliefs) within each agent, the degree of dissimilarity between the knowledge representation (including language) and inference mechanisms used by different agents, and the ability of agents to learn or adapt by exposure to an environment.

The broad approach of DAI dates back to the *Pandemonium* system of Selfridge [26], a brief description of which is worth describing here, to indicate the state of the art of the 1960s. While no single researcher can be credited with laying down the foundations for modern work on DAI, Selfridge's work is historically important, predating other work on the topic by about a decade.

Pandemonium

The *Pandemonium* system was a natural language processing system proposed in 1959 by Selfridge [26] and may be considered the ancestor of all modern DAI systems. This system was intended to parse English sentences, and accomplished this by using a large number of autonomous 'demons,' each of which may be considered an agent with a very small knowledge base. Each demon would gauge its applicability to the problem at hand, and would 'shriek' (send a message to the controller) with a 'loudness' (strength or gauged applicability to the problem) used by the central controller to determine which demon was the winner in the shrieking competition. Giving control to the winner demon enabled a rule (associated with that demon) to fire. The problem-solving approach is thus *opportunistic*, i.e., dependent on the most promising action based on evaluating the current state, rather than being preprogrammed.

Although the Pandemonium system was the forerunner of modern DAI systems, this model was of limited applicability. The agents were very simple, and physically located on the same machine. Each agent was analogous to a single rule in a production system, rather than having a non-trivial knowledge base. The next major step in DAI was the development of systems with multiple agents, each of which had a substantial knowledge-base. Such systems reached maturity with industrial application in the 1980s, using a 'blackboard' communication model, discussed in Section 10.2. More recent developments have been in the direction of increasing autonomy for each agent, leading to *MultiAgent*

Systems (MAS)[1] in the 1990s, discussed in Section 10.3.

10.2 Blackboard Systems

The blackboard (BB) framework is a general and flexible non-deterministic system architecture, a spinoff of the *Hearsay* speech-understanding project. Its origin is traced to the work of Selfridge [26] mentioned above, as well as the ideas of Newell [22] and Simon [27]. The name 'blackboard' comes from the simple paradigm of physical blackboards: a hypothetical collection of people solving a jig-saw puzzle on a blackboard in complete silence, examining and modifying the current state (partial solution).

A more 'realistic' example involves detecting a possible threat (such as an enemy plane) in a battlefield scenario. Signals and inputs from different sources may be analyzed in different manners, using different kinds of expertise. Best results are obtained if knowledge from the different *knowledge sources* can be combined effectively. Solutions may be partial and hypothetical (e.g., "there is an object whose response to this radar signal resembles that of a small fighter plane"). A solution consists of bits and pieces of information, supported by multiple lines of reasoning. Various separately identified components (of the object being detected) constitute a hierarchy.

Knowledge is partitioned into various independent agents referred to as *knowledge sources (KSs)* The system is heterogeneous: different KSs can operate through different internal mechanisms, e.g., the forward chaining steps of one KS may be interleaved with the backward chaining steps of another. KSs perform subtasks, interacting with the blackboard data structure. All communication proceeds through the blackboard, which contains globally accessible state data. In the simplest blackboard systems, each KS may read from or write to the blackboard, when permitted to do so by the control mechanism.

If only one KS can access the blackboard at a time, then the blackboard system may contain a control module or KS that implements a conflict-resolution strategy, scheduling various KSs. In general, control may reside in the KSs, on the blackboard, in a separate module, or some combination of these.

KSs contribute *opportunistically* towards incremental construction of solutions: each KS that can contribute to some fragment of the problem does so, unhindered by any rigid global plan. The system may invoke high level conflict-resolution strategies in case of contention of multiple KSs for simultaneous access

---

[1]The abbreviation 'MAS' is used to refer to both singular and plural forms of "MultiAgent System" in this book.

to the blackboard.

The language of each KS may be specialized: each KS is an expert system in its own right, and is responsible for knowing the conditions under which it can contribute to a solution. A KS is analogous to a large rule, whose condition part checks whether the rule can be applied.

The basic approach in blackboard systems is to divide the problem into loosely coupled subtasks that correspond to areas of specialization within the task. For a particular application, the designer defines a solution space and the knowledge needed to find the solution. Knowledge sources and solution space (including "what's on the blackboard") are often structured hierarchically, as appropriate for solving the problem. As in the CRYSALIS system [23], a BB can have multiple 'panels'; the solution space may be partitioned into multiple hierarchies.

The manner of dividing the problem into subproblems is crucial to the success of the approach. The solution space is often divided into regions (levels) containing partial or intermediate solutions, *e.g.,* word-level and syllable-level in Hearsay-II. The information in each region is globally accessible on the BB. In many cases, a KS receives information from one region and sends it to another. The decision to employ a particular KS is made dynamically using the current solution state.

With uncertain or limited available data, progress is still made, *e.g.,* by maintaining logically consistent alternative partial solutions.

The global effects of applying knowledge are minimized to highly structured and disciplined changes to the "current best hypothesis," often an explicitly maintained data structure. One of the KSs may indicate when termination criteria are satisfied, with or without successful completion of the main task.

The following are some important features of BB systems:

- BB systems use *dynamic control*: the method of taking the next incremental step towards the solution is chosen anew, rather than being predetermined. There is considerable flexibility in programming the control. Knowledge can be coded either in control rules or complex control regimes, even in separate blackboards that make control decisions.

- A control module may select a *Focus of Attention*, using information from the BB and the potential problem-solving contribution determined for each KS: there is no rigidity as to which part of the emerging solution should be attended to next. The focus can be a KS (so that objects on the BB are chosen for execution) or a blackboard object (so that a KS must be chosen to process that object), or a combination of both.

- BB systems often use a strategy called *island driving*: pieces of the solution are separately developed, followed by attempts to combine these pieces by building inferential bridges between them.

A BB model does not address the details of designing and building an operational system. Application-specific engineering decisions are needed regarding the questions: "How is knowledge to be represented? What mechanisms activate and determine appropriate knowledge?" In the 'BB1' system, for instance, the control problem is viewed as a problem-solving planning problem to be solved using the blackboard approach.

A few well-known blackboard systems are reviewed in the remainder of this section.

10.2.1 Hearsay

The *Hearsay* project had the ambitious goal of speech-understanding, and underwent three phases of development, with changes in architecture in each phase.

The first implementation, Hearsay-I [25], had an organization that addressed the following requirements:

1. The contribution of each KS to the overall problem had to be measurable. Adding a KS to the system should improve performance.

2. The system should recover gracefully from errors. Absence or removal of a KS should not cripple the system.

3. Changes in performance requirements should not necessitate major modifications to the model.

The control mechanism of Hearsay-I polled different processes, in order to choose and activate the one most confident in contributing to the region of sentence hypothesis currently in focus. This was followed by the testing of new hypotheses by KSs. However, Hearsay-I was plagued by the following problems:

1. The blackboard contained a description at only the word-level; multiple levels would have helped.

2. There was only a limited amount of parallelism in the control sequence.

3. There was no provision to express relationships among alternative sentence hypotheses.

4. The system used a built-in problem-solving strategy which made modifications awkward.

These deficiencies led to the development of Hearsay-II [12], a system of historic importance for the field of Distributed Artificial Intelligence. In Hearsay-II, the information used by each KS was uniformly represented and made globally accessible. At each potential KS activation, the appropriate KS was dynamically selected and activated by a scheduler. Control of KS activation is determined by the actions of other KSs on the blackboard, rather than explicit calls from a KS or a centralized sequencing mechanism. Both top-down and bottom-up problem-solving behaviors were accommodated in Hearsay-II, and each KS's inference mechanism was chosen independently of the others. The system allows competitive hypotheses that represent incompatible interpretations of the same portion of the utterance (spoken sentence being processed).

Hearsay-II uses a mechanism called *selective attention* to allocate computing resources to the actions considered most promising, based on:

- probable effects,

- global significance (deduced by analyzing its relationship with existing hypotheses), and

- relative desirability (compared to other actions).

Each KS receives information from some level of the blackboard and modifies the blackboard at some level, as described in Figure 10.1. Each KS consists of a *condition procedure* (that determines whether the corresponding action can be executed) and an *action procedure*. Some KSs influence the activities of other KSs, rather than directly modifying the blackboard, e.g., WORD-CTL creates initial goal hypotheses at the word level, interpreted by MOW as indicating how many word hypotheses to attempt to create at each time step. Such KSs also affect the search procedure, e.g., restarting the execution process with different initial goals if the search process stagnates without reaching the goal nor leading to further useful activation.

The Hearsay-II architecture is illustrated in Figure 10.2. Based on the status of the blackboard, the control module determines whether the condition procedure of some KS needs to be considered for scheduling. The scheduler calculates a *priority* value for each procedure currently being considered, using the focus-of-control database. Priority is calculated based on an estimate of the degree to which a procedure's execution would assist in the overall task being addressed by the Hearsay-II system. Priority also depends on the credibility and

SEG: Parameter→Segment Digitizes signal, measures parameters, produces labeled segmentation

POM: Segment→Syllable Creates syllable-class hypotheses

MOW: Syllable→Word Creates word hypotheses

WORD-CTL: Word→Word Controls the number of word hypotheses

WORD-SEQ: Word→Word-sequence Creates word-sequence hypotheses using weak grammatical knowledge

WORD-SEQ-CTL: Word-sequence→Word-sequence Controls the number of word-sequence hypotheses

PARSE: Word-sequence→Phrase Parses word-sequences, creating phrase hypotheses

PREDICT: Phrase→Phrase Predicts words that may precede or follow a phrase

VERIFY: Segment→Word Evaluates consistency between segment hypotheses and contiguous word-phrase pairs

CONCAT: Phrase→Phrase Creates phrase hypotheses from acceptable contiguous word-phrase pairs

RPOL: All levels→All levels Evaluates credibility of each hypothesis, using information from other levels

STOP: Phrase→Phrase Halts processing if an acceptable sentence has been found, or computational resources are exhausted; output is either a sentence or a set of complementary phrase hypotheses

SEMANT: Phrase→Database Interface Generates unambiguous interpretation for the information retrieval system

Figure 10.1: KSs mapping information between various levels in Hearsay-II system; POM and MOW were replaced in 1977 by NOAH, a more efficient KS

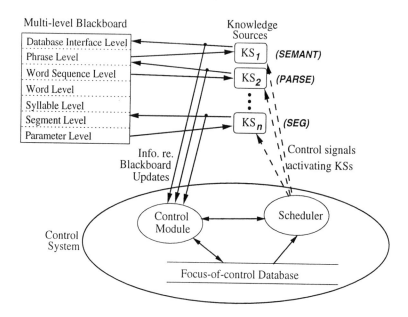

Figure 10.2: Hearsay-II Architecture

duration of the best hypotheses in each level and time region, and the amount of processing required from the time the current best hypotheses were generated. The priority of an existing hypothesis may be downgraded if no measurable progress (towards a more comprehensive hypothesis) has been achieved for a long time. The highest priority procedure is then executed:

1. If this happens to be a condition procedure, the effect is to determine whether the corresponding action procedure must be considered for scheduling.

2. If an action procedure is executed, the blackboard is modified, and the control module is also informed of the change. This is immediately followed by the execution of RPOL, a high priority KS, used to evaluate various hypotheses.

Example 10.1 *(adapted from [11])* The Hearsay-II system is presented with the spoken input

Are any by Feigenbaum and Feldman?

The following are some of the early steps of processing the speech signal using various KSs:

1. The first step is the extraction of four acoustic parameters by applying simple algorithms to the sampled speech signal; this is the task of SEG (a KS). Five classes of segments are produced: *silence, sonorant peak, sonorant nonpeak, fricative,* and *flap,* together with information such as duration, amplitude, and relative amplitude (compared with neighboring segments). Each segment is localized in time; the earliest segments for the given sentence are UW, AA, ER, AW, followed by ER, then AY, AE, IH, EY, and so on.

2. WORD-CTL and WORD-SEQ-CTL then create goal hypotheses at the word level and word sequence levels, respectively.

3. POM creates syllable-class hypotheses, identifying syllable nuclei and then parsing outward from each nucleus using a grammar whose rules are annotated with probabilities based on a preprocessed database of sentences. Each syllable-class corresponds to a sequence of segments. For the early part of the current sentence, one syllable-class is [Stop, I-Like, Nasal] and another is [Liquid, I-Like]. Each such sequence is associated with a credibility rating.

4. MOW creates word hypotheses from the syllable-class hypotheses, drawing on a vocabulary of 1011 words; each hypothesis is associated with a credibility rating. For instance, the syllable-class [Stop, I-Like, Nasal] leads to the generation of word hypotheses such as *PIN*. For the given sentence, 90 words were hypothesized, of which four were correct (ARE, BY, ANY, FELDMAN).

5. WORD-SEQ creates word-sequence hypotheses, using a table of frequencies of word-pairs in the language, acoustic and phonetic knowledge, and statistical knowledge generated from previous behavior of WORD-SEQ. For the given sentence, four word-sequence hypotheses were created, of which two are correct (ARE, AND FELDMAN) and two are wrong (EIGHT, SHAW AND MARVIN).

6. PARSE verifies that all four word-sequences are valid language fragments.

7. PREDICT suggests 292 possible candidate words that may follow ARE, of which VERIFY eliminates 277; of the rest, the highest rated are REDDY, ANY, HUGH, YOU. CONCAT then creates phrases such as ARE REDDY and ARE ANY, but the predicted words have low enough ratings that the

system searches for other possibilities. PREDICT and VERIFY then suggest a number of words that may follow AND FELDMAN, and EIGHT, including FEIGENBAUM. Although the sequence AND FELDMAN FEIGENBAUM is rejected, the word FEIGENBAUM receives high rating based on comparing it with the lower level data, and also because it is a long word that is preferable to shorter words given the long syllable sequences not yet associated with words. This leads to constructing and evaluating sequences such as FEIGENBAUM AND FELDMAN.

Eventually, the complete sentence is correctly generated, and STOP deactivates other competing hypotheses.

10.2.2   HASP

The HASP system [24] was developed to interpret continuous sonar signals passively collected by hydrophone arrays monitoring an area of ocean.

The first attempt was to use DENDRAL's plan-generate-test inference procedure [2]. This approach did not work, since it could not cope successfully with several serious problems:

1. Input data arrived in a continuous stream.

2. Analysis of activities had to be tracked over time: history is significant.

3. Conclusions were to be drawn by combining evidence from many types of relevant information.

4. There was no plausible generator of the solution space, and no simulator to generate all possible signal combinations.

This led to the exploration of a blackboard approach.

HASP represented the 'Current Best Hypothesis' explicitly, partitioned into levels of analysis (harmonic sets, sources, ship types) that correspond to the approach generally used by human analysts to solve the problem being addressed by HASP. Each KS consisted of rule-based knowledge that transformed information from one level to another. The architecture of HASP is illustrated in Figure 10.3.

The main characteristics of HASP are enumerated below:

1. Events (*e.g.*, appearance/disappearance of a signal) drive the system; *a priori* decisions were made about which events are significant.

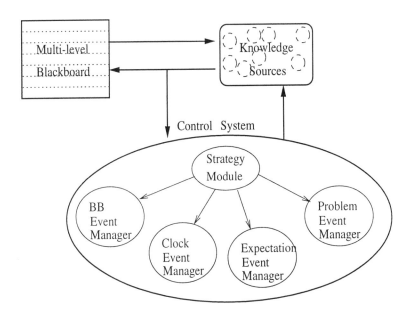

Figure 10.3: HASP Architecture

2. The system represents time and uses temporal notions to predict trends and to generate expectations of future events.

3. The system is capable of handling multiple input streams; in addition to inputs that are to be interpreted by the system, the system also accepts high-level model-based expectations as input.

4. Explanations are generated from the execution history with the help of templates that select appropriate rule activities in an understandable way.

10.2.3 GBB

The Generic Blackboard Development system (GBB) [3] is a commercial blackboard development shell of considerable practical importance; it has spurred the development of many modern industrial blackboard system applications.

GBB maintains a tree structure whose internal nodes are blackboards; each child node in the tree is a blackboard nested in the parent node blackboard. The leaves in the tree, called "spaces," represent simple blackboard elements.

GBB uses pattern-matching with a set of indexes to retrieve components of the system; the retrieval process can also utilize "filter" procedures to check for conditions that cannot be tested by pattern-matching alone.

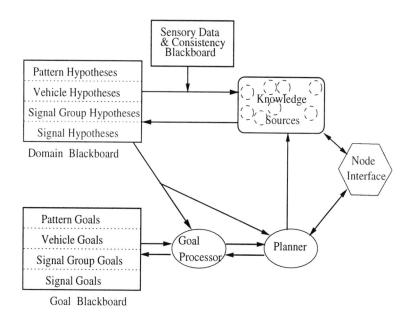

Figure 10.4: DVMT Node Architecture

GBB provides an environment that has been used to develop many blackboard applications, e.g., a crank shaft design system in use at Ford Motor Company [20]. Another interesting application, vehicle monitoring, is described in Section 10.2.4 below.

10.2.4   DVMT

The purpose of the *Distributed Vehicle Monitoring Testbed (DVMT)* [21] network simulation is to generate a map containing the identity and movement of vehicle patterns based on acoustic data. DVMT uses a *goal-directed* blackboard architecture, extending the architecture of Hearsay-II through the addition of a "goal processor" and a "goal blackboard" that are distinct from the domain blackboard. DVMT was implemented by tuning the blackboard data base of GBB (described in Section 10.2.3). Each node in the network is a complete blackboard system (a la Hearsay-II), sketched in Figure 10.4.

The main task of the goal processor is to instantiate goals on the goal blackboard. Hypotheses may be mapped to goals, goals may be mapped to subgoals, and goals may be mapped to domain knowledge sources, establishing the connection to the domain blackboard. Thus, in addition to a subgoaling facility, goal generation may be triggered by the creation or modification of hypotheses on the domain blackboard.

The "Data Blackboard" (D-BB) contains hypotheses regarding vehicle movements, refined by knowledge sources. The D-BB is partitioned into four levels of abstraction: signals, groups (harmonically grouped signal hypotheses), vehicle types, and patterns (containing spatially related vehicles, e.g., convoys). Each abstraction level is further subdivided into two levels: location hypotheses and track hypotheses (movement history).

KSs must process lower level hypotheses to obtain higher level hypotheses. The control component of DVMT creates goals on the Goal Blackboard, where each goal represents a request to create hypotheses on the D-BB. Execution of KSs results in achieving goals.

DVMT also includes two other blackboards: the "consistency blackboard" (C-BB) and the "ghyp blackboard" (GH-BB). The C-BB evaluates the developing solution using simulation measurement tools. The GH-BB contains a complete set of the sensory data.

Each hypothesis on the D-BB, C-BB and GH-BB describes an event class, time locations, and an estimate of the confidence in the accuracy of the hypothesis. Each goal is characterized by time regions, event classes, and a rating to estimate the relative importance of achieving the goal. Time-regions are geographical regions connected along the time dimension, e.g., representing possible geographical location ranges of a vehicle in different time intervals.

10.2.5 BB1

Hayes-Roth [14] proposed a "control blackboard" architecture that has come to be known as "BB1." In BB1, a blackboard approach is applied not just to the domain problem, but also to the problem of control and coordination among the knowledge sources (agents) that solve domain-specific problems. This is accomplished by using a separate "control blackboard" used for communication among "control knowledge sources" (CKSs).

Each CKS incrementally modifies "control plans" at three levels of abstraction:

1. "Strategies" are long-term control plans, possibly consisting of several levels of sub-strategies.

2. Lowest level sub-strategies consist of "foci," goals to be achieved by the system.

3. Each focus is associated with a set of "heuristics" used to judge the relevance of a possible action to the focus.

These control plans can be changed by the user, allowing for considerable flexibility and responsiveness to changing problem-solving environments.

If there is no single most important goal, BB1 can maintain multiple active foci; the system must then judge the tradeoffs between the relative importance of different goals and the relative quality of actions.

Control KSs are also placed on the same agenda as domain KSs, and selected using the same scheduler. But most applications give higher priority to control KSs; no clear mechanisms exist for BB1 to judge the relative value of domain KS activations vs. control KS activations.

We observe that the control plans of BB1 implement problem-solving strategies only through rating functions that select knowledge source instances, not directly identifying actions. This implies that only some restricted forms of subgoaling can be implemented. No explicit record is maintained of the relationships between subgoals that have to be pursued.

10.3 Multiagent Systems

In the blackboard model, work is divided among agents that divide and share knowledge, and the manner in which agents communicate follows an approach that requires the availability of a centralized (shared) blackboard to which all agents have access. By contrast, recent years have seen an explosion of work on "multiagent systems" (MAS) wherein each agent is considerably more autonomous, and no predetermined communication scheme (such as a blackboard) is assumed. Whereas the primary question in blackboard systems addresses task decomposition and solution synthesis, behavior coordination is the major issue of concern in MAS. Blackboard systems may be considered to be special cases of MAS.

The essential respect in which MAS are distinguished from other approaches is the far greater degree of autonomy granted to each agent. Further, it is almost always assumed that each agent operates on a different machine, and that communication is initiated and carried out independently by each agent. Indeed, developments in internet technology have led to considerable experimentation and developments in MAS.

In a typical MAS, each agent has its own goals, but is also able to recruit other agents to help solve its own problems. Agents cooperate in problem solving, share expertise, work in parallel on common problems, exhibit fault-tolerance through redundancy, and represent the viewpoints as well as knowledge of multiple experts.

Knowledge must be represented declaratively, defining what each agent knows, and how an agent can use and access the knowledge of another agent.

A distributed computing system with multiple processors may be considered to be a multiagent system when the candidate agents are capable of interacting and sharing knowledge, and can perhaps cooperate in solving a joint task.

Example 10.2 Huhns and Stephens [16] give an example of a kitchen with multiple "smart" appliances: although the coffee-maker and the toaster may each be equipped with a computer (processor), it is only when they "know" (and accomplish the goal) that both coffee and toast must be ready at the same time, that we may consider the collection of these systems to be a multiagent system.

An agent may be defined to be an active object with the ability to perceive, communicate, reason and act, which can explicitly represent knowledge, and which has a mechanism for operating on knowledge or for drawing inferences from knowledge.

The system designer must determine how agents must decompose goals and tasks, and allocate subgoals and subtasks to other agents. Each agent must also be equipped with the capability of combining partial results and partial solutions gathered from other agents.

10.3.1 MAS Architectures

The most general MAS architecture allows direct arbitrary interactions among all agents, with no prespecified controller. The structure of each agent may vary, with some agents possessing sufficient complexity to warrant an agent possessing an MAS architecture internal to itself. Each agent may have its own goals, intentions, and beliefs. Each agent may have its own knowledge base and representation language; however, each agent must also be capable of using languages known to agents with which it communicates, or must be equipped with translators for the languages used by all such agents; the latter solution requires $O(n^2)$ translators for n agents, an expensive alternative.

Such vast generality implies considerable complexity, avoided sometimes by restricting the degrees of freedom of the MAS in some manner. For instance,

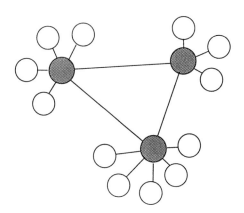

Figure 10.5: Multi-Hub Architecture with three hubs, denoted by shaded circles

a specific system may impose a single controller agent that determines the goals for a set of agents, and the relationship among the agents may be a "master-slave" relationship.

A *multi-hub* system, shown in Figure 10.5, partitions agents into groups, with a single agent in each group serving as group controller, group coordinator, or primary communicator with the agents outside the group.

A generalization of the multi-hub system, shown in Figure 10.6, divides the collection of agents into subsets that are not completely disjoint; each agent may belong to several groups with which it establishes communications. The choice of its groups may be dictated by the needs of each agent, or by the communication network. Such a system is more robust than a multi-hub architecture in which failure of a group controller/communicator disables many agents.

An MAS may be hierarchically organized using either a "horizontal" or "vertical" organization, illustrated in Figure 10.7. A horizontal layered structure is one in which system inputs are supplied to each layer and system outputs may be generated by all layers. A vertical layered structure is one in which each layer is restricted to interact with only the layers immediately above and below it, with system inputs being supplied to only one layer, and system outputs being generated by only one layer. Each higher layer may correspond to a higher level of abstraction.

However, such a system need not preclude feedback cycles; higher layer agents may generate expectations, plans, or goals to be satisfied by lower layer agents; or lower layer agents may pass on tasks beyond their ability to higher layer agents.

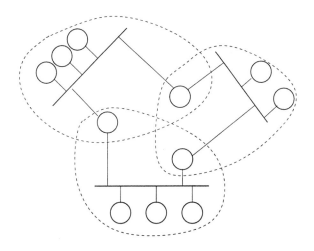

Figure 10.6: Overlapping Clusters Architecture

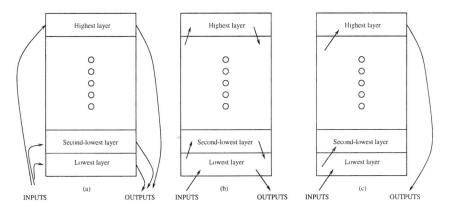

Figure 10.7: (a) Horizontal Layering; (b) Vertical Layering with feedback; (c) Vertical Layering without feedback

10.4 Agent Interactions

This section describes mechanisms used in MAS to ensure that agents interact effectively. Agents must determine goals they share with other agents, determine common tasks, avoid unnecessary conflicts, and pool knowledge and data. Agents must also have some agreed upon arrangements that will be obeyed, to enable them to seek each others' services.

We first address the nature of communication needed between agents. The goal of a message may be to transfer information, or to ask for some action to be performed by another agent. The terms used in the message may be interpreted in various ways, taking into account the perspective and the possible private or personal nature of communication. The meaning of a message may be distinguished from the context and framework of the agents communicating. The target of a message may be more than one agent, possibly even all the agents in the system. Messages may be categorized into assertions, queries, and variations of these (reply, request, explanation, command, permission, refusal, offer, bid, acceptance, agreement, proposal, confirmation, retraction and denial message types). Some agents may be restricted in their ability to send or receive some of these message types, classified as follows [28]:

- a "basic agent" can only receive assertions;

- a "passive agent" sends assertions and receives both assertions and queries;

- an "active agent" receives assertions and sends both assertions and queries; and

- a "peer agent" receives and sends both assertions and queries.

A protocol for communication among agents must determine the manner in which agents exchange messages, especially given that their internal languages may be different. A common language for the messages must be agreed upon in advance.

10.4.1 KQML

Knowledge Query Manipulation Language (KQML) is a language for inter-agent communication that is sufficiently high-level and general to be used by most MAS. The first component of a KQML message is called a "performative"[2] (a term borrowed from speech act theory), identifying the meaning and force

---

[2]Some authors refer to the message itself as the performative.

Table 10.1: KQML Performatives in which S conveys information to R

Performative	Intent
tell	the :content is in S's knowledge base
deny	the negation of the :content is in S's knowledge base
advertise	S will process a message matching :content
error	R's previous message is incorrect in some respect
sorry	S cannot provide a more informative response to R
ready	S is ready to respond to a message received from R
register	S announces its name to R
transport-address	S associates its name with a transport address

associated with an utterance. Examples of performatives are *promise, report, convince, insist, tell, request,* and *demand.*

Each KQML message has the following syntax:

(<performative-name> { :<keyword> <expression>}*)

where the asterisk denotes repetition (zero or more), and the keywords (necessarily preceded by a colon) identify the sender, receiver, language, ontology, and content (message body), in any sequence. An expression (following a keyword) may be a word, string, or a parenthesized sequence of expressions, of which the first is a word.. A word is a sequence of characters. The *ontology* refers to the specification of all the objects, concepts, and relationships of interest, e.g., inheritance hierarchies and relational schema specifications.

A subset of KQML performatives, extracted from Table 2 of [19], is listed here. In the descriptions, 'S' refers to the sender, 'R' refers to the receiver, and :content refers to the main content of the message being sent from S to R. Table 10.1 describes performatives where S conveys information to R, and Table 10.2 covers cases where S makes a request to R. In addition, there are a number of performatives intended to reverse the actions of previous messages, e.g., *untell, uninsert, undelete, unachieve, unadvertise,* and *unregister.*

KQML message contents are often expressed using *KIF*, a formal language that expresses first order logic.

Example 10.3 The following KQML messages (using KIF and Prolog languages) tell a simple story, illustrating the syntax and nature of communication between agents. We define a *Spies-World* ontology in which there are unary predicates such as *Spy, Resign, Send-to-heaven, Medal-of-honor-recepient* and *Country,* and binary predicates such as *Works-for.*

Table 10.2: KQML Performatives in which S requests R to take some action or to send some information (each ellipsis denotes the obvious omitted phrase "S asks R to")

Performative	Intent
ask-if	. . . inform if :content is known to R
ask-all	. . . send all instantiations of :content true in R's knowledge base
ask-one	. . . send one instantiation of :content true in R's knowledge base
stream-all	A multiple-response version of ask-all
eos	end-of-stream marker to stream-all
insert	. . . insert :content into its knowledge base
delete-one	. . . remove one sentence matching :content from its knowledge base
delete-all	. . . remove all sentences matching :content from its knowledge base
achieve	. . . perform actions that have a specified result
subscribe	. . . send updates to R's response to a performative
standby	. . . announce its readiness to provide a response to the message identified by :content
next	. . . send next response (reply) to a message from S
rest	. . . send remaining responses to a message from S
discard	. . . discard remaining responses to a message from S
forward	. . . forward the message to a specified addressee (agent)
broadcast	. . . forward the message to every agent known to R
broker-one	. . . find one response to a performative, *via* some other agent who will send the response
broker-all	. . . find all responses to a performative, *via* some other agent who will send the response
recommend-one	. . . recommend an agent that may respond
recommend-all	. . . recommend all agents that may respond
recruit-one	. . . recruit an agent that will respond
recruit-all	. . . recruit all agents that will respond

```
(tell
        :sender      Agent007
        :receiver    M
        :reply-with  id0
        :language    KIF
        :ontology    Spies-World
        :content     (AND (Spy Carl) (Country Toonland)
                          (Works-for Carl Toonland))
)
```

```
(achieve
            :sender       M
            :receiver     Agent007
            :in-reply-to  id0
            :reply-with   id1
            :language     KIF
            :ontology     Spies-World
            :content      (OR (Send-to-heaven Carl) (Resign Agent007))
)
```

```
(ask-all
            :sender       Agent007
            :receiver     M
            :in-reply-to  id1
            :reply-with   id2
            :language     KIF
            :ontology     Spies-World
            :content      (AND (InCity Carl X) (Incity Y X)
                               (Works-for Y MI5))
)
```

```
(tell
        :sender        M
        :receiver      Agent007
        :in-reply-to   id2
        :reply-with    id3
        :language      Prolog
        :ontology      Spies-World
        :content       [InCity(Carl,Syracuse),
                            InCity(Ada,Syracuse),  InCity(Brad,Syracuse),
                            Works-for(Ada,MI5), Works-for(Brad,MI5)]
)

(achieve
        :sender        Agent007
        :receiver      Ada
        :reply-with    id4
        :language      KIF
        :ontology      Spies-World
        :content       (Send-to-heaven Carl)
)

(sorry
        :sender        Ada
        :receiver      Agent007
        :in-reply-to   id4
)

(achieve
        :sender        Agent007
        :receiver      Brad
        :reply-with    id5
        :language      KIF
        :ontology      Spies-World
        :content       (Send-to-heaven Carl)
)
```

We assume that Brad can do the needful, and does it right away. Although the preceding and the next message have the same :content, 'achieve' asks for this goal to be satisfied, whereas 'tell' asserts that the goal has been satisfied.

```
(tell
        :sender      Brad
        :receiver    Agent007
        :in-reply-to id5
        :language    KIF
        :ontology    Spies-World
        :content     (Send-to-heaven Carl)
)
(tell
        :sender      Agent007
        :receiver    M
        :in-reply-to id1
        :reply-with  id6
        :language    KIF
        :ontology    Spies-World
        :content     (Send-to-heaven Carl)
)
```

Note that agents have only partial information about other agents, e.g., agent M is unaware that Agent007 did not do the required work (Send-to-heaven Carl) himself.

```
(tell
        :sender      M
        :receiver    Agent007
        :in-reply-to id6
        :reply-with  id7
        :language    KIF
        :ontology    Spies-World
        :content     (Medal-of-honor-recepient Agent007)
)
```

Although the above story is unreal, it illustrates many of the essential mechanisms in communication using KQML: agents send information, recruit other agents to carry out specific actions, and respond to previous messages.

10.4.2 Agent coordination protocols

At a high level, we may consider agents as searching in an AND-OR graph whose nodes represent goals and subgoals. Indirect dependencies may also exist among subgoals, due to sharing of resources. Agents may communicate results to one another, allowing other agents to make progress in the problem-solving process.

The following coordination activities need to be performed:

1. Defining the goal graph

2. Mapping goals and subgoals to the set of agents available

3. Making decisions regarding which goals or collections of subgoals should be explored next

4. Graph traversal

5. Reporting results of solving some goals

For coordination to occur, agents must be willing to make "commitments" to other agents, pledging to perform certain actions or solve certain subgoals. These commitments should be consistent with each agent's capabilities and availability, and its understanding of its future needs. "Conventions" must also exist, regulating commitments in environments that change with time, e.g., determining what is to be done if an agent declares that it cannot meet a prior commitment, perhaps because of a new, more urgent need for its resources [28]. One example is the "Limited Bandwidth Social Convention," with the following three rules, where "LC" abbreviates "Local Commitment."

LC satisfied   ⇒ Inform all related commitments
LC dropped   ⇒ Inform all strongly related commitments
LC dropped   AND communication resources not overburdened
      ⇒ Inform strongly and weakly related commitments

Another is the "Basic Joint Action Convention," with the following rules:

Commitment to   joint action changes
      ⇒ Inform all other team members of the changes
Status of   commitment to present team changes
      ⇒ Inform all other team members of the changes
Status of   joint commitment of a team member changes
      ⇒ Determine whether joint commitment is still viable

Note that joint action implies joint commitments from two or more agents.

"Coherence" denotes how well a system behaves as a unit; indeed, optimal performance can be assured if all of a system's components are operating according to a predetermined and carefully choreographed sequence of actions;

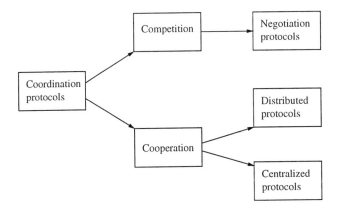

Figure 10.8: Classification of coordination protocols

unfortunately, this is contrary to the spirit and capabilities of DAI systems. The general problem addressed by coordination protocols is to maintain some semblance of global coherence without explicit global control.

Coordination protocols, as illustrated in Figure 10.8, depend on whether agents cooperate (to help each other solve problems of common interest), or compete (with each agent pursuing its own goals). The nature of the coordination mechanisms used depends on the relationships of agents:

- *Cooperation* is coordination among non-antagonistic agents.

- *Negotiation* is coordination among competitive or self-interested agents.

Protocols for these two kinds of interactions are described below.

10.4.3   Cooperation protocols

These are special cases of coordination protocols in which agents are motivated to work together for joint goals. To cooperate successfully, each agent must maintain a model of other agents and how future interactions may occur. The overall strategy is to decompose tasks and distribute them to different cooperating agents. Indeed, blackboard systems may be considered a special case of this paradigm.

Task decomposition may be performed by the system designer, or by agents using hierarchical planning methodologies; in some cases, the decomposition may be inherent in the problem description itself. One out of many possible decompositions must be chosen. Problems may be decomposed based on the difference in functions, or on considerations such as which subproblems belong together most naturally.

The task distribution phase must account for the limitations and capabilities of different agents. Agents with a broader perspective should be in charge of assigning tasks. Care should be taken to ensure that critical resources and capable agents are not overloaded. Coherence is sometimes achieved by allowing agent responsibilities to overlap; however, this may cause contention problems, requiring a conflict-resolution step. Communication and synchronization costs should be minimized, taking advantage of the geographical proximity within clusters of agents. For important tasks, periodic monitoring may be necessary; a task may need to be reassigned to a different agent in case the original agent appears to make little progress. For increased fault-tolerance, multiple agents may be allocated the same task, with the final decision depending on which agent completes the task first, or with a voting process implemented after several agents return their results.

Cooperation protocols can be based on market mechanisms, or metaphors drawn from human social interactions. In some cases, the existence of a predetermined organizational structure implies that the responsibilities for each agent are fixed beforehand. The *contract net protocol*, described below, is one such frequently used protocol.

Contract Net Protocol

A "manager" agent needs a task to be performed, and asks which "contractor" agents would be willing and able to perform the task, selecting one among these. In the simplest case of "Directed Contracts," the manager may query a small number of agents in some sequence, and the latter may reply with "Accept" or "Refuse" responses. In the more general case, the manager sends a message announcing the task, receives some bids, evaluates the bids, awards the contract, receives the results from the chosen contractor, and synthesizes these results with other relevant information. The task announcement includes a set of addresses, a specification of the eligibility criteria, a high-level description of the task, a specification of constraints about the bid, and an expiration time before which the bid must be received. The contractor receives the task announcement, evaluates its capability to respond, then sends a message either declining or bidding for the contract, performs the contract if the bid is accepted, and reports results to the manager. In some cases, a manager may request "immediate response" bids; the contractors may then respond with "busy," "ineligible," or "uninterested" messages, possibly causing the manager to alter its planning strategy.

10.4.4 Negotiation

When each agent has its own goal or self-interest to be pursued, coordination protocols require negotiation. Agents must first agree about the language, protocol, and decision process to be used in the negotiation. A good negotiation protocol must be efficient, stable (agents should benefit by sticking to the agreed-upon policies rather than by reneging on commitments), simple, and unbiased (not unduly favoring one agent).

Example 10.4 A collection of agents may need to download a collection of documents from the worldwide web, where inter-agent document-sharing is much less expensive than downloading. A simple protocol involves each agent declaring which documents it needs. Whenever multiple agents require the same document, one of them is chosen randomly to download the document, and others are given access to the downloaded document. This is a stable policy, and it is in the best interest of all agents to abide by the protocol.

Some other negotiation strategies are derived by principles of economic rationality; each agent performs decision-making using the tools of utility theory (discussed in Chapter 3), and negotiation may result in a "pareto optimal" deal, such that no other deal is better in all respects.

An important concern of multiagent systems is "Belief Maintenance" – the maintenance of a consistent internal belief structure in each agent, including mechanisms to keep track of the reasons for drawing conclusions. Certain assumptions may be made at first, but may turn out later to be incorrect, when it is necessary to withdraw the conclusions made using these assumptions. This issue has been explored, extending Doyle's "Truth Maintenance System" [9] to the context of multiagent systems [15]. Each agent must have a stable knowledge base: beliefs must be supported (i.e., there must be some reason to assert a belief), and must be logically consistent, as discussed in Chapter 2.

Voting mechanisms are simple to describe but involve considerable communication overhead and too much prior organization, and are hence not popular in MAS.

Market mechanisms can be used to derive certain MAS protocols. These follow a producer-consumer model, with prices and profits driving the entire negotiation. Equilibrium conditions assume that consumers bid to maximize their utility, producers bid to maximize their profits, and net demand is zero. The greatest difficulty in these protocols is that preference structures of individual agents cannot always be captured easily by simple numeric estimates. Hidden assumptions may distort the numbers chosen in an implementation.

Agents must function in *societies of agents*, interacting with each other in well-defined ways according to set protocols. This often necessitates that agents must exist for significant periods of time, interact with other agents to achieve personal (and common) goals, explore their environment, and learn from it. Agents may join groups and accept group-imposed constraints willingly. One agent may depend on another to achieve subgoals, when the latter is more capable of doing so. Conversely, an agent may commit to perform some task required by another agent, with the expectation that such favors may be returned in the future. Reciprocal dependence relationships and cooperative behavior may come to exist.

10.5   Example Applications

This section discusses several practical applications of MAS to large and complex real-life problems.

10.5.1   Sensor Net

Davis and Smith have applied the contract net protocol to the *Distributed Sensor Net Establishment* (DSNE) problem [8]. An agent has to monitor a wide geographic area, and uses its task structure representation to determine that sensor information from remote areas is required, for which it requires the assistance of other agents. It uses the contract net protocol to find suitable agents that can perform the sensing subtasks. To be eligible, a bidding agent must have a sensor position in the desired geographical region, and must have the desired sensing capabilities. Each such agent examines the task abstraction to determine whether it can perform the task and is interested in doing so; if so, it submits a bid. If one or more of such bids is acceptable to the manager agent (that asked for the bids), it awards the contract to one such potential contractor agent. Otherwise, the manager agent may modify its requirements to target a larger or different pool of bidders.

10.5.2 Emergency Management

Cuena and Ossowski [7] present an Environmental Emergency Management System motivated by several such systems in use for specific emergencies [13, 4, 1]. This system would contain the following agents:

- Local Emergency Management Agents (LEMA), one per region, responsible for local decisions;

- Dam Management Agent (DMA), for dam control;

- Fire Brigade Management Agent (FBMA), responsible for fire protection safeguards and population evacuation; and

- Transport and Ambulance Management Agent (TAMA).

Each LEMA maintains communications with FBMA, TAMA and DMA agents. Task assignment is based on the specialization of each agent. Every agent receives information from the environment and the society of agents. For example, each LEMA receives information about rainfall and water levels in different parts of the relevant region. A LEMA must have diagnostic knowledge to enable it to determine whether a potential emergency may arise in the relevant region. The LEMA may then invoke repair knowledge to help eliminate or alleviate problems, possibly by requesting the services of the DMA, FBMA or TAMA. A domain model is used to determine what messages to send to these agents.

10.5.3 Traffic Management

Cuena and Ossowski [7] present another decision support example, based on the European KITS [5] and Spanish TRYS [6] projects, addressing the tasks faced by traffic control centers (TCCs) that manage urban transport. Information handled by a TCC includes messages transmitted by human observers (including urban police), visual information obtained by videocameras, and different kinds of sensors (detecting vehicle speeds, rates of vehicle flow, etc.,) at strategic parts of the network, that generate a continuous flow of numerical data about traffic conditions. Traffic control is accomplished by varying the lengths of green and red time periods for traffic lights, and by using "variable message signs" (VMSs) that modify traffic signals, including panels to inform drivers about problems ahead. The traffic management problem involves identifying problematic situations, diagnosing causes, and generating plans to improve traffic conditions.

In the proposed system, agents are homogeneous, and each agent focuses on a single geographical region. Each agent possesses area-specific knowledge that helps decision-making. Agents perform:

- data abstraction (transforming raw data into qualitative measures such as whether the average speed is high or low),

- problem type identification (e.g., identifying incident congestion, overload congestion, etc.),

- solution refinement,

- demand estimation (time-varying),

- effect estimation (to determine the effect of a traffic flow on a problem),

- signal plan selection, and

- short term prediction (estimating the results of changes).

Agent regions overlap to some extent, causing possible conflicts in their plans, to be resolved by peer-to-peer communication, or by a coordinator. Conflicts may be resolved by allowing the agents with the most severe problems to maintain its signal plan.

10.6   Bibliographic Notes

Blackboard Systems, edited by Engelmore and Morgan [10], is a very useful introduction to the topic, including articles on Hearsay-II [11] and other historically important blackboard systems. Another useful source of information on the same topic is the collection of articles in *Blackboard Architectures and Applications*, edited by Jagannathan, Dodhiawala and Baum [17].

The collection of articles in *Multiagent Systems*, edited by Weiss [28], is an excellent and comprehensive overview of the field of multiagent systems. *Intelligent Information Agents*, edited by Klusch [18] focuses on the use of agents in the internet world. The complete specification of KQML has not been finalized, at the time of writing of this book; for a proposal, the interested reader is referred to the internet site http://www.cs.umbc.edu/kqml

Bibliography

[1] N.Avouris, "Cooperating Knowledge-based Systems for Environmental Decision Support," *Knowledge-Based Systems* 8(1):39-54, 1995.

[2] B.G. Buchanan, G.L. Sutherland, and E.A. Feigenbaum, "Heuristic DENDRAL: A program for generating explanatory hypotheses in organic chemistry," in B. Meltzer and D. Michie (Eds.), *Machine Intelligence 4* Edinburgh University Press (U.K.), 1969.

[3] D.D. Corkill, K.Q. Gallagher, and K.E. Murray, "GBB: A Generic Blackboard Development System," in *Proc. National Conf. on Artificial Intelligence,* Philadelphia (PA), 1986, pp. 1008-1014. Also in R.S.Engelmore and T.Morgan (Eds.), *Blackboard Systems,* Addison-Wesley, 1988, pp.503-518.

[4] J.Cuena, "The use of simulation models and human advice to build an expert system for the defense and control of river floods," in *Int. Joint Conf. on Artificial Intelligence (IJCAI-83),* Morgan-Kaufmann, 1983.

[5] J.Cuena, J.Hernandez, M.Molina, "Case Presentation for the Use of Knowledge-Based Models for Traffic Management – Madrid," in *Proc. First World Congress on Applications of Transport Telematics and Intelligent Vehicle-Highway Systems,* 1994, pp. 564-571.

[6] J.Cuena, J.Hernandez, M.Molina, "Knowledge-based Models for Adaptive Traffic Management," *Transportation Research,* 1995, 3(5):311-337.

[7] J. Cuena and S. Ossowski, "Distributed Models for Decision Support," Ch. 11 in G. Weiss (Ed.), *MultiAgent Systems,* MIT Press, Cambridge (MA), 1999.

[8] R. Davis and R. Smith, "Negotiation as a metaphor for distributed problem solving," *Artificial Intelligence,* 20:63-109, 1983.

[9] J. Doyle, "A Truth Maintenance System," *Artificial Intelligence,* 1979, 12 (3): 231-272.

[10] R. Engelmore and T. Morgan (Eds.), *Blackboard Systems,* Addison-Wesley, 1988.

[11] R. Engelmore, A.J. Morgan, and H.P. Nii, "Hearsay-II," in R. Engelmore and T. Morgan (Eds.), *Blackboard Systems,* Addison-Wesley, 1988, pp.25-86.

[12] L.D. Erman, F. Hayes-Roth, V.R. Lesser, and D.R. Reddy, "The Hearsay-II Speech-Understanding System: Integrating Knowledge to Resolve Uncertainty," *Computing Surveys,* June 1980, 12(2):213-253.

[13] European Commission: Telematics Applications Programme (1994-1998), in *Guide to the 1995-1996 Telematics Projects,* European Commission, Directorate-General XIII, Telecommunications, Information Market and Exploitation of Research, 1996.

[14] B. Hayes-Roth, "A Blackboard Architecture for Control," *Artificial Intelligence,* 1985, 26 (3): 251-321.

[15] M. N. Huhns and D. M. Bridgeland, "Multiagent Truth Maintenance," *IEEE Trans. on Systems, Man and Cybernetics,* 1991, 21(6):1437-1445.

[16] M. Huhns and L.M. Stephens, "Multiagent Systems and Societies of Agents," Ch. 2 in G. Weiss (Ed.), *MultiAgent Systems,* MIT Press, Cambridge (MA), 1999.

[17] V. Jagannathan, R. Dodhiawala, and L.S. Baum (Eds.), *Blackboard Architectures and Applications,* Academic Press, 1989.

[18] R. Klusch (Ed.), *Intelligent Information Agents,* Springer, 1998.

[19] Y. Labrou and T. Finin, "A Proposal for a new KQML Specification," TR CS-97-03, Computer Science and Electrical Engineering Department, University of Maryland Baltimore County, Feb. 3, 1997.

[20] S.E. Lander, S.M. Staley and D.D. Corkill, "Designing Integrated Engineering Environments: Blackboard-Based Integration of Design and Analysis Tools," in *Concurrent Engineering: Research and Applications Special Issue on The Application of Multi-agent Systems to Concurrent Engineering,* March 1996, 4(1):59-72.

[21] V.R. Lesser and D.D. Corkill, "The Distributed Vehicle Monitoring Testbed: A Tool for Investigating Distributed Problem Solving Networks," *AI Magazine*, 1983, 4(3):15-33. Also in R. Engelmore and T. Morgan (Eds.), *Blackboard Systems*, Addison-Wesley, 1988, pp.353-386,

[22] A. Newell, "The knowledge level," *Artificial Intelligence*, 1982, 18:87-127.

[23] H.P. Nii and E.A. Feigenbaum, "Rule-based understanding of signals," in D.A. Waterman and F. Hayes-Roth (Eds.), *Pattern-Directed Inference Systems* Academic Press, NY, 1978.

[24] H.P. Nii, E.A. Feigenbaum, J.J. Anton, and A.J. Rockmore, "Signal-to-Symbol Transformation: HASP/SIAP case study," *AI Magazine*, Spring 1982, 3(2):23-35.

[25] D.R. Reddy, L.D. Erman, R.D. Fennel, and R.B. Neely, "The Hearsay speech understanding system: an example of the recognition process," in *Proc. Third International Joint Conf. on Artificial Intelligence*, 1973, pp.185-193.

[26] O. Selfridge, "Pandemonium: A Paradigm for Learning," *Symposium on the Mechanization of Thought*, London: HM Stationery Office, 1959.

[27] H.A. Simon, *The Sciences of the Artificial*, MIT Press, Cambridge (MA), 1969.

[28] G. Weiss (Ed.), *MultiAgent Systems*, MIT Press, Cambridge (MA), 1999.

10.7   Exercises

1. How does a knowledge source in a blackboard system differ from an agent in a multiagent system?

2. How may Distributed A.I. systems make use of the availability of parallel computers, as opposed to distributed computing systems?

3. What are the advantages and disadvantages associated with the use of a hierarchical control scheme, as opposed to a truly distributed control scheme?

4. Does the existence of control strategies negate opportunistic problem solving?

5. Modify the KQML interaction in Example 10.3, illustrating that not everyone who works for MI5 is a spy; some of the agents whom *Agent007* asks for help may not be capable of doing so.

6. Modify the KQML interaction in Example 10.3, illustrating the use of *recruit-one, recruit-all, broker-one* or *broker-all* performatives.

7. Consider a special case of the SpyWorld ontology, where each agent is aware of only two other agents in its organization, other than M. Modify the KQML interaction in Example 10.3 so that *Agent007* can still ensure that Carl is sent to heaven, without letting M know who did it (so that *Agent007* still receives the medal).

8. Construct KQML interaction sequences to model the following multi-agent interactions:

   (a) Agents conduct an election to determine the current "controller."

   (b) After (a) above, the controller fails and agents detect this fact and conduct another election.

   (c) After (b) above, the previous controller that was temporarily disconnected comes back and must determine that it is no longer the controller.

   (d) An agent conducts an auction for a single item, with constraints on the minimum price.

   (e) An agent conducts a simultaneous auction for multiple items; each bidder may be bidding for multiple items, but may have constraints on the total amount each bidder can spend.

9. Discuss the possible design of a DAI (blackboard or multiagent) system for each of the following problems:

   (a) Finding useful information over the internet

   (b) Distributing consumer products in a supermarket chain

   (c) Monitoring activities of financial firms (e.g., stock exchanges, brokerage firms)

   (d) Monitoring crime and criminals in a geographically large region

   In each case, discuss whether a centralized approach would be equally feasible.

10. Evaluate the feasibility of automating the part procurement process for an industrial concern using autonomous agents that navigate the internet, with authority to negotiate and make purchases on behalf of the industrial concern. What would be the major roadblocks to implementing such a mechanism?

Index